Macromedia
FLASH INTERFACE DESIGN

Twelve effective interfaces and why they work

> Darcy DiNucci

Macromedia Flash Interface Design: A Macromedia Showcase

Darcy DiNucci

Published by Peachpit Press, a division of Pearson Education,
in association with Macromedia Press.

Peachpit Press
1249 Eighth Street
Berkeley, CA 94710
510/524-2178 • 800-283-9444
510/524-2221 (fax)

Find us on the World Wide Web at: **http://www.peachpit.com**
http://www.macromedia.com

Editor: Serena Herr
Production Coordinators: David Van Ness, Kate Reber
Copy Editor: Jill Simonsen
Technical Editor: Chris Jones
Proofreader: Elissa Rabellino
Art Preparation: Carla DiNucci
Interior Design: Celery Design and Wolken Communica
Cover Design/Layout: Wolken Communica
Index: Karin Arigoni

ISBN 0-321-12399-9
9 8 7 6 5 4 3 2 1
Printed and bound in the United States of America

ACKNOWLEDGMENTS

Thanks to all of the development teams who relived, rebuilt, and recounted their experiences and strategies for retelling here. This book would have been impossible without their cooperation and endless patience.

Thanks to Serena Herr, my editor at Macromedia Press, who made me do the hard stuff (those blasted sidebars) to make this a better book, and to Chris Jones of Small Pond Studios, Web developer extraordinaire, who vetted the technical stuff.

And finally, thanks to my husband, Kevin Radley, for his patience as I replayed Flash sites over and over (with the sound on); to Heather, who cared for Jackson Sphere as I toiled; and to Jackson, who made it fun by playing, jabbering, and hollering all the while.

TABLE OF CONTENTS

INTRODUCTION

Everyone knows you can create exciting Web sites using Macromedia Flash. This book sets out to prove that, despite rumors to the contrary, Flash sites can also be examples of great interface design.

The sites profiled here exemplify the cardinal rule of interface design: Know what the user is trying to accomplish, and make it easy for them to accomplish it. But saying that a site must help users succeed at their tasks is like saying the site should load without crashing the user's computer. It's simply a given of good design.

Just as a site's programmers have to design working code, a site's creators must design for usability. The really interesting thing is how good designers create usable Web sites that must also meet a variety of other goals. By analyzing the interfaces of a dozen sites—running the gamut from corporate marketing to experimental comics—we show that good interface design can take many forms and that what makes an interface "good" differs in each situation.

> Innovation and Usability

You could argue that a Web site is easiest to use if it simply adheres to the conventions—and the limitations—of HTML. But while the rules of good interface design apply to Flash, the rules of HTML design often don't, and if you wanted to do only what's possible in HTML, you wouldn't be using Flash in the first place.

Flash has gotten a bad rap for usability, partly because Flash sites don't follow the rules of HTML Web pages, and partly because designers can get carried away with Flash's capabilities.

MINI USA: Great information design and playful asides convince users that the car, like the site, is fun and reliable.

R!OT MANHATTAN: QuickTime is embedded in Flash using new features of Flash MX and a sophisticated approach to interaction.

HELLO DESIGN: A straightforward structure, simple cues, and a light dusting of wit create an image of playful trustworthiness.

It's tempting to throw in animation, sound, and other effects because you can, and not because those effects further the site's goals.

Used well, though, Flash's capabilities can enhance, not detract from a site's usability. Its quick response (without calls back to the server for the next page or graphic), plus its ability to demonstrate an action with an animation or to trigger one action with another can add to a user's understanding of a site's content and its rules of interaction. Designers are free to create effective interfaces that not only make sense to the user but also are actually fun to use.

> Examples Broad and Wide

No site has a "perfect" interface (though I think some of these come close). But each of the sites profiled here has aspects that I think are inspired. And it's not just me who thinks so. Several of these sites have carried off the field's top design honors.

Some of the sites (Hello Design, the HandSpring ad) exemplify simplicity, consistency, and clarity—the hallmarks of usability. Some (the NCAA Final Four Brackets, MOMA's Russian avant-garde books site, MINI USA) show how thoughtful information and interaction design can clarify complex sets of information. iHotelier's OneScreen shows how a Flash interface can simplify interactions that depend on databases.

SLEEPING GIANTS: An artful combination of music, voice-over, and animated stills engross visitors on this virtual tour.

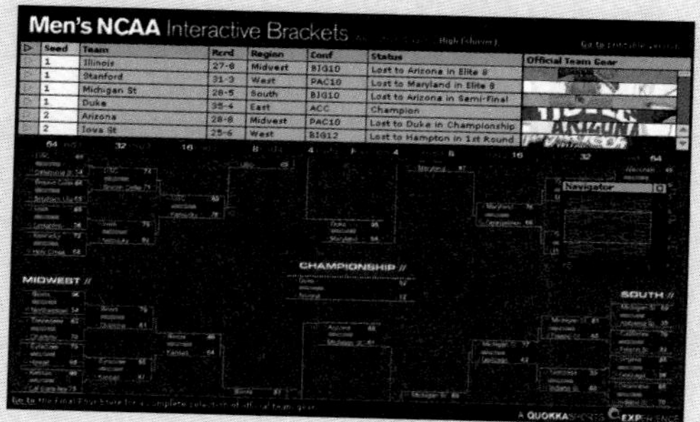

NCAA FINAL FOUR BRACKETS: The designers fit a time-honored interface to the Web with thoughtful design and some custom-designed controls.

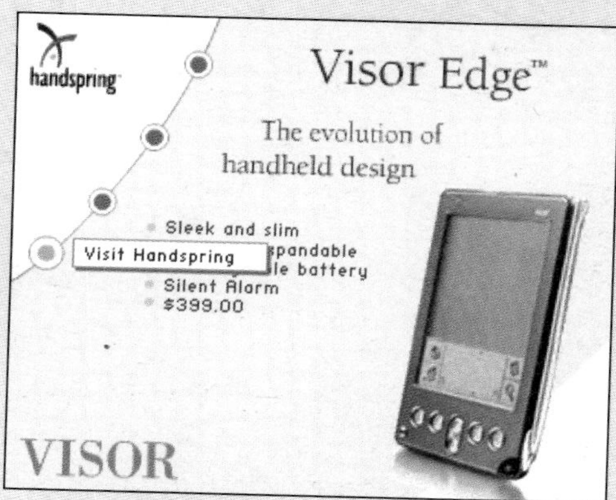

HANDSPRING AD: A banner ad becomes a mini-site when done in Flash.

Others are more surprising. The MINI USA site, for example, pulls some shenanigans that work *because* they're unexpected, an attribute that would be fatal to another site's success. In The Collective Unconsciousness Project, the designer meets his goals—and engages site visitors—by *withholding* control from the users, a mistake in most situations.

In each case, though, these sites adhere to that cardinal rule: their every element is designed to help users understand and interact with the content. They manage to engage the user without getting in the way.

> Steal This Idea

Creating a site that delights rather than frustrates users is easier said than done, of course. Everyone wants to do it. Everyone intends to do it. So why are so many Web sites—in Flash or in any other format—so maddening to use? And how can this book help you avoid the usability pitfalls that trip up interaction designers in general and Flash designers in particular?

First, the site profiles analyze the best features of the site in question. The site's designers explain their thinking, and I add my own comments about how the sites work and how their interactions further their creators' goals. (In some cases, I point out missed

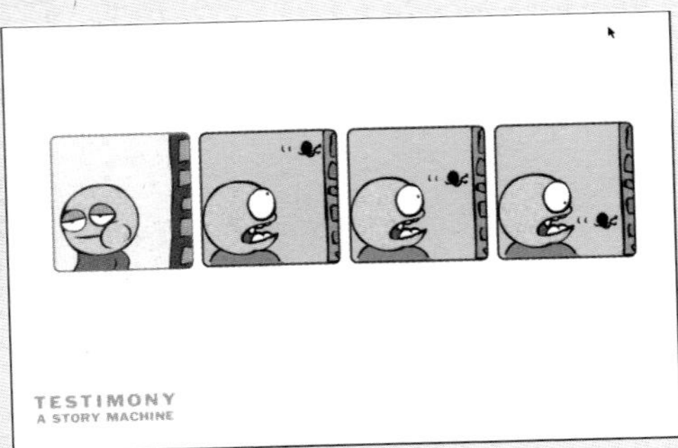

TESTIMONY: A STORY MACHINE: Click anywhere and see what happens. A simple interface frees the user for a more important task: constructing the storyline in this interactive comic book.

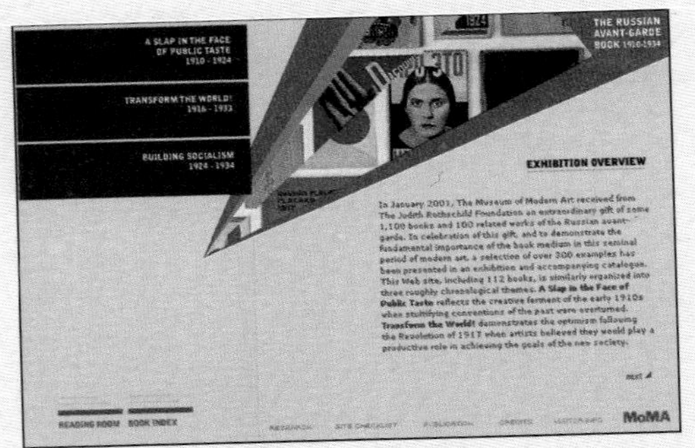

MOMA: The Russian Avant-Garde Book 1910-1934: Vivid illustrations and scholarly text, combined in careful proportions, explain an era.

THE COLLECTIVE UNCONSCIOUSNESS PROJECT: Keeping the user disoriented creates the proper state of mind for this database of dreams.

cues and missed opportunities as well.) Full-color illustrations show the site's features in action.

"Spotlight" sidebars between the chapters highlight aspects of Flash sites that require special attention from designers. And "Under the Hood" sidebars in each chapter look at how some of the effects shown here were accomplished in Flash. For each project, we focus on one effect—the one we think is the niftiest, the cleverest use of Flash, or the most useful in a range of applications—and describe how the developers did it. They provide an insight into how top Flash developers work with ActionScript—and a head start on your coding, in case you want to try something similar in your own work. (The original developers have updated their code, as necessary, to bring it up to date for Flash MX.)

Taken together, these features offer inspiration, practical guidelines, and down-to-earth pointers on how to create sites that skillfully carry their users along on the kinds of journeys that are possible only in Flash.

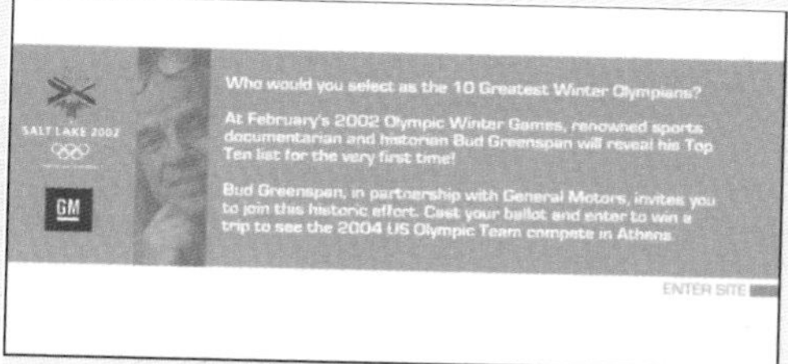
SALT LAKE 2002
GM
Who would you select as the 10 Greatest Winter Olympians?
At February's 2002 Olympic Winter Games, renowned sports documentarian and historian Bud Greenspan will reveal his Top Ten list for the very first time!
Bud Greenspan, in partnership with General Motors, invites you to join this historic effort. Cast your ballot and enter to win a trip to see the 2004 US Olympic Team compete in Athens.
ENTER SITE

BUD GREENSPAN'S TEN GREATEST WINTER OLYMPIANS: An economical and innovative interaction design packs four activities plus all the emotions of the Olympics into three pages.

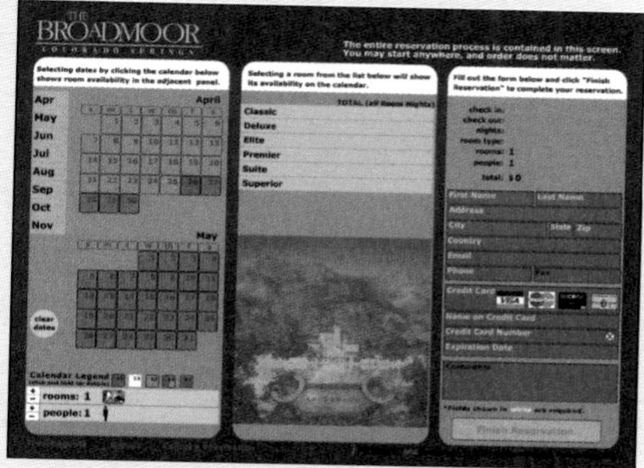
THE BROADMOOR
COLORADO SPRINGS
The entire reservation process is contained in this screen. You may start anywhere, and order does not matter.
Selecting dates by clicking the calendar below shows room availability in the adjacent panel.
Selecting a room from the list below will show its availability on the calendar.
Fill out the form below and click "Finish Reservation" to complete your reservation.
Apr
May
Jun
Jul
Aug
Sep
Oct
Nov
April
May
Classic
Deluxe
Elite
Premier
Suite
Superior
check in:
check out:
nights:
room type:
rooms: 1
people: 1
total: $0
First Name
Last Name
Address
City
State
Zip
Country
Email
Phone
Fax

IHOTELIER ONESCREEN: Hotel bookings become easy when five pages of HTML become one, instantly responsive page of Flash.

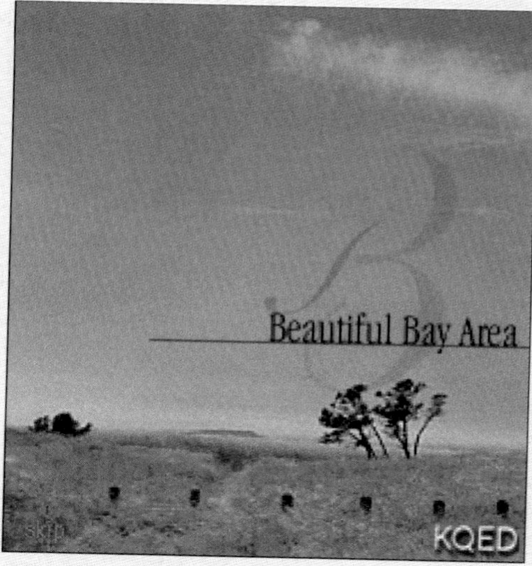
Beautiful Bay Area
skip
KQED

BEAUTIFUL BAY AREA: Repackaging a Web site for a PocketPC handheld computer requires a new look at the interface.

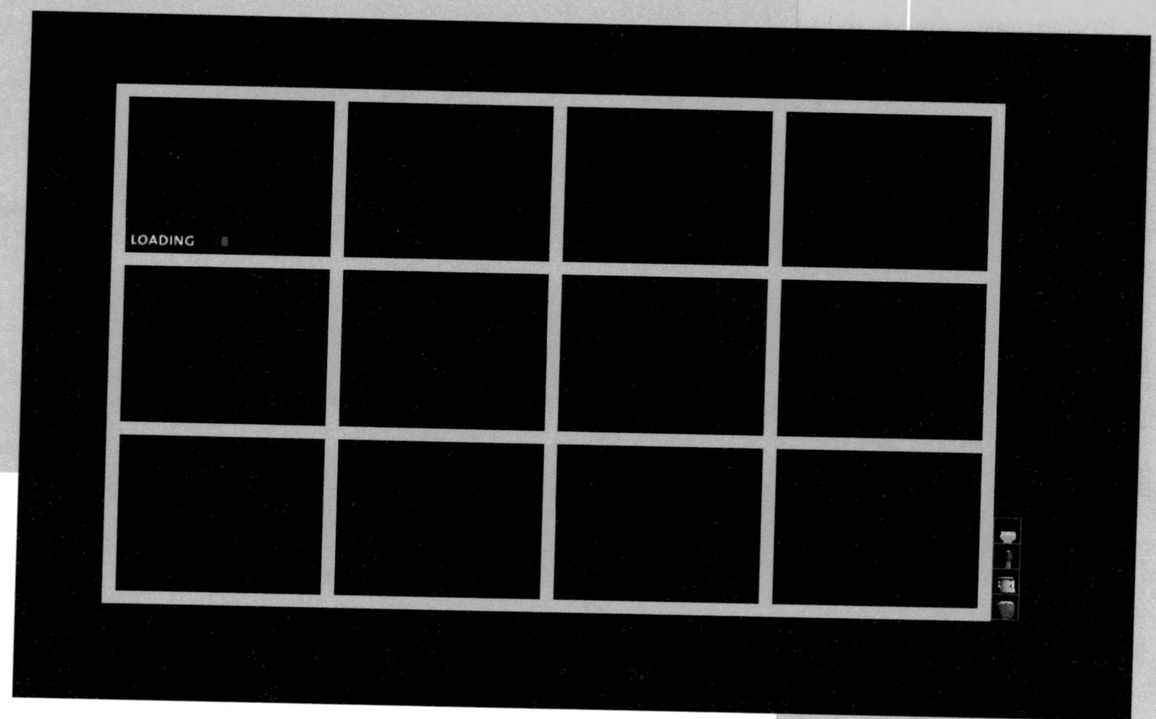

CHAPTER

MINI USA

EURO RSCG CIRCLE

DESIGN: Euro RSCG Circle
CLIENT: BMW
URL: www.miniusa.com

ASSOCIATE CREATIVE DIRECTOR: Birch Norton
FLASH DESIGNER AND PROGRAMMER: Nat Wales
ART DIRECTOR: Jamie Bakum

CHAPTER

MINI USA

INTRO

How do you make a Web site "motor"? Euro RSCG Circle created a site for BMW's new MINI Cooper that features fast acceleration, quick turns, and a sense of adventure—all in an interface that speaks of intelligent engineering.

Pictured: (from left) Sister Jamie Bakum, Nat "Chicken Leg" Wales, Birch Norton the Really, Really Awful

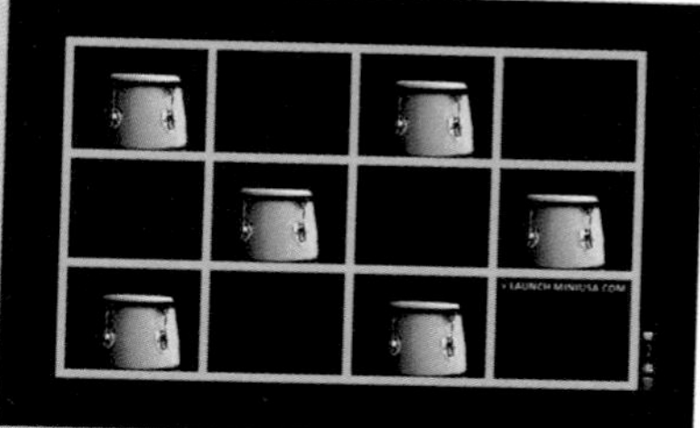

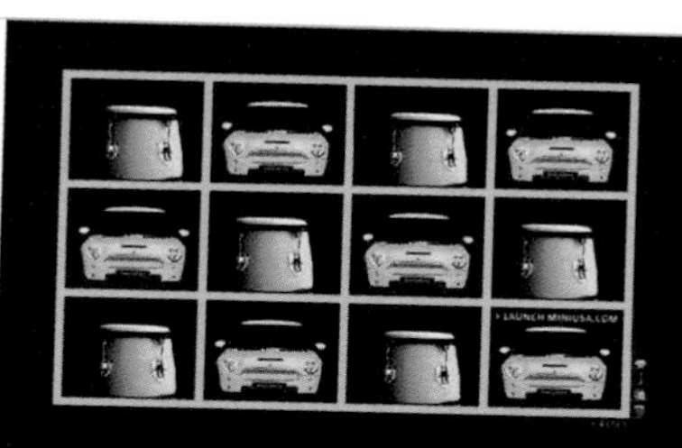

The first screen to appear starts the fun with a quick game. Rolling over the images produces a startling animation and sound effect (a drum-roll for the drums, a "pow-pow" for the boxing gloves). Clicking an image brings up the matching cars. The effect establishes the site as a place to have fun and to expect the unexpected. It also associates the cars with other graphic, fun objects. The page is based on a poster campaign by MINI's agency, Crispin, Porter + Bogusky, brought to life with Flash's multimedia effects.

Most people have only seen the Mini Cooper in cool old English films from the '60s. Maybe, once in a while, you'll see one rolling down a big city's street as some collector's retro-chic ride. The car's tiny size and hip mystique won it legions of fans, but Minis hadn't been sold in the United States since 1968. When BMW decided to reintroduce the car (now to be called the MINI) in America for the new millennium, it announced its plans far in advance of the car's actual introduction. To keep the MINI in the public eye during the interim, BMW approached Euro RSCG Circle, an international digital-marketing firm (www.circle.com), to build a Web site that would not only offer information about the car and how to get it, but build on the MINI mystique.

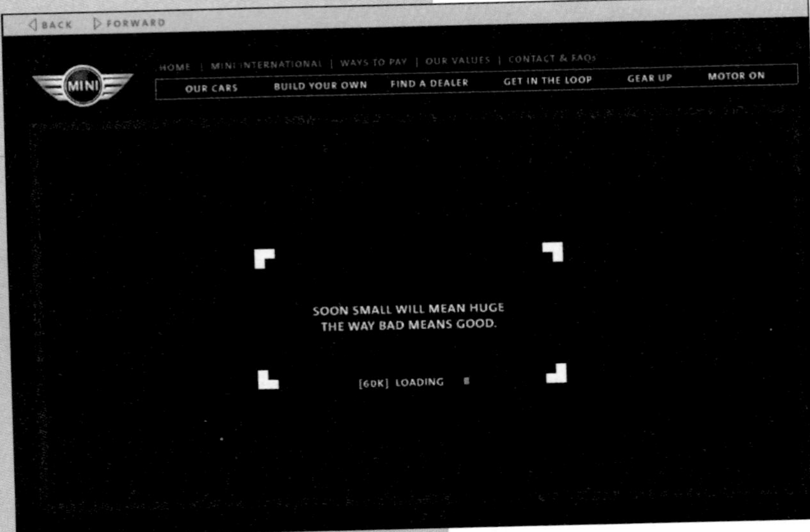

Launching the site opens a new window. More attitude is displayed in the messages that pop up as the site loads (along with a considerate note about the size of the file you're waiting for).

The site's graphic branding, based on strong outlines, is established in a lively way as the boxes are drawn with carefully paced animation.

The MINI home page is fairly traditional. The primary navigation elements occupy a box at the top of the screen, with secondary destinations listed above. The main portion of the screen offers a glamour shot of the car and introduces its slogan, "Let's Motor," as well as providing space for timely promotions. The fun tone is hinted at in the writing and in some unexpected action: The subline ("Let's remember...") moves with your pointer.

> The MINI Brand

Since MINI's ad agency, Crispin, Porter + Bogusky (CP+B), had masterminded the new MINI's initial launch, and Interbrand Zintzmeyer & Lux München had developed the MINI's corporate identity, Circle wasn't exactly starting from scratch on the Web site. Interbrand had already established a strong graphic identity for the MINI, using bold outlines to surround all content, and CP+B had come up with the slogan "Let's Motor" for the car's launch. In addition, the ad agency had created several catchphrases and images to define just what motoring was all about—for example, "Let's remember that automobiles were invented to advance civilization" and "Take a left turn when you're supposed to go right." Circle's job was to extend that brand into the MINI Web site.

> Choosing Flash

"If there was a software equivalent to the MINI, it would be Flash," says Birch Norton, the project's creative lead at Circle's Boston office. "It can be incredibly quick and let you do things that you think would take a lot more money." For a site focused on branding, like MINI's, Norton felt that Macromedia Flash was essential. "If a brand can be encapsulated by music, with pacing and tone and stuff, you can do the same thing in Flash. In HTML you can play with design and content. But with Flash, you can play with the emotion, too."

Making the site universally accessible wasn't a top priority for MINI, Birch says. "MINI would say themselves that the car is not for everyone. It's for people who aren't afraid of technology and who appreciate good design. And those people would probably already have the Flash plug-in."

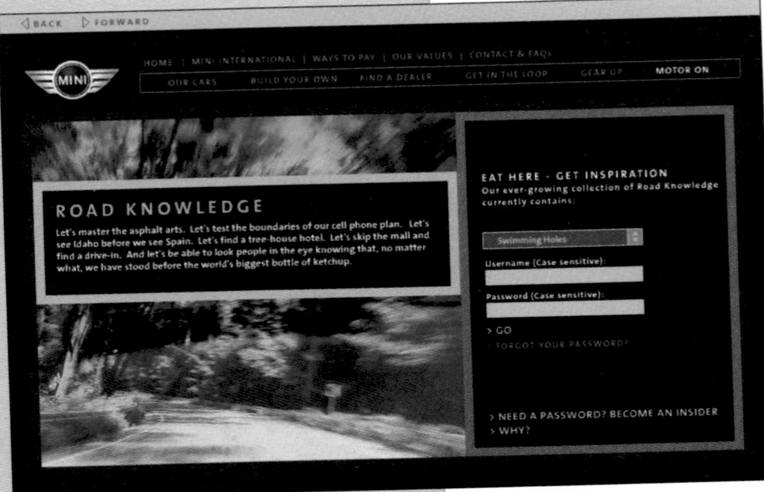
BACK
FORWARD
HOME | MINI INTERNATIONAL | WAYS TO PAY | OUR VALUES | CONTACT & FAQs
OUR CARS
BUILD YOUR OWN
FIND A DEALER
GET IN THE LOOP
GEAR UP
MOTOR ON
MINI
ROAD KNOWLEDGE
Let's master the asphalt arts. Let's test the boundaries of our cell phone plan. Let's see Idaho before we see Spain. Let's find a tree-house hotel. Let's skip the mall and find a drive-in. And let's be able to look people in the eye knowing that, no matter what, we have stood before the world's biggest bottle of ketchup.
EAT HERE - GET INSPIRATION
Our ever-growing collection of Road Knowledge currently contains:
Swimming Holes
Username (Case sensitive):
Password (Case sensitive):
> GO
FORGOT YOUR PASSWORD?
> NEED A PASSWORD? BECOME AN INSIDER
> WHY?

BACK
FORWARD
HOME | MINI INTERNATIONAL | WAYS TO PAY | OUR VALUES | CONTACT & FAQs
OUR CARS
BUILD YOUR OWN
FIND A DEALER
GET IN THE LOOP
GEAR UP
MOTOR ON
MINI
1957 A STAR IS BORN
Sir Leonard Lord's challenge falls to Alec Issigonis, designer of the Morris Minor. His self-appointed goal: a fuel efficient car capable of carrying four adults, within economic reach of just about anyone.
<<<< Click and drag the Mini to navigate throught the timeline...

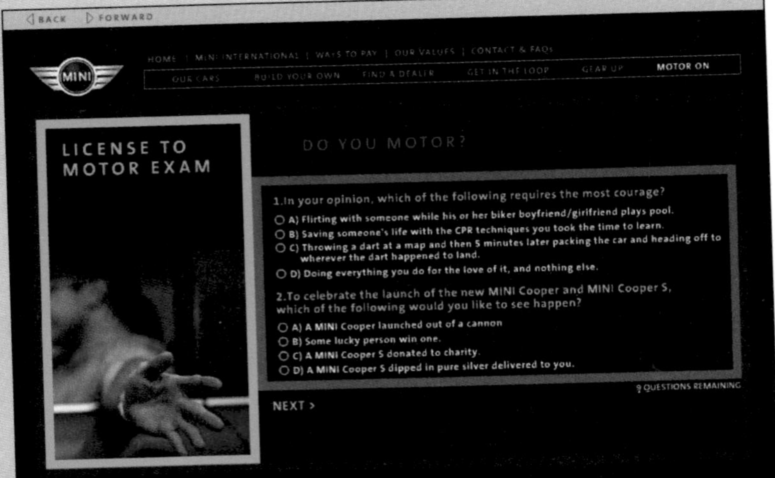
BACK
FORWARD
HOME | MINI INTERNATIONAL | WAYS TO PAY | OUR VALUES | CONTACT & FAQs
OUR CARS
BUILD YOUR OWN
FIND A DEALER
GET IN THE LOOP
GEAR UP
MOTOR ON
MINI
LICENSE TO MOTOR EXAM
DO YOU MOTOR?
1.In your opinion, which of the following requires the most courage?
A) Flirting with someone while his or her biker boyfriend/girlfriend plays pool.
B) Saving someone's life with the CPR techniques you took the time to learn.
C) Throwing a dart at a map and then 5 minutes later packing the car and heading off to wherever the dart happened to land.
D) Doing everything you do for the love of it, and nothing else.
2.To celebrate the launch of the new MINI Cooper and MINI Cooper S, which of the following would you like to see happen?
A) A MINI Cooper launched out of a cannon
B) Some lucky person win one.
C) A MINI Cooper S donated to charity.
D) A MINI Cooper S dipped in pure silver delivered to you.
9 QUESTIONS REMAINING
NEXT >

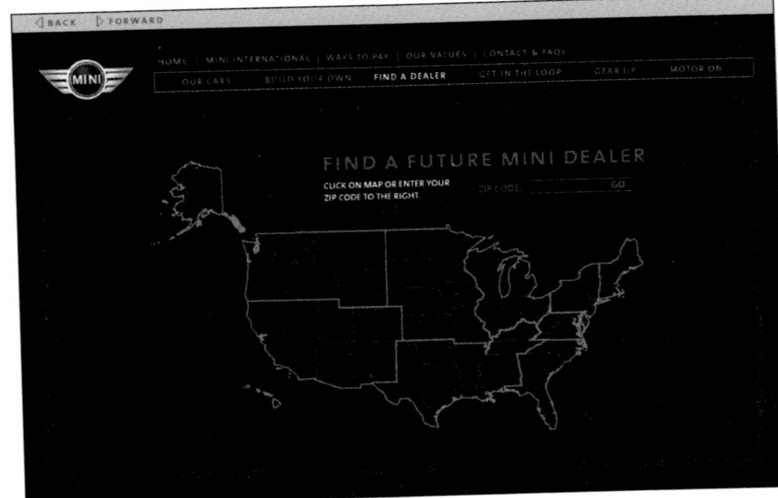
BACK
FORWARD
HOME | MINI INTERNATIONAL | WAYS TO PAY | OUR VALUES | CONTACT & FAQs
OUR CARS
BUILD YOUR OWN
FIND A DEALER
GET IN THE LOOP
GEAR UP
MOTOR ON
MINI
FIND A FUTURE MINI DEALER
CLICK ON MAP OR ENTER YOUR ZIP CODE TO THE RIGHT.
ZIP CODE:
GO

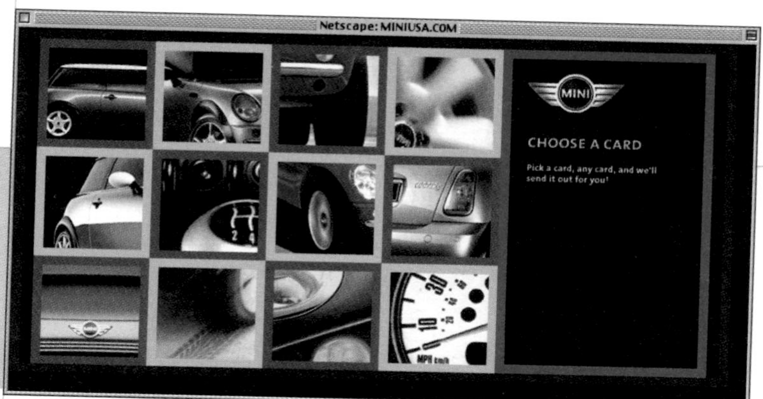
Netscape: MINIUSA.COM
MINI
CHOOSE A CARD
Pick a card, any card, and we'll send it out for you!

A selection of section openers shows how the Circle team used MINI's graphic standards to create fairly straightforward, simple pages. Custom interfaces for sections such as the Timeline (facing page, top right), the eCard creator (above), and the Dealer Finder (facing page, bottom right) impress with their elegant, well-thought-out interfaces.

> How Far to Go?

The Circle team started the design process by looking for ways to give the site the attributes associated with the car it described: "It's an icon for personality, charisma, character, cheekiness—a bit of a bulldog," says Norton. "It's fun, tight-handling. It's not about speed, it's about being nimble."

"On the Web site, we wanted to give people the feeling that they could just hop in and drive. As the site's copy says, take a left turn when you're supposed to go right. And when you're 'motoring,' sometimes getting lost is a fantastic thing," says Norton. After some consideration, the team decided not to take that last idea too far. Says Norton, "We were thinking, 'Do we actually get people lost on the site?'" Eventually they backed away from the concept because of the newness of the brand: "In the beginning, we thought we'd better keep it pretty straightforward," he says.

The Web site also had to strike the right balance between fun and the information suitable to a car site. "In the end, people don't come here for entertainment, they come here for information," says Norton. The challenge, then, was to find a way to make the site fun without making it silly or getting in people's way.

The result is a Web site that's remarkable for its clean, intelligent, and finely tuned interface—yet still manages to delight users.

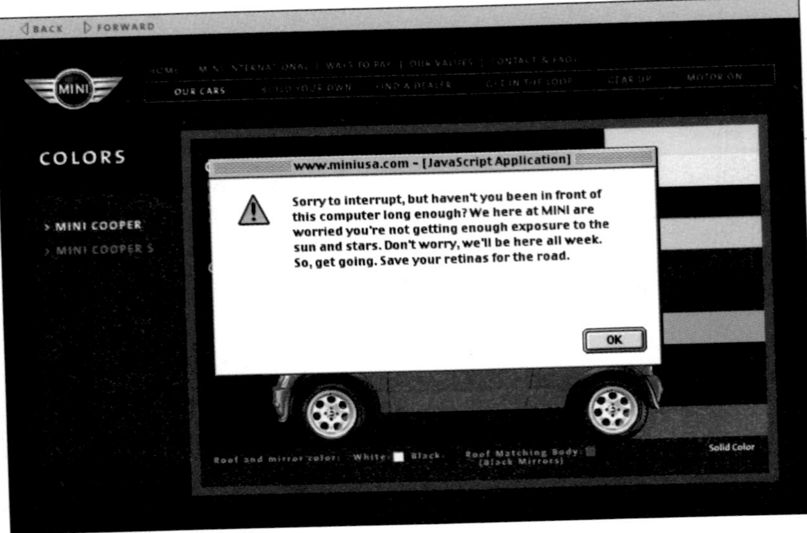

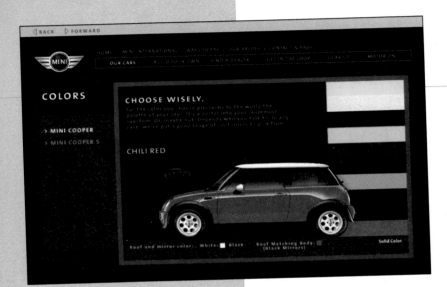

"Embedded motoring moments" surprise visitors at unexpected intervals. The arrival of the helicopter (left) is announced by its sound. Then it swoops across your screen and back again, where it hovers until you click it: It then displays a message telling you that the MINI shares technology with Blackhawk copters.

The error message (right) pops up after you've been on the site for several minutes.

> The Medium Is the Message

Circle found surprising ways for the Web site to embody the MINI brand, one of which was the pace of the animation. On the site, screens are built element by element: As each screen loads, blocky dots flash, then fly into position to establish the corners of the prescribed content boxes. As the blocks extend into lines, expand, and finally find their final shape, other boxes are drawn in similar fashion and filled in, with quick choreography that—surprise!—feels like the movement of a fast-cornering car. The moving elements decelerate smoothly as they reach their position on screen. The animations resolve into straightforward gridded pages, but the brand message has been subtly planted: quick, smooth, and clever. And it all happens too fast to be annoying.

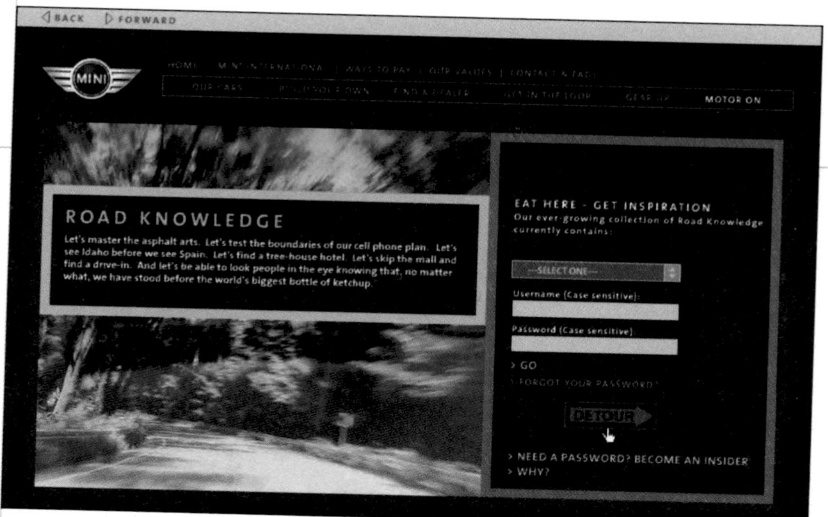

More unexpected touches. The detour sign (above) doesn't appear until you mouse over it. When you click it, it opens a window onto a site explaining a project that uses pigs to control traffic lights in Europe.

> Motoring Moments

Circle found another way to inject fun without causing delays by using what the team calls "embedded motoring moments." These are surprises that turn up while users are going about their information-finding business on the site.

The Circle team brainstormed a long list of possible moments, then decided where to place them on the site. They were helped by the corporate identity guidelines, which specified framed content. "With all the content boxed up like that, it's easy to have things happen in the boxes," says Norton. And if the boxes are the same size, you could have the same things happen anywhere on the site."

The list of "motoring moments" includes randomly placed items like hidden detour buttons ("Detour" road signs that appear only when the user's pointer is over their position on the page and that, when clicked, take users to an unexpected location on the Web); surprising effects in the feature descriptions (for example, a lightning flash when you click the description of the automatically activated windshield wipers); and an error message that pops up after you've spent awhile on the site, asking whether you don't have something better to do.

Norton says the team considered adding a hint page, providing clues to where viewers could find the motoring moments, but in the end decided to leave it to chance. Again, a subtle message: nonchalant cool.

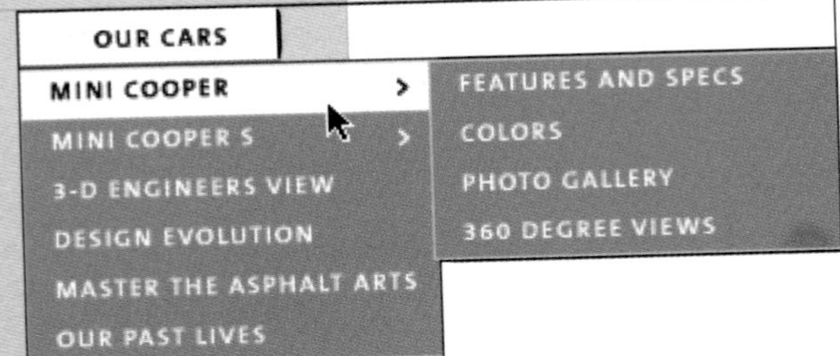

The Our Cars section of the site offers a multitude of ways to find out about and dig into the MINI Cooper's features.

A handful of the hottest features are displayed as the balance of the Features and Specs section loads (right). When the section has finished loading, the copy cleverly changes to "Fully Loaded" and offers you a choice of views.

In the detail views (facing page, top), rolling over a spot pops up a label for the feature. Clicking the feature dot opens a window with more information (facing page, bottom).

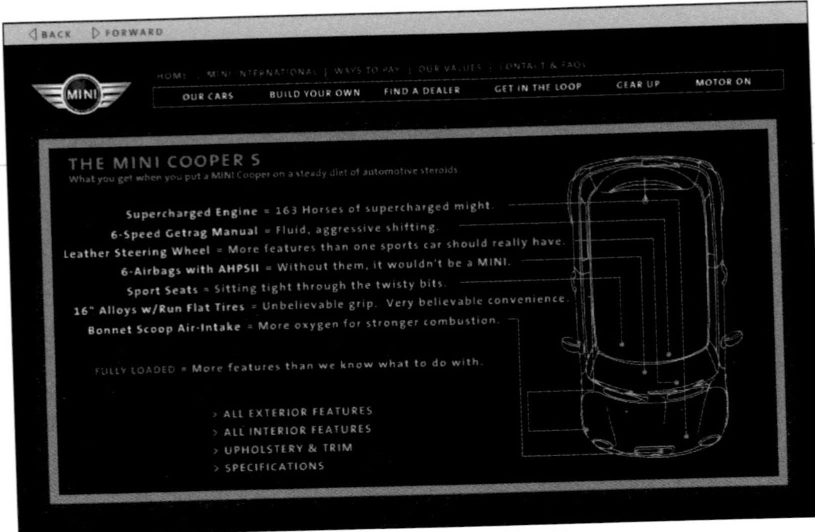

> Features and Specs

The heart of the site is Features and Specs, the first item in the Our Cars section. Here, visitors are invited to explore nearly 100 individual features of the two models: the Cooper and the Cooper S. Each feature is named in a callout. Click the feature name, and a box opens with more information.

"This section is all about these little stories," says Norton. "Why does this part exist? Why is the speedometer mounted in the middle of the dash?" To focus on the details rather than the car's overall appearance, the autos are presented in outline drawings.

The sheer number of callouts is almost overwhelming. When you see the detail offered in every box—complete with interactive elements, graphics, and motoring moments—you begin to understand the astonishing amount of work that went into this section. Norton knows that people probably won't make it through every feature, "but that's OK," he says. "The message here is that there are a lot of features."

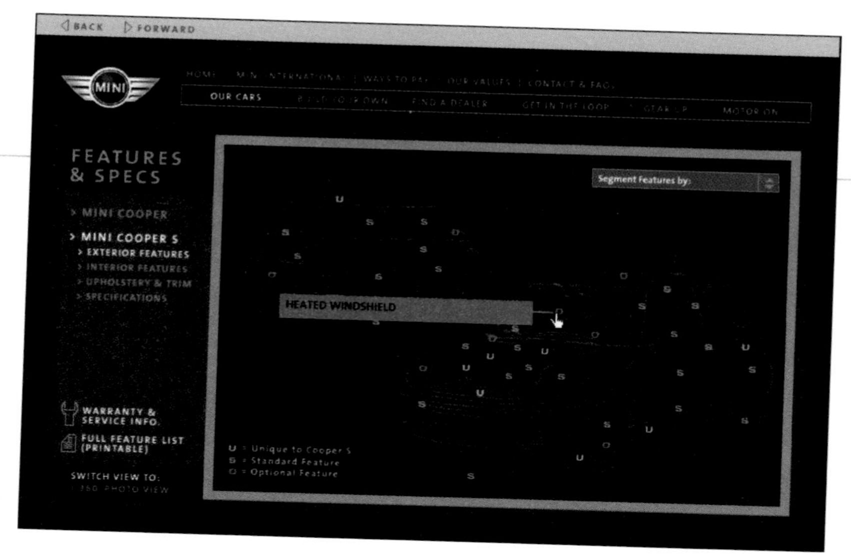

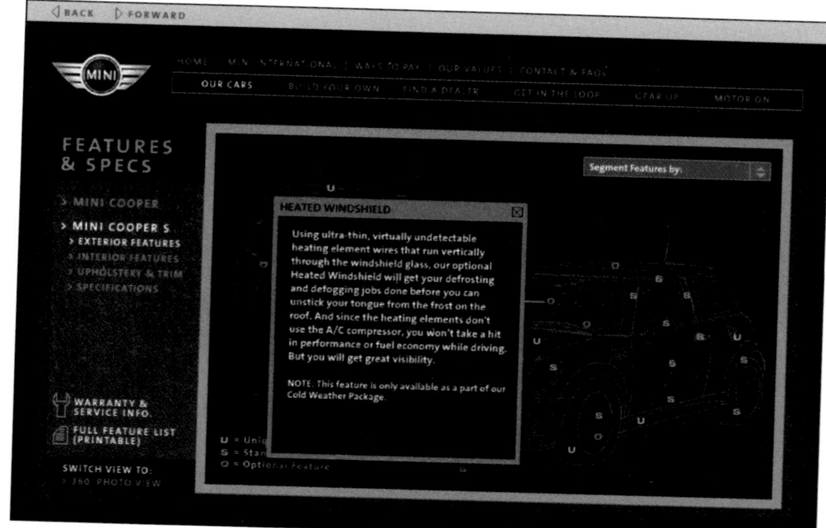

For the impatient, a summary feature list is available, and a pull-down menu lets visitors view features by category (Safety, Performance, and so on). The hoped-for interaction is that visitors will keep discovering new details as they visit the site again and again. Remember, MINI launched the site long before the actual car, and part of the strategy was to keep potential buyers interested during the waiting period.

"There are cool features here that people won't learn about for six months," says Norton. "That's good. When people think they have the full story, and then they find out there's more, that's what we want." Mere volume, however, isn't enough to keep people interested. The text has to offer real information. "If you clicked on one or two or three links and just found fluff, you wouldn't go through any more," Norton explains. "You would think, 'Oh, they're just babbling.'" Here, as throughout the site, the copy upholds the brand, dishing out information in short, pointed paragraphs that are enlivened by snappy verbs and a few surprises.

Nat Wales, the team's Flash programmer, says that the challenges in this section had more to do with organization than technology. Each window is a reused movie clip with variables that describe its position and how it opens. Wales gave each piece of content its own ID, which the movie clip then uses to call it. All of the information in the windows was saved in Flash. "It's as easy to change SWFs as it is to change entries in a database," says Wales.

Circle is proud that the Build Your Own section takes into account all the rules that go into configuring a car with a combination of features that is actually available. As you go through the four steps of building your MINI, the feature list builds in the right-hand frame, along with the total cost.

> The Configurator

The Circle team is especially proud of the Build Your Own section, which they refer to as the "Configurator." "We were able to condense what might be 40 steps into just a few pages," Norton boasts.

At 270 K, this section is one of the slowest to load, but Norton says the trade-off is worth it. "You have to sit and wait for the 270 K, but if it were HTML, you'd wait 15 seconds for each page." The size here comes from layers of images, he explains. "We wanted to show what you were actually getting." (And because the cars weren't in production yet, the upholstery and other details in all those images had to be mocked up in Adobe Photoshop.)

"The hard part of this was that you had all sorts of rules: If you order this, you can't get that, and if you order a package, it's added in a different way," says Wales. Each item has four states—selected, deselected, part of a package, or disabled. The developers needed to know what state each item should be in depending on the state of several other options. Otherwise, they'd run the risk of doing what Norton says he's seen other auto sites do: give viewers the ability to configure cars they can't actually buy.

Again, Wales says the secret of the MINI site's success was its crafty architecture, which the team completed before coding began. "We had all the rules in an Excel file, and we sorted everything out before we started building it."

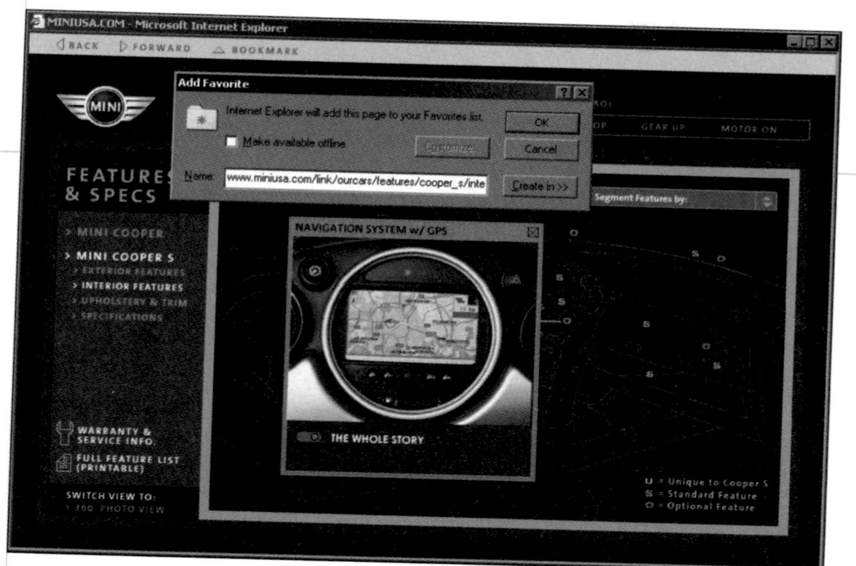

Back and Forward buttons and the ability to bookmark pages aren't common on Flash sites. They not only allow users extra navigation features, but also give MINI the ability to send people directly to one of the site's sections from other marketing materials such as emails.

> Deep Linking

The site's navigability is boosted by a feature that most users won't find remarkable, though Flash developers may. Although Back and Forward buttons are commonly available on the Web, they're not on Flash sites. On a computer using Microsoft Internet Explorer, you can even bookmark individual sections (a JavaScript feature not available on other platforms). Although the site is a single Flash movie, Wales did some tricky programming to allow users to access different sections of the movie as if they were separate pages. He created identifiers for each section that act like Web-page URLs (but that he calls "nodes"). A section identifier can be appended to the movie URL when it's loaded. Then, each clip is responsible for calling the proper node beneath it, passing the variables down the tree structure until the proper section is found. By using a global link function that calls on the node identifiers, the site is able to track the viewer's every move—which is necessary in order to have functioning Back and Forward buttons.

The Back and Forward buttons still don't work exactly like they do in a browser—after all, there's still no "page" here—but at least they give users the option of going directly to the last section viewed or to the beginning of the current section without navigating the movie from the beginning. As for the buttons' limitations, Norton is philosophical: "It's better to have buttons that kind of work in Flash than none at all."

UNDER THE HOOD
DEEP LINKING IN FLASH

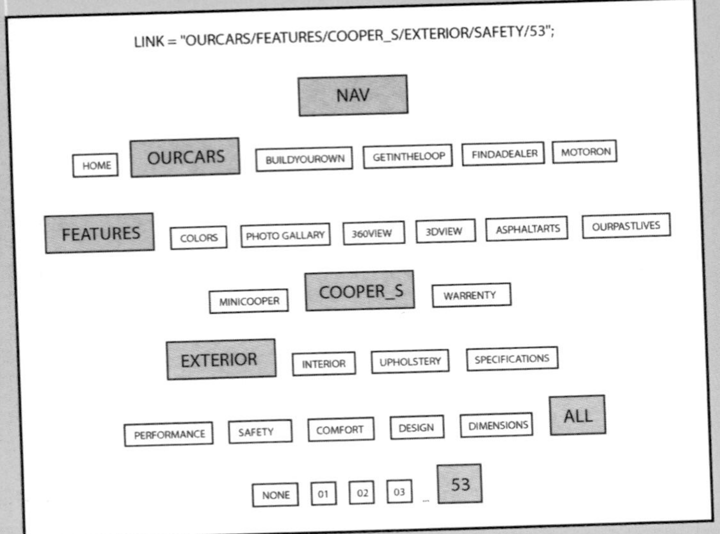

Figure 1
The MINI USA identifiers use levels of the site's hierarchy as in the directory structure of a standard URL. This figure shows the point on the site referred to by the identifier ourcars/features/cooper_s/exterior/safety/53.

```
//sets global link variable to the passed parameter.
_global.gGotoLink = function(urlstring) {

    gLink = urlstring;
    gParseLink();
    var targetclip = gCompareLink();
    eval(targetclip).linkAction();
}
```

Figure 2
The `gGotoLink` function manages links from inside the movie (as opposed to calls that go through the server). The `gCompareLink` function is used by `gHistory` (Figure 6).

The MINI USA site combines the fluid interaction of a Flash site with the random-access benefits of HTML. The ability to link from outside the site to specific content inside it, to track the level of interest in different pieces of content, and to move back and forth through just-viewed content without starting over from the home page are unusual in Flash, and the Circle team had to create a special movie structure and special programming to achieve it.

HTML has the above-described capabilities because each piece of content has its own URL. To make the Flash-driven MINI site work the same way, Circle implemented its own system of URL-style identifiers for the site. The MINI USA identifiers refer not to a directory structure on a server but to the site's internal hierarchy (**Figure 1**). To call up specific content from outside the site, the identifier would be appended to the minusa.com URL and called via the `SRC=` parameter in the HTML `<EMBED>` tag. For example, to bring up Feature 53 in the MINI Cooper S's exterior safety features, the `SRC=` URL would look like this: `http://www.miniusa.com/link/ourcars/features/cooper_s/exterior/safety/53`.

In the MINI USA system, this assigns the value `/ourcars/features/cooper_s/exterior/safety/53` to a global `gLink` variable. (A Java servlet parses the URL and passes the value from external links. A global `gGotoLink` function [**Figure 2**] does the same for links from inside the movie.) When the `gLink` changes, a `gParseLink` function (**Figure 3**) turns the parts of the `gLink` path into an array called `gLinkArray`. For example, the above identifier would result in a `gLinkArray` value with six parts: `ourcars`, `features`, `cooper_s`, `exterior`, `safety`, and `53`.

```
_global.gParseLink = function() {
    //removes an extra slash at the beginning
    var myLastChar = gLink.length - 1;
    if (gLink.charAt(0) == "/") {
        gLink = gLink.slice(1);
    }
        //removes an extra slash at the end
    var myLastChar = gLink.length - 1;
    if (gLink.charAt(myLastChar) == "/") {
        gLink = gLink.slice(0,myLastChar);
    }
    //splits link variable into new array.
    gLinkArray = gLink.split("/");
}
```

Figure 3

The `gParseLink` function turns the section identifier stored in `gLink` into an array that can be accessed by other functions.

```
linkAction = function() {
//pass GetNode method possible sections
var mynode = GetNode("minicooper","minicoopers","warranty");
//loads a swf with same node name into a place holder movie clip.
loadMovie(mynode + ".swf","content_mc");
}
```

Figure 4

The `linkAction` function, used in the movie wherever different paths are possible, employs the `GetNode` function (described in Figure 3) to check an array (`gLinkArray`) that holds the new node request. If `gLinkArray` holds one of that section's options, the `linkArray` executes an action, such as loading a new movie (as shown here) or going to a new frame.

```
MovieClip.prototype.GetNode = function(){
    //loop through linkArray
    for (var l = 0; l < gLinkArray.length; l++) {
        //for each item in link array... loop through arguments
        for (var a = 0; a < arguments.length; a++) {
            //if linkArray and arrgument are equal..
            if (gLinkArray[l] == arguments[a]) {
                //will set target path at same node as the link in link array.
                gNodeTarget[l] = targetPath(this);
                //if this is the last node in the link array then update history
            var linkLastIndex = gLinkArray.length - 1;
                if(l == linkLastIndex) {
                    gUpdateHistory();
                }
                //returns value of node found in link array.
                return arguments[a];
            }

        }
    }
}
```

Figure 5

The `GetNode` method, used by `linkAction` to check `gLinkArray`, is defined as a method of the MovieClip class in the movie's first frame. (According to Nat Wales, Circle's programmer, defining it as a global function had unexpected results on the scope of the `targetPath`.) In addition to returning the value of the matching node to the statement that invoked `linkAction`, the `GetNode` method updates two other variables: `gHistory` (used in `gUpdateHistory`, Figure 6) and `gNodeTarget` (used in `gCompareLink`, Figure 7).

```
_global.gUpdateHistory = function() {
   if(gHistoryAction) { //bypass History update when using browser control
      gHistoryAction = false;
   }else { //updating history for non browser control navigation.
         //chop off everything after current position in History Array
         var nextentry = gHistoryPosition+1;
         gHistory.splice(nextentry);
         //next entry added to history array
         gHistory.push(gLinkArray);
         // set HistoryPosition = last index of History array.
         gHistoryPosition = gHistory.length - 1;
   }
   //reset gLink to reflect new array. This is also where tracking info would be sent.
   gLink = gHistory[gHistoryPosition].join("/");
}


   _global.gHistoryStep = function(direction) {
   //Steps through history according to parameter. ("back" or "forward").

   if(direction == "back") {
      if(gHistoryPosition != 0) {
         //sers new value of gLinkArray
         gLinkArray = gHistory[gHistoryPosition - 1];
         // determine path to node
         var targetclip = gCompareLink();
         //reduce history position
         gHistoryPosition--;
         //set Hisoty action to true to disable gHistoryUpdate
         gHistoryAction = true;
         //reset node according to result of targetclip.
         eval(targetclip).linkAction();
      }
   }else if (direction == "forward") {
      if(gHistoryPosition != gHistory.length -1) {
         gLinkArray = gHistory[gHistoryPosition + 1];
         var targetclip = gCompareLink();
         gHistoryPosition++;
         gHistoryAction = true;
         eval(targetclip).linkAction();
      }
```

Figure 6

The `gUpdateHistory` function updates the `gHistory` variable, keeping an up-to-date log of the user's path through the movie. The `gHistoryPosition` variable, used by the Back and Forward buttons, records the current position in the `gHistory` array. A final function, `gHistoryStep()`, accepts `"back"` or `"forward"` as arguments and steps through the `gHistory` accordingly, referring to `gHistoryPosition`. The `gHistoryAction` variable ensures that the action of stepping through the history by Flash itself will not be recorded in the `gHistory` array.

```
//this function retrieves the appropriate target path for the node that needs to be reset.
_global.gCompareLink = function (){

    //check each array and find first array position at which they do not match...
    var currentLinkArray = gHistory[gHistoryPosition];
    for(var l = 0; l < currentLinkArray.length; l++) {
        //when they don't match...
        if(gLinkArray[l] != CurrentLinkArray[l]) {
            //set thePath = to the TargetPath for that same node.
            return(gNodeTarget[l]);
            //clear invalid nodes in gNodeTarget
            gNodeTarget.splice(l);
            }
    }
}
```

Figure 7

The gCompareLink function is called by gGotoLink (Figure 2) to pinpoint exactly where the new path (stored in gLinkArray) differs from the last (stored in gHistory), so that the section only rebuilds from the point at which the two paths differ.

Every point in the movie where a number of paths are possible includes a linkAction function (**Figure 4**), which uses a method called GetNode (**Figure 5**) to check whether the values in gLinkArray match any of GetNode's own possible paths. If they do, linkAction tells Flash what to do with the information (usually a gotoFrame or loadMovie action).

Another set of global variables and functions (**Figure 6**) create, update, and check a gHistory array, which is used to control the movie's action when a Back or Forward button is clicked, as well as to track user paths through the site. The gUpdateHistory function, called by GetNode, updates the gHistory array each time the user selects a new section of the site.

The MX code used here has almost exactly the same functionality as the Flash 4 code used to create the original site, though the coding and the memory use are more efficient in MX. One difference in behavior is capitalized on by the gCompareLink function (**Figure 7**). In Flash 4, the movie had to rebuild an entire section to reach an embedded node. In contrast, the gCompareLink function, called by gGotoLink (Figure 2), compares a new value of gLinkArray with gHistory to find out where the first difference in the path occurs, and then rebuilds only from that point for cleaner, faster switches between sections.

NAVSTATE:
ourcars
NUMOFSECTIONS:
34
WHATTODO:
timeline
lINK:
null
CANBOOKMARK:
false
PLATFORM:
MAC
FEATUREVISIT:
FEATURELINK:
false
OPENEDFEATUREWINDOW:
true
CURRENT NODE:
ourpastlives/timeline
BACKACTION:
0
BACKNUM:
7
BACK1:
home
BACK2:
ourcars/features/cool
BACK3:
ourcars/features/cool
BACK4:
ourcars/performance
BACK5:
thevaluesection/ourv
NUMOFSTEPSFORWARD:
0
MAC 5,0,41,0
17
34
DISPLAY VAR:
GO

A debugger, which can be called up from any screen on the site if you know where to click, shows the variables currently in use. (This screen shows the variables from an instance of the Timeline.) The entries in the center column show how the deep linking works. The variables labeled in blue are those the programmers set in Flash. Orange codes the variables used for the Features section. Red identifies the user's machine; in the future, they might be used to fine-tune the user's experience with movies appropriate to the user's machine and connection speed. The Display Variable section allows the programmer to test different variables by typing them there.

This setup offers advantages for the site's owners as well as its users. Part of MINI's marketing plan was to send emails to registered users. The ability to call different parts of the site made it possible to send people directly to specific information from those emails. "If we send out an email that talks about windshield wipers, we can send out a URL that sends them to Features and Specs with the windshield wipers window open," says Norton.

It also allows MINI to figure out where people are going on the site—a "tracking" function—again common in HTML but not in Flash movies. By seeing what items are called, the carmaker can figure out, for instance, what options and colors are drawing the most interest.

> Sound Decisions

Sound is used minimally on the MINI site. Subtle clicks signal a user's choices from a menu. Bouncy music plays for a couple of seconds as sections load, and appropriate sounds accompany a few of the motoring moments (the helicopter blades, thunder with the lightning flash). Norton is a bit sheepish about the dearth of sound. "The sound effects aren't an afterthought, but they are the last thing on the priority list," he says. "I think the sound could be a little bit richer." Even the spot sounds used for interaction feedback could be better developed, he says.

According to Norton, the team may offer options for a site sound track in the future. Currently, though, the sounds are used primarily for humor and brand. His favorite bit? The tension-building James Bond–type sound you hear when you click Contacts—what Norton calls "the most boring thing on the site."

> Fine-Tuning

Prior to launching the site, the Circle team rounded up ten people to put it through its paces: Two were from MINI enthusiast clubs, four were simply car shoppers, and another four generally fit MINI's target demographic—though just what defines that demographic is hard to say, according to Norton. MINI is not just going after youngsters looking for an inexpensive, hip car. The company recognizes that there's a whole set of older folks who remember the Classic Mini from the 1960s and '70s and who, they hope, will be among the car's early adopters. Norton says the testing recruiters did their best to find "open-minded, free-spirited, tech-savvy people."

During the testing, the brand message was evaluated extensively, yielding encouraging results: People wanted the car. Once this had been determined, the testers ran the sample users through a few tasks: Find out whether the car has air bags. Does it come in green?

The site proved easy enough to navigate, but users were overlooking some of its niftiest features. For example, in the Features and Specs section, they didn't understand that a window with more information would open in response to clicking a feature's name. To make it more clear, the team inserted a few helpful hints.

The team is still fine-tuning the site in response to user feedback. Case in point: I was enchanted by the site and wanted the car—until I took the License to Motor exam and was told not to bother: I wasn't up to the challenge. I was annoyed, and my earlier goodwill began to fade.

The reason for my rebuke? Apparently the Circle team weighted the response to the first question very heavily—which meant that if you didn't get it right, you would be told you weren't ready to motor. I complained, and apparently I'm not the first. The team will be changing the scoring mechanism. ■

HAVE YOU TRIED CLICKING THE MATCHES?
<<<< Click and drag the Mini to navigate through the timeline...
Rollover icons to find features. Click icons for full details.

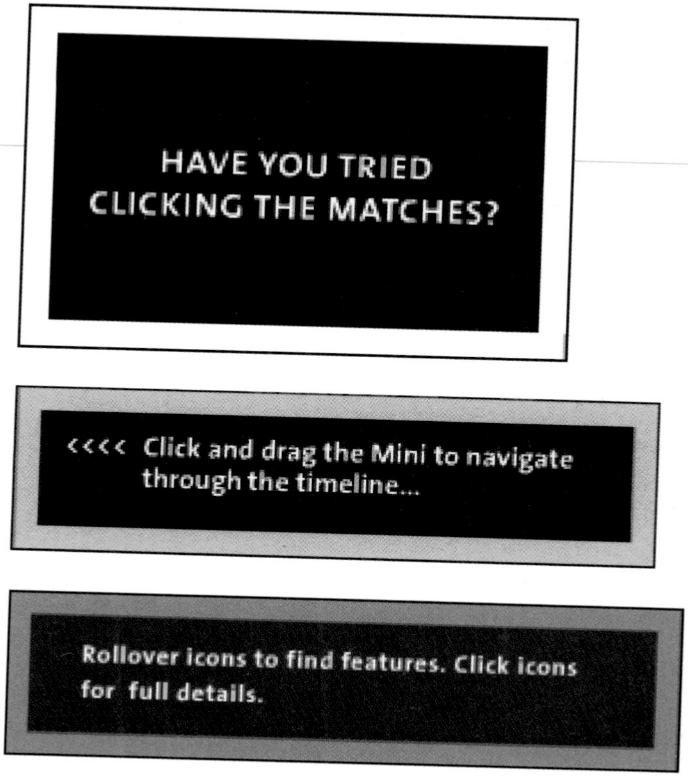

User testing showed that users weren't finding all the features. Pop-up boxes were added to clue them in.

SPOTLIGHT

USER INTERFACE AND BRAND

Companies spend millions of dollars in efforts targeted at creating and reinforcing their *brand*—the image they evoke in the minds of the public. Those efforts can take the form of sponsoring charitable events or being associated with star athletes. A large part of it, though, is honing the combination of words, pictures, and other media that will represent the company, conjuring up a carefully measured mix of associations, impressions, and emotions.

Some company Web sites have the sole purpose of communicating and reinforcing the company's brand. But user interface specialists who have done tests on how different types of content and user experiences affect a user's perception of the company behind a site found that the old ways of communicating and reinforcing a brand don't work on the Web. A study by the usability experts at User Interface Engineering (www.uie.com) found that the words and pictures on a site—the traditional branding tools—had a relatively minor effect on the user's impressions. Much more important was the user's experience interacting with the Web site itself. If users were successful in finding out what they came to find out or doing what they came to do, they thought better of the company. When asked whether they considered the site "fun," the same effect applied. If they achieved what they came to do with the site, they considered the site fun. Colors, animations, images all had little effect on their impression.

The MINI USA site uses all the bells and whistles of traditional brand messaging, but they never stand in the user's path. On this site, the brand is really communicated through the well-engineered, snappy interface.

It makes sense. Traditional media are all about sending a message. Their users are essentially passive, absorbing words, images, music, and other sensory stimuli. The Web, though, is about interaction. Users aren't being told about the company, they're actually experiencing it firsthand, through its Web site. UIE says, "Because the direct experience is so powerful, the effects of indirect messaging can disappear." Someone telling you about someone or something is beside the point when you have actual experience by which to judge it.

The implications of this are important for any Web site, of course, but perhaps even more so for Flash sites. For many designers and their clients, it's tempting to put Flash's capabilities to work enhancing the message with sound, animation, video, and other whizbang effects. You can create the equivalent of a television commercial on the Web. But why waste the time? Users aren't there to see a commercial. If you're a car company, they're there to find out about your cars. If you're a hotel-booking site, they're there to book a hotel room. A lot of excess messaging isn't leading them to that goal, and it's probably getting in their way. The best investment in brand is putting all your effort into getting users to their goals.

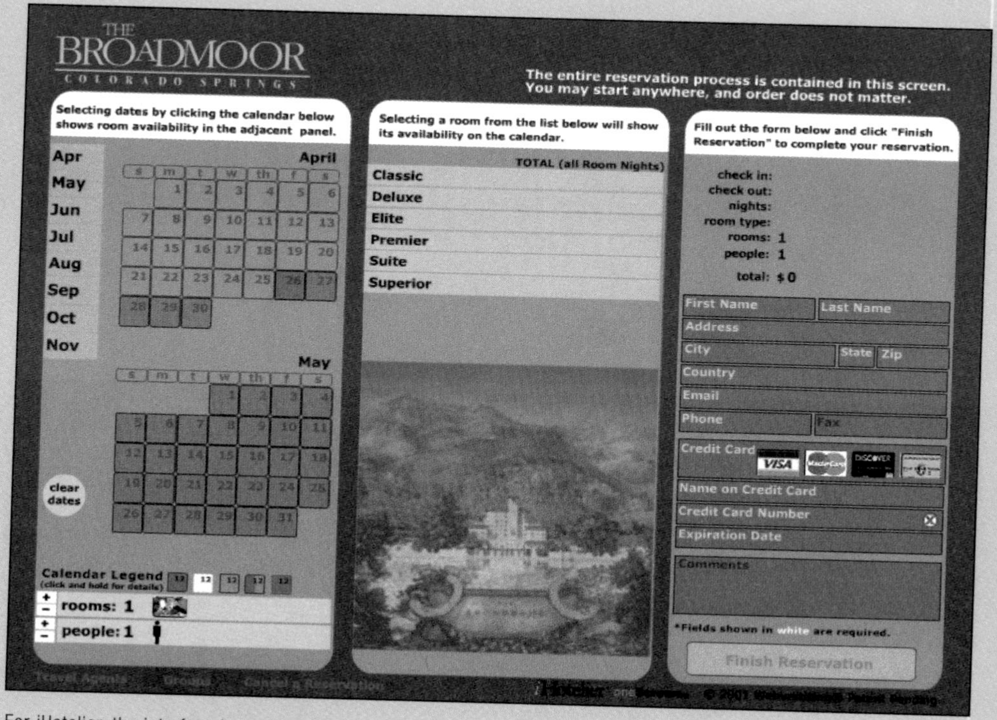

For iHotelier, the interface is the brand. The entire product is sold on its nifty ability to make hotel booking easier. Even its name, OneScreen, refers to its interface design.

CHAPTER

R!OT MANHATTAN

NATZKE & GRIDPLANE
R!OT MANHATTAN
DESIGN: Natzke & Gridplane
CLIENT: R!OT Manhattan
URL: www.riotingmanhattan.com
DESIGN & FLASH PROGRAMMING:
Erik Natzke, JD Hooge
CREATIVE DIRECTOR: Jeremy Hollister
ART DIRECTOR: Judy Wellfare
PRODUCER: Luis Ribeiro
EXECUTIVE PRODUCER, DESIGN & BRANDING: Sari Rosen

CHAPTER

R!OT MANHATTAN

INTRO

In the minimal but surprising design of R!OT Manhattan's Web site, Erik Natzke and JD Hooge applied Flash MX's embedded QuickTime and dynamic drawing features with sophistication.

Pictured: (from left) Erik Natzke, JD Hooge

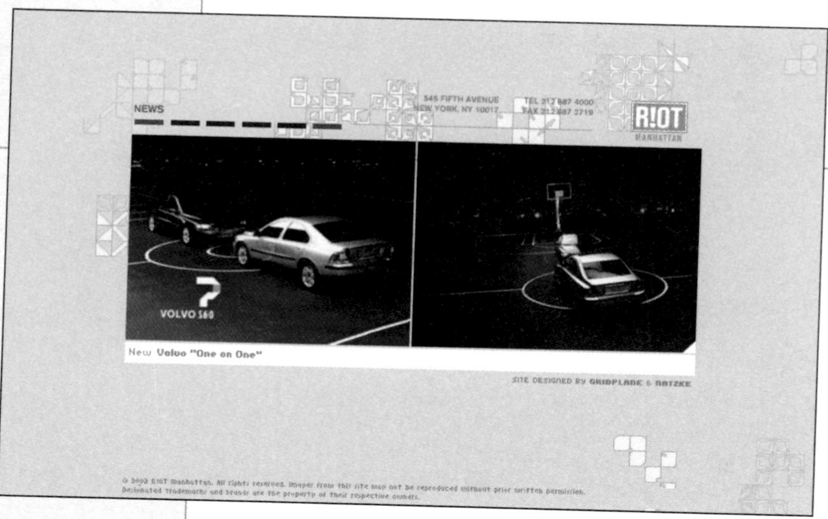

R!OT's home page features its latest client work, plus a dynamic pattern the studio has adopted in its branding program.

After creating a new branding program in early 2002, R!OT Manhattan, a design, visual effects, and editorial finishing studio, needed a new Web site to reflect that brand. Acting on a colleague's recommendation, creative director Jeremy Hollister approached Flash designer Erik Natzke to do the job.

R!OT's goals were fairly simple: In addition to incorporating the new branding graphics, says Hollister, "we wanted a Web site that would act as a gallery to showcase our work," referring to the firm's corpus of commercial and broadcast video. "We wanted to keep the site interesting enough that it was fun to look at, but also keep it simple enough to make the work pop out."

Although Flash MX hadn't been officially released, Natzke, working with a prerelease version of the software, realized that its ability to embed QuickTime video and draw shapes controlled by ActionScript could be just what this client needed. The site he and partner JD Hooge created for R!OT is a stellar example of how these features can effectively advance a site's goals.

Wellfare created rules for using the pattern in different media, such as the print ad shown here. She provided Natzke and Hooge with examples of the pattern's use in works like this to clarify its character.

> Regrowth and Rebuilding

Judy Wellfare, R!OT Manhattan's art director, says the company's redesigned logo graphics were meant to reflect a theme of new growth and rebuilding. They were, she says, a symbol of the direction envisioned for the studio, as well as of the studio's hopes for its hometown of New York after September 11.

The core of the branding system is a complex, abstract pattern that Wellfare describes as "a series of lines that form shapes and tear away from each other, always evolving." It suggests the grid of a city, or building blocks, or new life growing in a Petri dish, or any number of things, depending on the user's own associations. The pattern was designed to work across a variety of media from video and print to the Web. In dynamic media, the pattern becomes an animated cellular system that extends itself in both mathematically controlled and random ways.

R!OT had created the pattern in Adobe AfterEffects and composited and choreographed it with Inferno (a high-end video editing system made by Discreet). Now it was up to Natzke to see what he could make of it in Flash.

R!OT gave Natzke and Hooge the brand rules and style guide, along with samples of the pattern used in different media. Those included a dynamic version used in the studio's show reel, some examples of its use in print, and a set of 33 iterations of the pattern that could be used in an animation. Natzke, a master at turning mathematical constructs into artful Flash animations, set to work with a prerelease copy of Flash MX.

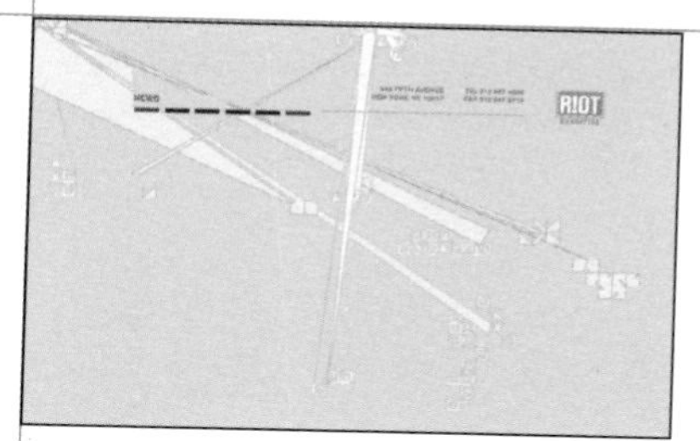

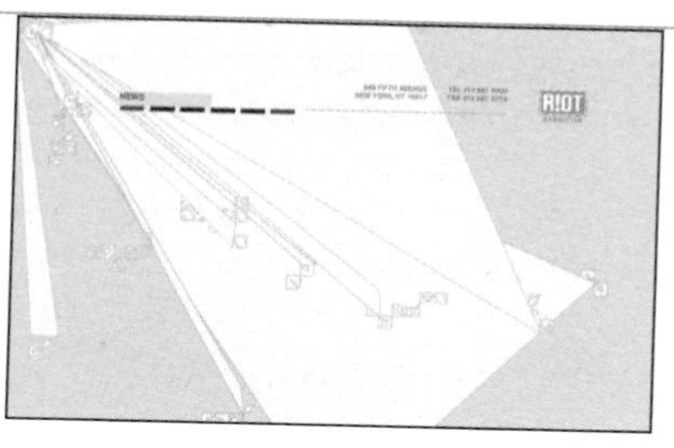

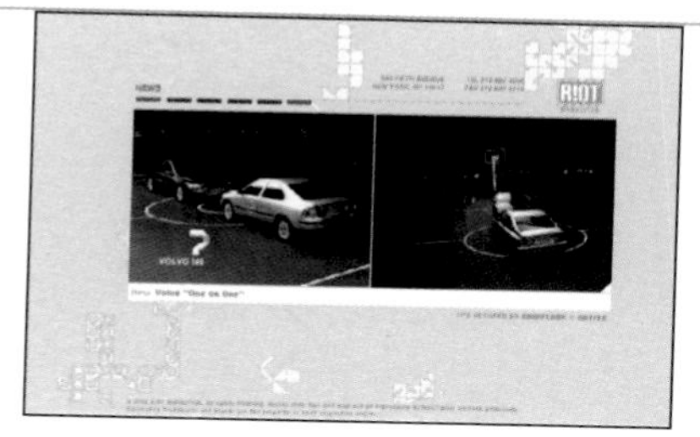

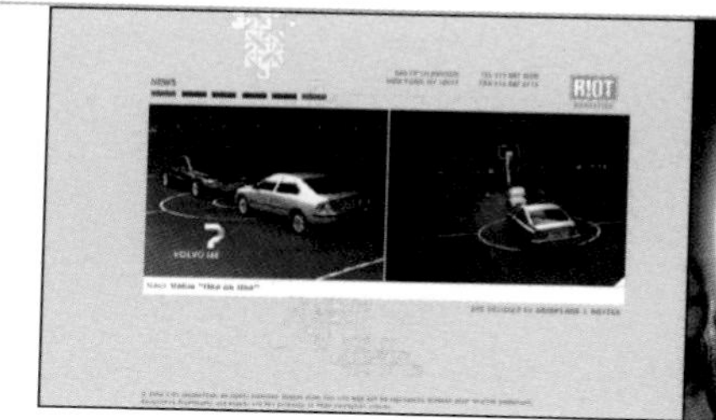

R!OT's branding graphics play throughout the browser window, building up in one area, then shooting off in an unexpected direction to start a new colony. The two left-hand screens show some pattern effects as the site loads. When the content block is onscreen, the pattern continues its animation around and behind it, as seen in the two right-hand images.

As in all of his work, Natzke's goal was to create animations that would have a life of their own. "I didn't want them to have the sterile, cold feel of a computer. I wanted them to have a feeling of life," he says. That proved a good match for R!OT's goals. "They described what they wanted as a 'genetic' system," Natzke says. "You plant a seed, and it grows and spreads out."

Accordingly, Natzke created a system that first figured out where each "seed" would be planted, and then, communicating with the neighboring cells, decided how each would grow. The system even plotted the death of cells. "It's constantly counting how many [iterations] are onscreen, and it has a maximum population it can't exceed," he explains.

To create the raw material for the process, Natzke built a Flash-based drawing tool. Using the tool, the designers then drew each of the 33 shapes and their mirror images. As they drew, using screen grabs of the shapes as patterns, the tool captured the coordinates of each point into a series of arrays, recording a mathematical description of each shape. The tool also created transitions between the iterations, via a slider that manipulated the movie clip. ActionScript then manipulated those coordinates to create the animation.

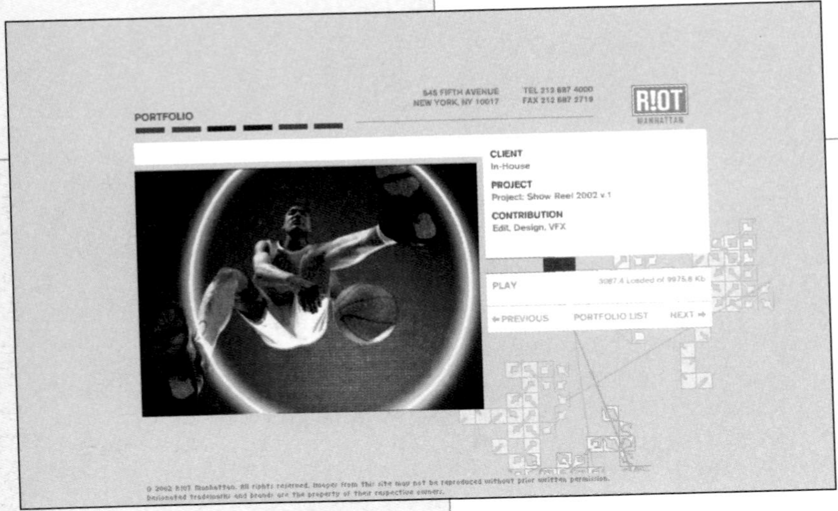

The site's almost monochrome graphic design and simple structure put the attention where it's wanted: on the videos.

The pattern begins promulgating as the site loads, beginning at a random point and following its mathematical rules of multiplication and rebirth until loading is complete. The animation halts as the initial screen comes into view, then starts playing again as the site waits for the user's first click. The animation stops again when another action is in the foreground—for example, a video playing or a new screen loading. According to Natzke, this is done primarily to ease the load on the processor, though it also focuses the user's attention—part of the team's aim of making sure the site doesn't distract the viewer from the content.

Natzke and Hooge played with many variations of the animation before settling on the current one. "It's a big part of what both of us do," says Hooge. "Play with math and see what will happen visually." They went through hundreds of variations, including animations based on just squares, variations that played with different colors and alpha levels, and one that used a magnifier factor to change the size of the squares. Hooge says the use of same-size squares in the final version reflects their decision to keep the pattern in line with the other screen elements. Even with the uniform size, Hooge says, "it took a lot of pain and struggle to get everything to add up. The ActionScript got really crazy." Wellfare says that the experiments conducted by Hooge and Natzke taught her more about her own creation. "Erik sent us lots of tests—'happy mistakes,' he called them. We learned a lot about the pattern's animation potential from them." In her own design process, Wellfare had built the animation rules only to a certain point, so, she says, "to see it grow beyond that was really exciting."

The inspiration worked in both directions. In one meeting, Hooge relates, someone from R!OT mentioned that at one point the animation seemed to "attack his mouse." That led to the development of one of the animation's most interesting actions: Once in awhile, it jumps to the current mouse position, giving the user a momentary feeling of control over it. That feeling disappears quickly if the user tries clicking again. Natzke explains the effect: "If you move your mouse while the pattern is plotting a new position to generate, it will jump to the current mouse position." Since the program checks for the mouse position only every third time it generates a new position, however, the action can't be controlled or predicted. It seems alive. Besides its intrinsic interest, Wellfare points out another advantage of this interactivity: "If you're tired of waiting for a video to load, there's something to play with."

For all its complex activity, Hollister is pleased to note that the pattern is unobtrusive. It's nearly the same color as the background, and once the site has loaded, it's always secondary to the main content window, running behind the window and never overshadowing it. As Hollister describes it, "The body of the navigation sits in the middle of the frame, while the pattern explores the whole area of the browser."

> A Simple Structure

The structure of R!OT's site is quite simple—a classic architecture for a studio, featuring news, a portfolio of work, case studies, contact information, and a client area. It hasn't changed much, in fact, from the site's former incarnation.

The site's graphic design is likewise simple. The pattern animation provides the only design graphics; all other content is text-based. And all of the site's elements—from the pattern to the navigation bar to the text content—are styled in a very simple, almost monochromatic palette of gray and white, with subtle touches of bronze for accent.

These are, in fact, the colors of R!OT Manhattan's logo (though in print, the gray is a metallic silver impossible to achieve on the Web). It's also a color scheme that designer Hooge is very much at home in, reminiscent of his work on other sites such as miniml.com and his old company's site, fourm.com. "I'm a huge fan of white space, simplicity, and contrast," he says, "and of using white with another color that's more vibrant. Even if it's an unsaturated color, against white you always have contrast." Like the white walls of a physical gallery, the site's color scheme provides a neutral background against which the work can be appreciated.

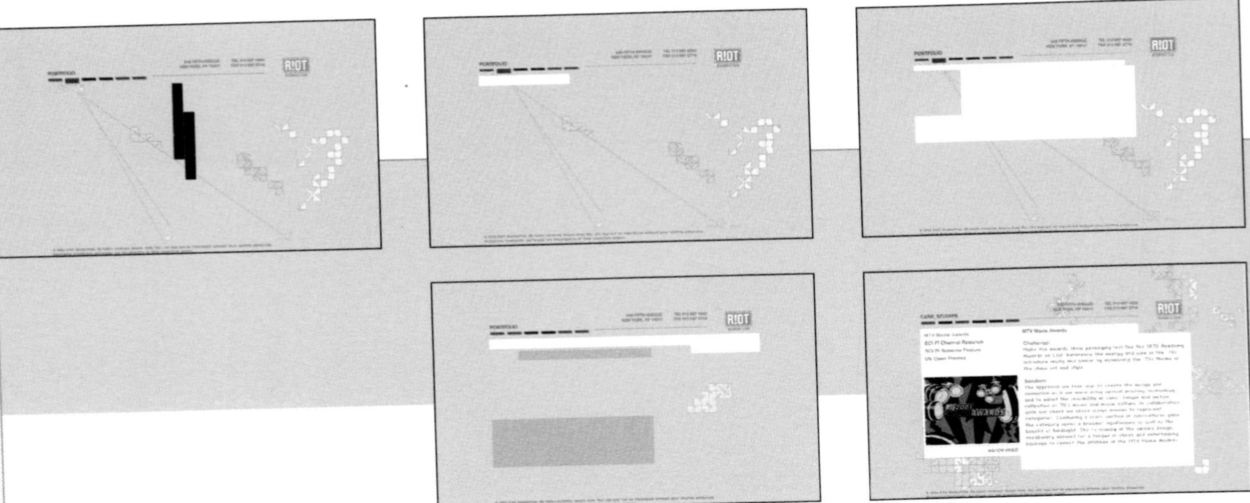

Each new section is drawn using a complex choreography of color blocks, resulting in an asymmetric final grid. The top row shows a transition to the main Portfolio page. The bottom row shows a transition from that page to a work sample.

> Surprising Motion

The site's graphic simplicity is balanced by its complex motion. No action works simply, or as expected. Rolling over the navigation bar doesn't result in a pop-up of the section name, but rather in a playful overlapping of section names as one exits and another enters stage left.

Clicking a new section triggers a complex choreography of background, foreground, and text, as blocks of color extend, retreat, speed around corners, and then come slowly to rest in their final positions. The process is mesmerizing—and speedy enough to build the page in just a few, fascinating seconds.

Natzke compares creating these transitions to writing music: "You have a certain set of rules to your score: how wide things are and how long they should play. Most of the animations happen over eight frames, so there's sort of a tempo created."

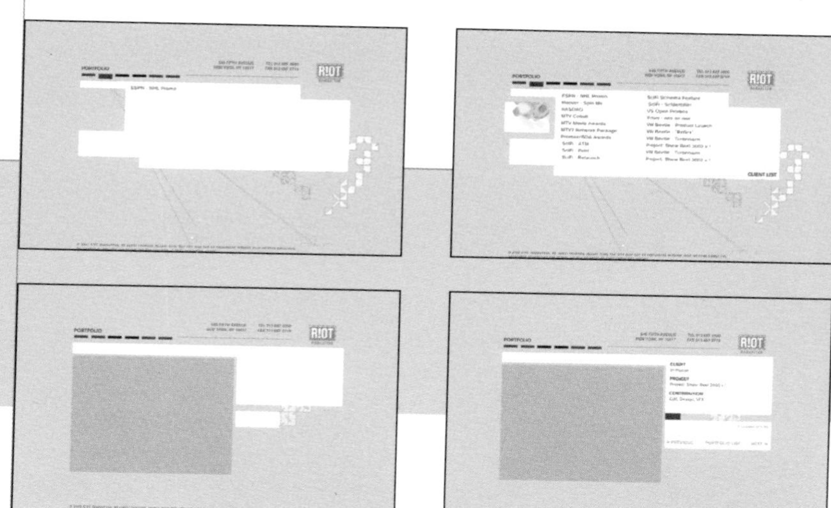

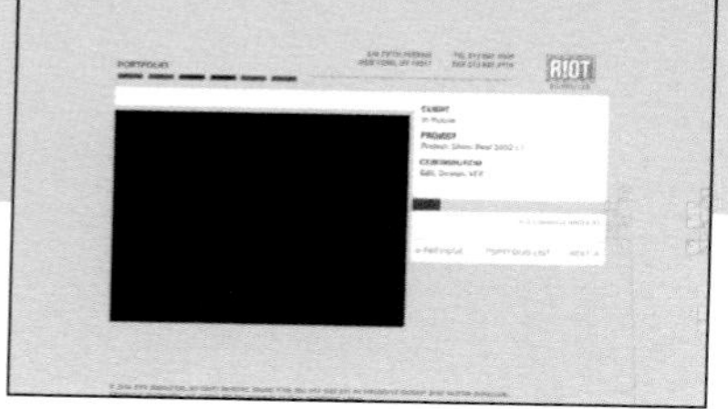

The animations evolved over several experiments and rounds of fine-tuning. "I was given the stills of one section and another section, then it was up to me to figure out, 'How do these things resolve themselves?'" Natzke explains. After trying more obvious approaches, such as sliding in the background blocks or having them fade up, he hit upon the approach of drawing the shapes with "ribbons" (as he calls them). "It felt right; it felt like what R!OT was doing in other places," he says. In fact, the movement is reminiscent of the motion of the pattern itself: After a period of what seems like logical growth, the animation suddenly shoots off in a new direction and begins growing from there.

The result looks random, but in fact it is painstaking art. Natzke says he spent four weeks fine-tuning the transitions. "It's weird how timeline animation tends to become the most difficult thing," he muses. "As I built it out, I'd think, 'Well, that's cool,' and I'd have to go back to the other sections to make it work there."

The timing of the transitions is as important as the movement itself. Natzke says a key part of the fine-tuning was making sure the animations didn't become annoying. "You have to balance how long people will be willing to wait versus what's important to the animation," he says. It's a line he says he often judges by his own reactions: "If the animation isn't doing anything tricky, you get tired. You say, 'Come on, let's get to the point.'"

The transition animations were coded simply, using tweening. "Most of it is done by going forward and backward with the playhead, using ActionScript to control the movement," Hooge explains.

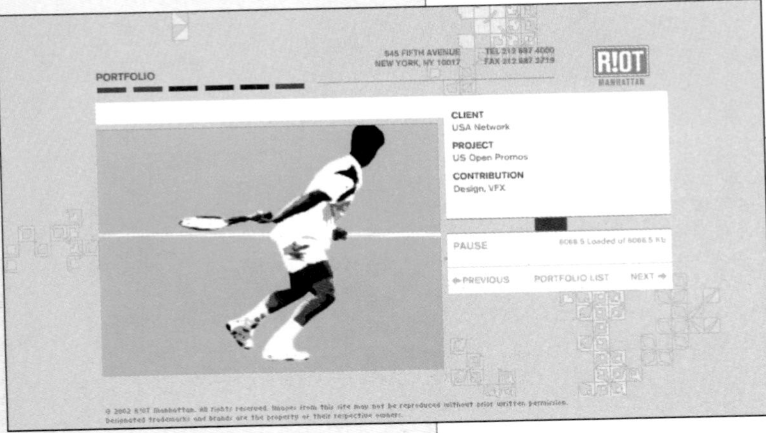

That's a video (from R!OT's work for the U.S. Open) playing in the Flash window.

> Video in Flash

The pattern animation is impressive, the transition sequences virtuoso, but the quiet revolution on the site is hidden deeper —it's reflected in the playback of R!OT's sample videos within the Flash window.

Videos are featured in two places on the site: in the Portfolio and Case Study sections. Each section sets aside a portion of the page for the video. After the page appears, the video begins to load. A loading counter begins running below the playback bar. Ever so subtly, a loading gauge—in the form of thin, bronze rules above and below the bar—begins to move. Playback begins when Flash has calculated that the time left to load equals the time left to play on the video. When that point comes, a Pause button (simply indicated by the word *Pause*) appears just below the bar. Click Pause, and the button toggles to read *Play*.

As the video is loading, very little is happening onscreen. The only movement is the slow crawl of the bronze loading gauge, the quicker ticking of the tiny byte count, and the ongoing animation of the pattern. "Something like a loading animation would be overkill," says the ever-minimal Hooge. "There's already lots going on with the animation." The result, again, is understated elegance.

The video player is, by design, as simple as can be. The dark gray bar (the playback head) appears immediately. The thin bronze lines at the top and bottom take longer to notice. They create the loading gauge. When they make it to the end of the bar, the video begins to play, and a Pause button appears at left. Click Pause and it changes to Play.

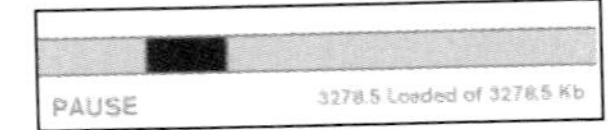

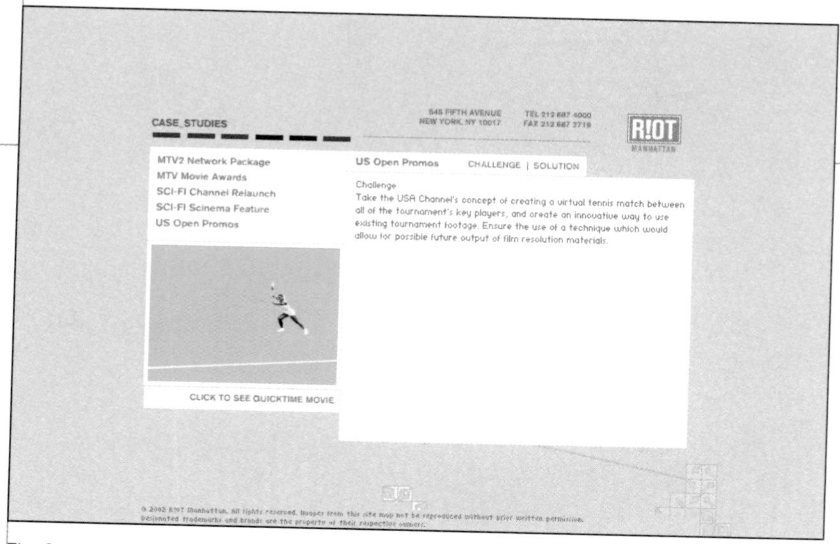

The Case Study section features a smaller video playback window.

Natzke credits Hooge for the simplicity of the playback controls: "I came up with a menuing system that was very user-difficult but interesting to do, and he came up with this easy one."

"I thought I wanted to take the player and move it around, or have the animation go over the top of it," says Natzke. However, he found that much of this activity simply wasn't feasible. In an earlier design, the playhead also acted as a loading gauge, growing only slowly to its full size. It was clever, and even more elegant in its simplicity, but confusing the first time you used it. Since it wasn't clear exactly how far the bar would eventually reach, the gauge failed to give users an idea of the relative completion of the download—a crucial part of its function.

The designers found themselves without much help when it came to figuring out what was needed in a QuickTime player. Sans any useful documentation, they just spent time with the Apple QuickTime player, analyzing what its functions were and then designing an interface for them. In the end, they purposely left out certain functions common to video players. For instance, they determined that since the playhead can be dragged to move back and forward through the video, a fast-forward control would be redundant.

> A Match of Client and Technology

Natzke and Hooge began working on the R!OT site in February 2002, a month before Flash MX was released—and long before most people would have the required Flash Player 6.

Hollister says it wasn't hard to make the decision to move to MX. "For us, the fact that it could deal with movies was the deciding factor," he says. The site offers the option of downloading the Flash player or going to an HTML version of the site.

"If we'd used Flash 5, we probably could have gotten away without the HTML site," says Natzke. Given R!OT's needs for the pattern animation and the video playback, though, it would have been hard to pass up MX's advantages. "This just seemed to be the perfect client for MX," Natzke says. ■

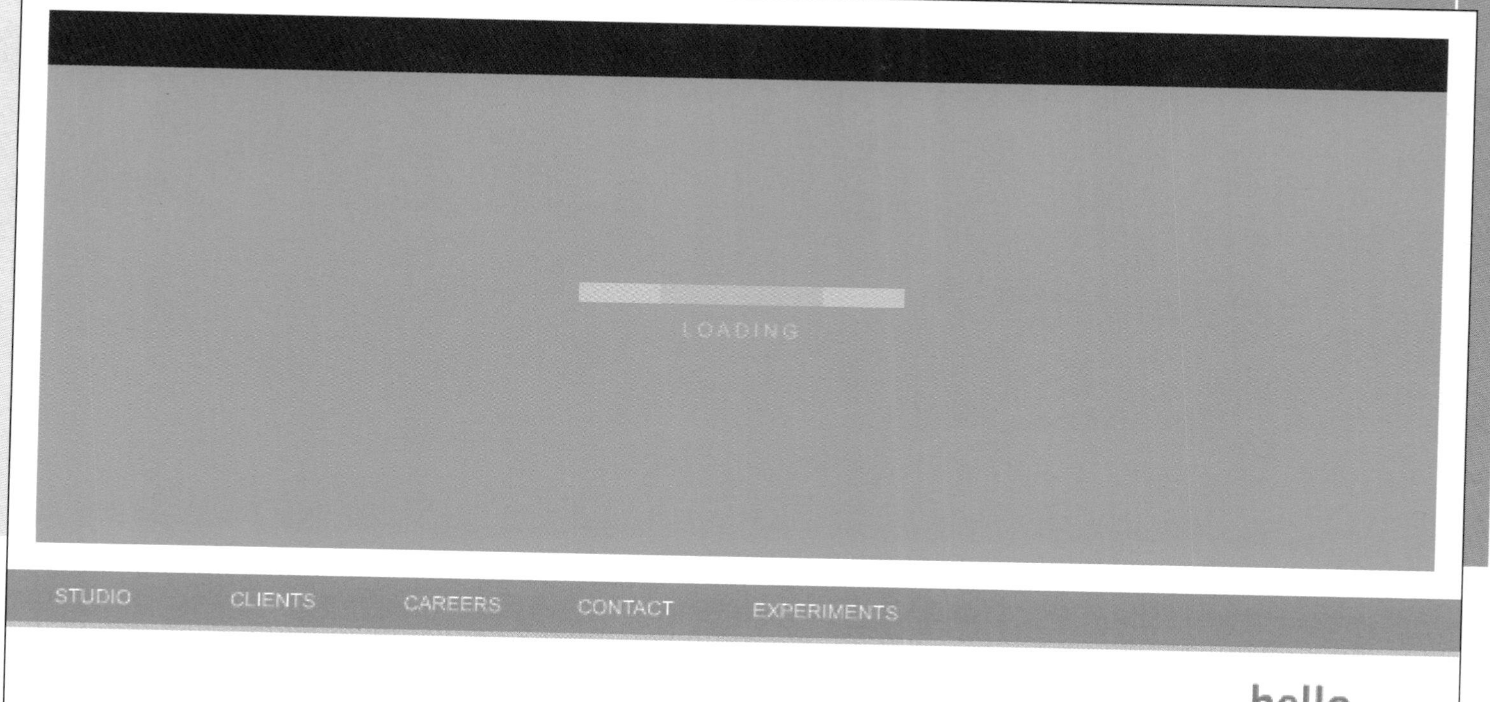

CHAPTER

HELLO DESIGN

HELLO DESIGN

DESIGN: Hello Design
CLIENT: Self
URL: www.hellodesign.com

DESIGN DIRECTOR: Hiro Niwa
CEO: David Lai

CHAPTER

HELLO DESIGN

INTRO

A design studio known for its experiments in cutting-edge interfaces makes sure its own site is as clear and easy to use as a toy for a three-year-old.

Pictured: [from left] Hiro Niwa, David Lai

Like a newspaper's front page, Hello's home page has a clear hierarchy. The first thing you see is a featured success story—in this case, about the firm's work on Sony's ImageStation. Next are some highlighted news features, and last, the site content structure. "We didn't want it to be overwhelming," says Hello co-founder David Lai. "We were thinking: 'What's the first read? What's the second read?'"

David Lai and Hiro Niwa founded Hello Design in 1999, leaving cutting-edge design firm Cow to try their hand at their own business. First step: set up a Web site.

The firm's first, HTML-based, site was followed quickly by this one, in Flash. At the time, the site's low-key, utilitarian interaction was a real departure from the usual Flash sites, which tended to use every attention-getting bell and whistle the program offered. The fact that the first Flash version of the site (created in Flash 4) still speaks for the studio today is a testament to the staying power of simple, well-thought-out interface design.

Of the site's groundbreaking simplicity, Lai, Hello's CEO, says, "Part of it was reaction, part of it was looking at our need. We wanted people to be able to read our information without being overwhelmed. We wanted something that would help people focus on the information."

Hello's site not only shows that simple interfaces are effective, it shows they don't have to be boring. Subtle details in graphics and interaction add humor and surprise.

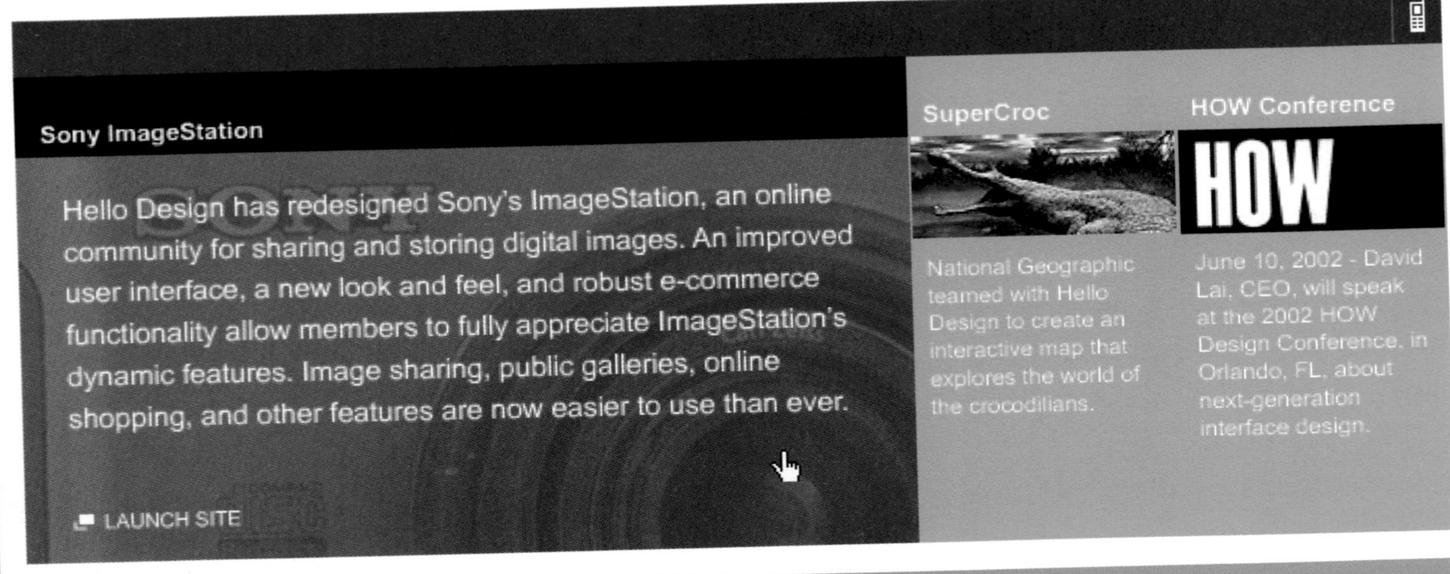

Almost the entire home page is active. Rolling over any part of the large content squares triggers a response: text that tells more of the story. You can click anywhere to take the next step.

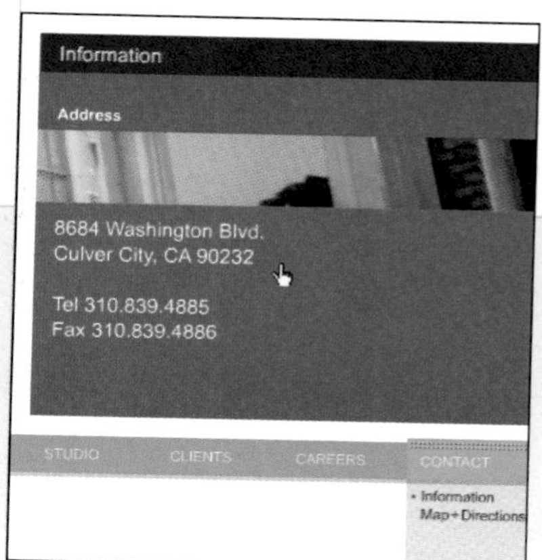

The simple "point anywhere and click" interactivity extends throughout the site. In some cases, as here, what exactly you'll get if you click is mysterious. If you guessed a map and directions, you'd be right.

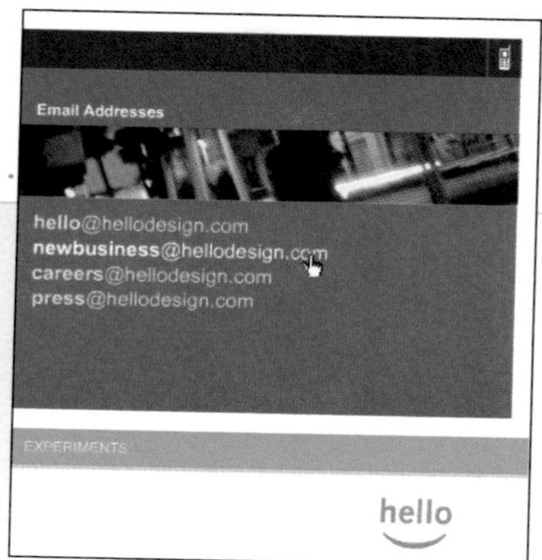

In the few places where precise placement of the pointer is required, a double rollover is used. The whole section highlights as you roll into it, but the pointing hand appears only when you roll over a link, which highlights to show that it's active.

> Clicking into the Information

The site takes advantage of only the simplest interface clues: rollovers to clarify what you're pointing to, and a pointing finger to tell you that you can click now.

You don't have to look for something to click. Chances are, as soon as you move your pointer into the browser window, something will happen. This is because every point in the blocky color tiles that make up the home page is live. As soon as your pointer enters any section of the page, rollover text appears to explain what you're pointing to.

This simple page structure and simple interaction are repeated on every page of the site. The message is: "easy," like the child's toy that Niwa, Hello's design director, had in mind when he created the site. Like the toy, the site feels somehow tactile when the user is interacting with it. "It feels like you're clicking into content," says Niwa. The same principle is used throughout most of the site.

Such simplicity can be risky, however. In many cases, you aren't told just what you'll get if you click. The assumption is simply "more." Informal testing among friends convinced the designers that this would be enough. If the action is unusual, like launching an outside site, information is added to explain it.

Lai says the idea for the site's interaction model grew partly out of its graphic design. In 2000, when the site was created, the designers wanted to make it fit into the 800-by-600-pixel screen that was standard at the time. They also felt that anything in an area this size couldn't be too complicated. So the site's content is laid out in a flexible grid of solid-colored squares. The home page is asymmetrically split into three sections. Other pages use two, three, or four equal parts.

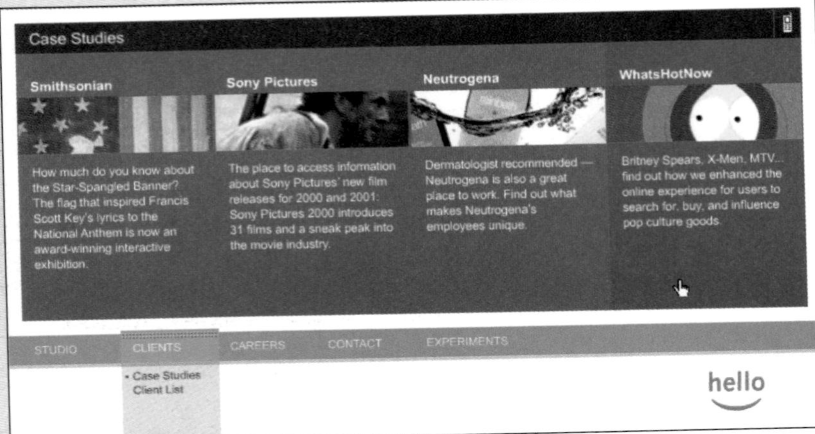

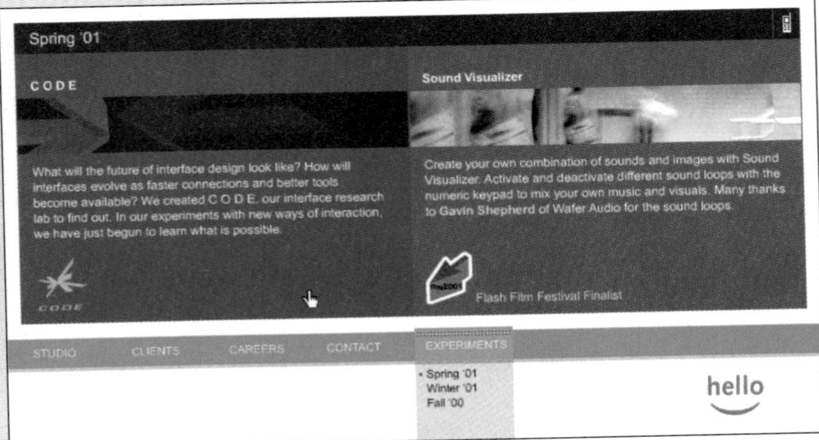

The site's pages are built on a grid of solid-colored rectangles, with two, three, or four sections per page.

"The question then came up of how do you navigate quickly into these sections," says Lai. "It made sense to just use these panels as something you could enter into."

> Simple, with Subtlety

Focus is the keyword for both the navigation system and the home page. The designers didn't want too much distracting detail on the page, but they wanted users to be able to view and jump directly to any section of the site from any other.

When you first arrive at the home page, you see only the top-level section headings. Rolling over a section name displays the subsections, which can be clicked to navigate to them. So far, so normal. The unusual detail is revealed when you attempt to navigate from one subsection to another. Rolling over another section name highlights the submenus while keeping the current section's menu active and in view. An extra dollop of surprise is added by the way in which the highlight moves into place: It seems to peel out of the active menu like a shadow and flit across the intervening sections, providing a momentary view of their subsections as it passes. All of this happens fast, and it takes a few viewings to notice just what's going on. (It's done with masks; see "Animating the Navigation Bar," page 42.)

Another surprising detail of the navigation bar is the drag bar that appears on the active menu's highlight. You can, in fact, drag the highlighting to a new position on the menu bar. The designers admit that few people actually notice this, but, says Lai, "we put it in because it's a nice feature."

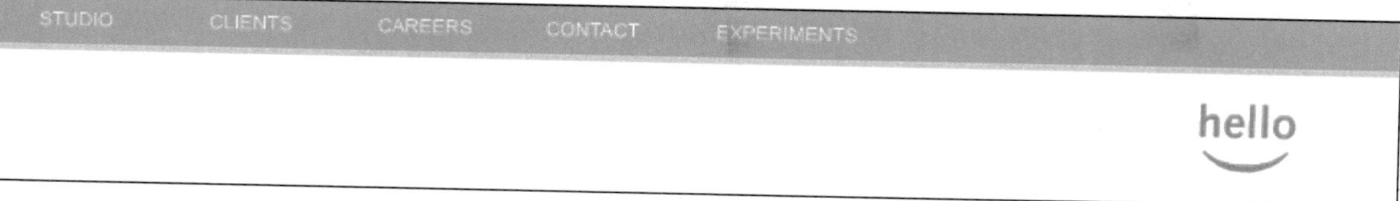

On entering the site, the visitor sees only the top-level navigation (top). Rolling over a section name displays the subsections beneath it (second). Clicking a subsection activates the page, darkens the highlight, and marks the current section (third). If you roll over other menu sections, the current section keeps its "active" highlight, but another rollover highlight moves across the menu bar (fourth) into position (bottom) to show the second section's subsections. Clicking the Hello logo takes you back to the home page.

UNDER THE HOOD

ANIMATING THE NAVIGATION BAR

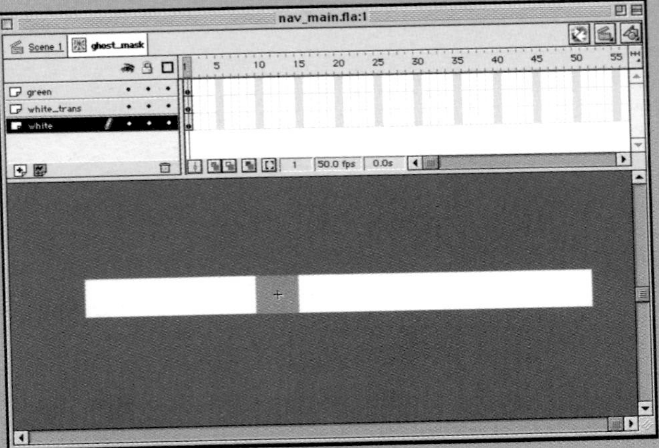

Figure 1

The movie clip ghost_mask will hide and reveal the site's submenus.

```
on (rollOver) {
    _root.ghost._visible=1;
    _root.ghost._x= 14;
    _root.active_x1 = 14;
    _root.active_x2 = 100;
    _root.active_y1 = 296;
    _root.active_y2 = 400;
}

on (press) {
    _root.action.gotoAndPlay("load_01");
}

on (rollOut) {
    _root.ghost. _visible= 0;
}
```

Figure 2

When the user points to a section title, this script moves ghost over the submenu. The ghost_mask movie clip moves to the same position.

The secrets behind the elegant animation of Hello Design's navigation bar are a sense of humor and a set of synchronized masks. ActionScript choreographs the movement of text, bullets, two masks, and a drag bar to hide, reveal, and highlight the site's subsections as the user moves the pointer across the navigation bar.

A layer of text containing a list of all the site's subsections is on the stage at all times. By default, though, the subsections are hidden by a mask. The mask, a long rectangle with a green-tinted opening in the middle (**Figure 1**), is created by a movie clip called ghost_mask.

A second movie clip, called ghost, creates a highlight effect. When the user points to a section title in the menu bar, a script (**Figure 2**) moves ghost into position over the submenu, while a custom function uses a simple formula to glide the opening in ghost_mask to the same position (**Figure 3**). With the two masks in position, the submenu is revealed and highlighted. (Bullets are added to submenu items when they're active or rolled over, courtesy of another movie clip.) When the pointer leaves the menu area, ghost becomes invisible and ghost_mask flits back to its original position, revealing the menus to its left as it goes.

Another set of movie clips creates the selected, active state of a section. An active section is highlighted in a somewhat darker green, with a drag bar attached to the title. The movie clip menudrag covers the portion of the active menu that intersects with the menu bar, while the movie clip menu covers the submenu portion. When the user clicks a section title or submenu, the movie clips move into position over the active section. Once they're in place, the submenu is placed on top. The script also controls the loading of the selected section.

```
ghost_x = ghost._x;
ghost_mask_x = ghost_mask._x+43
distance = ghost_x-ghost_mask_x;
speed = distance/2
x = ghost_mask_x+speed;
ghost_mask._x=x;
menu_x = menu._x;
distance2 = menu.destination-menu_x;
speed2 = distance2/2;
x2 = menu_x+speed2;
menu._x=x2;
menudrag_x = menudrag._x;
distnace3 = menu_destination-menudrag_x;
speed3 = distance3/2;
x3 = menudrag_x+speed3;
menudrag._x=x3;
drag_x = drag_control._x;
drag_y = drag_control._y;
if (drag_x<active_x1 or drag_x>active_x2) {
    ghost._x=menu_x;
}
if (drag_y,active_y1 or drag_y>ative_y2) {
    ghost.X=menu_x'
}
```

Figure 3

This function moves the ghost_mask movie clip to the current position of ghost. To create an organic, sliding movement, the function measures the distance between ghost_mask and ghost and moves ghost_mask half that distance, looping through that action until the two meet.

Just for fun, the designers added a second way to move to a new section. In addition to clicking on a section title, you can also move the menu highlighting to a new section by dragging it there. The movie clip menudrag includes a button that activates a function called startDrag when clicked. StartDrag makes the movie clip draggable within the menu-bar area (**Figure 4**). Dragging menudrag brings ghost_mask along as well, so that the submenus in its path are highlighted as they are passed over. When menudrag is released, a series of conditionals determine whether to move the active state of the menu to a new position or to leave it where it is.

```
on (press) {
    _root.gotoAndPlay("menudrag");
    startDrag("_root.menudrag", false, 14, 297, 358,297);
}

on (release) {
    stopDrag();
    _level0.menudrag_x = _level0.menudrag._x;
    if (Number(_level0:menudrag_x)<57) {
        _root.action.gotoAndPlay("load_01");
    } else if (Number(_level0:menudrag_x)<143) {
        _root.action.gotoAndPlay("load_02");
    } else if (Number(_level0:menudrag_x)<229) {
        _root.action.gotoAndPlay("load_03");
    } else if (Number(_level0:menudrag_x)<314) {
        _root.action.gotoAndPlay("load_04");
    } else {
        _root.action.gotoAndPlay("load_05");
    }
    startDrag("../drag_control", true);
}
```

Figure 4

The startDrag function lets the user drag the menu highlight over the menu bar.

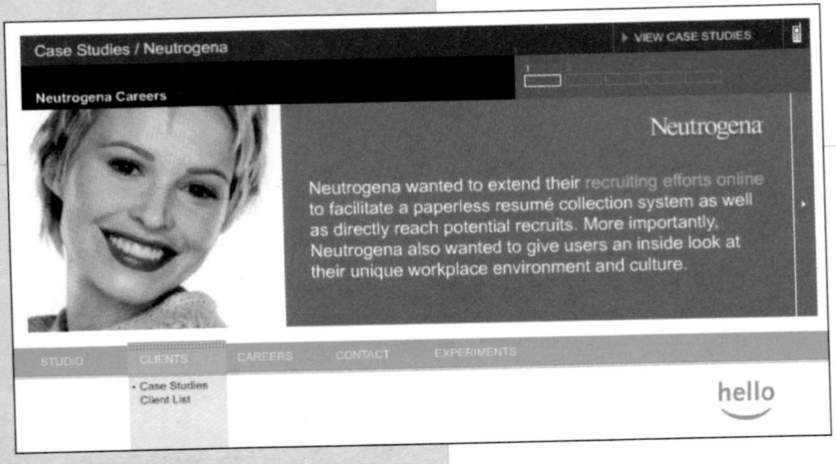

The top-level Case Studies page links to individual stories, told page by page. Sadly, the boxes at the top, which represent story pages, cannot be used to scroll forward through the story, and the highlighted text doesn't link to anything else. Nobody's perfect.

> Two Ways of Telling Stories

Like many design studio sites, Hello's offers a selection of case studies as well as a more complete client list. Unlike most sites, though, this one's client list links to deeper, more complex stories behind almost every name.

The Case Studies stories, which take visitors through the development process of the featured projects, use a straightforward navigation style. An arrow at the right of each page lets you scroll forward. As you do so, squares above the text representing the pages of the story are highlighted to show you where you are.

The Client List section reveals a more complex storytelling system. Names in the client list are clickable (or at least most of them are; a few are dimmed to signal that they're inactive). Clicking a name reveals a client story just as detailed as the one you'll find in the case studies, but in a different form.

Here, highlighting and pointing fingers let users know what actions are available. The subtitle Challenge is highlighted; beside it, Solution is dimmed. The first screen in the graphics window is bright; the half-revealed one next to it is dimmed. Rolling over the dimmed items highlights them, letting you know that clicking will bring the expected, but not explained, action.

The client story page also includes an element illustrating that even the simplest interface may not be clear to everyone. A page palette, with numbered boxes representing the pages in the story, was added when informal testing revealed that some users weren't sure how to scroll between the screen illustrations. The page palette seemed to solve the problem. It also adds information: Now users know how many pages are in the sequence.

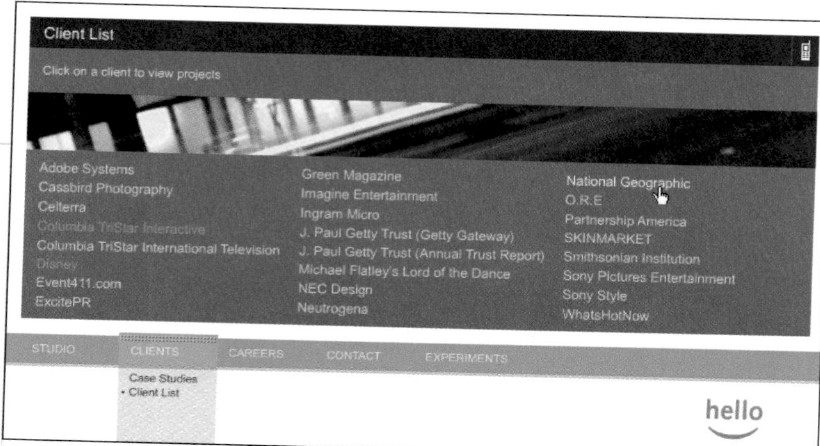

The Client List page uses three levels of highlighting: Names displayed in normal brightness are clickable; dimmed names are not. Rolling over a clickable name highlights it.

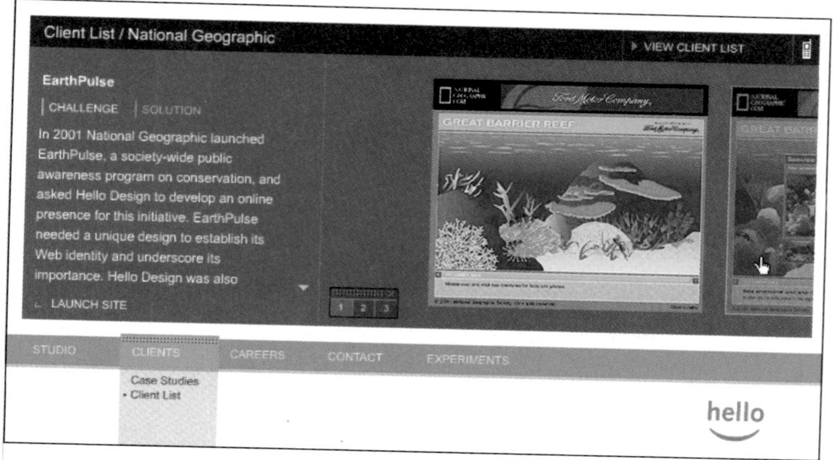

Clicking a client name reveals the site's most complex interface. You can click the half-revealed screen that follows to scroll to it, or you can click a number in the page palette to view screens in any order.

Lai and Niwa say they like to provide different ways of accomplishing a single task—as they've done on this portion of their site. "Why not give people multiple ways of doing something?" asks Lai. "If someone is trying to find a piece of information, why force them into a linear model?"

Users also get a choice when they want to leave a client story. They can return to the client list by clicking the always-available menu at the bottom of the screen, but they can also click the Client List menu that the designers added at the top-right corner of the screen. This drops a transparent menu over the current screen. The transparency, says Lai, lets people know they haven't lost their place, and that they're still at the same screen.

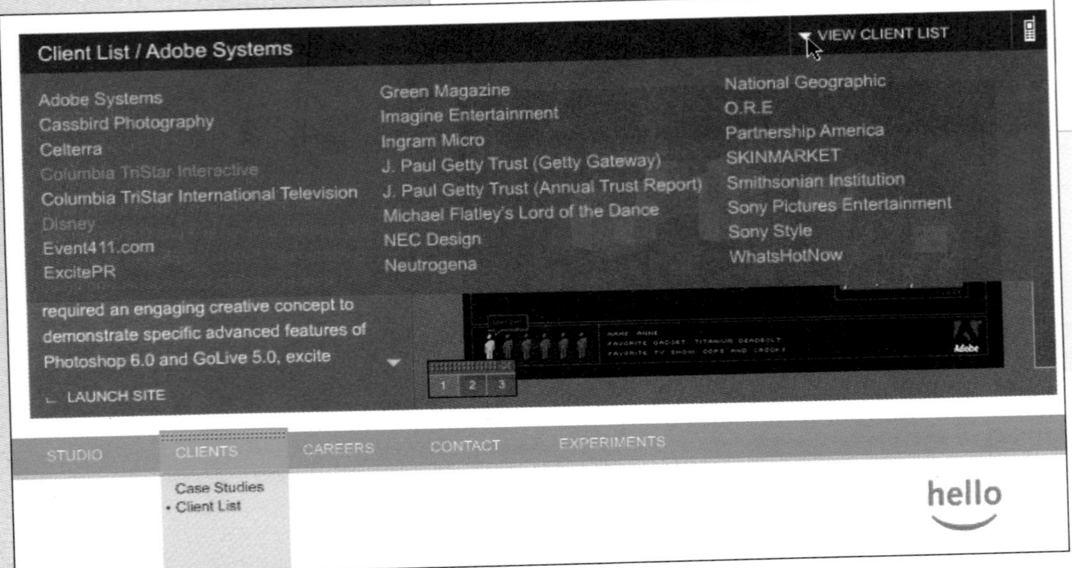

When you're ready to move on, clicking View Client List drops down a transparent menu that lets you select your next story.

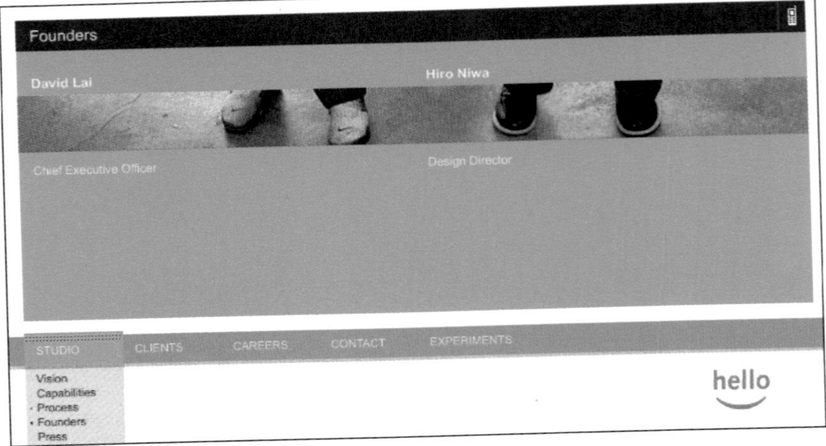

Bright colors, unexpected interactions, and a humorous graphics style, as in this screen identifying the founders by their shoes, keep the mood light.

> Underplayed Fun

Although straightforward, the site is far from staid. "We wanted to offer some sort of delight, something that people didn't expect," says Lai. That lightheartedness comes through in subtle ways.

You see it in the surprising mask that flits across the menu bar when you roll over a new selection. And you see it each time the pointing hand appears with no explanation—creating a mini-mystery that would frustrate if clicking didn't reveal what the user wanted, but delights when it does. The playfulness also comes through in the site's use of graphics: Click Founders (under Studio), and you see not a standard posed shot of Lai and Niwa, but a slice of their shoes.

Another example of the site's hidden wit can be found under the cell phone icon at the top-right corner of the screen. Pointing to it reveals the label Wireless Enabled. Is the site really available for handhelds? Explains Lai, "We wanted to learn the technologies and show that we were capable of developing for wireless." Since they didn't think people would actually want to view the studio's case studies on a cell phone, they created the "Mobile Survival Guide" instead, offering information they thought would be more useful on the road. Entries include topics like "What to do if you're stuck in a car that's sinking in water."

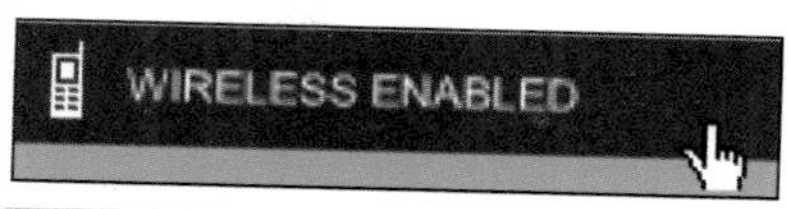

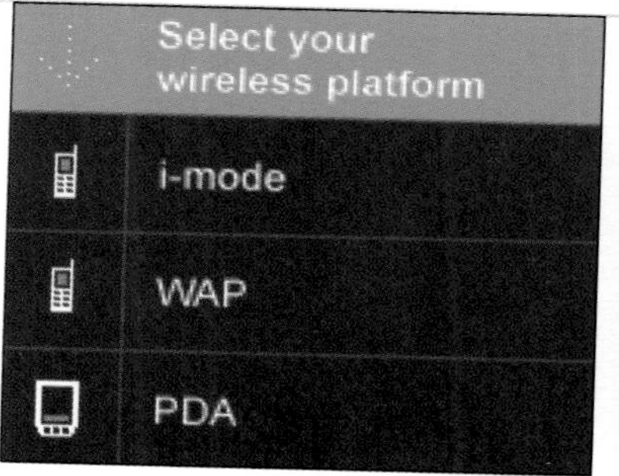

The one time the site doesn't give you what you expect: Downloading its wireless information gets you Hello's Mobile Survivial Guide—sort of like the best-seller *The Worst-Case Survival Guide*, but created for those on the go. It offers lighthearted instructions for handling unlikely disasters you may encounter in your travels.

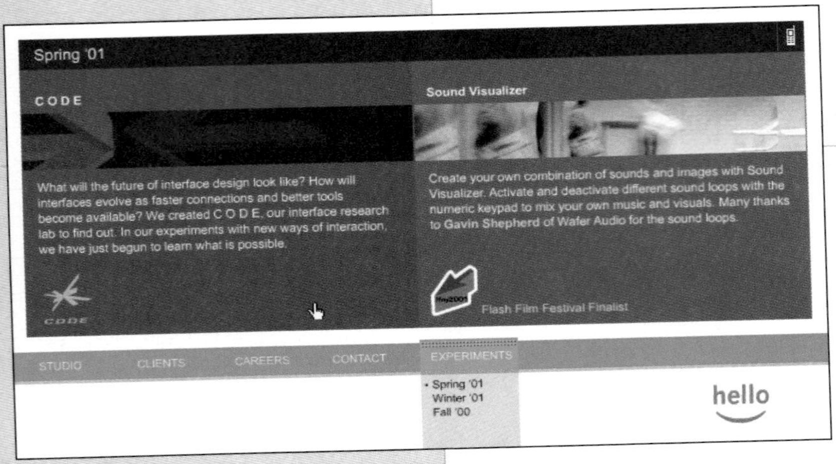

The Experiments section showcases Hello's forays into experimental interface design.

> A Fenced-Off Playground

After holding back on the rest of the site, the studio's designers pull out all the stops in their electronic playground, a section called Experiments. Here, Hello's designers showcase "whatever we feel like playing with," according to Lai.

The Experiments section is divided into seasons, with two "experiments" per page. The latest, titled CODE, is actually a separate Web site featuring the studio's experiments with interactive interfaces. Here, the designers show what they can do when the brief is simply, "Think about interface design."

"It's an extension of what we do in our work," says Lai. "The thing we like to do is just put away what we think we know and start from a higher perspective: What might work here?"

All the experiments, like Hello's site as a whole, are notable for three things. The first is their elegantly logical approach to the information they display. Calendar[3], for example, rethinks the basic desk tool for the electronic display. It combines the month-at-a-glance, week-at-a-glance, and day-at-a-glance versions in a series of zooming views that put all that information into a single screen. Second, the experiments all have simple, discoverable interfaces based on direct manipulation. There are no menu commands here, only rollovers, clicks, and drags, which trigger sophisticated feedback to help the user understand the effect of each action. And third, all the experiments provide visual delight as well as intellectual interest.

The Experiments section does more than just show off the studio's interface chops. It also garners information the designers can use in their work. "We have all these ideas, and we wanted to put them up there and get feedback on them," says Lai.

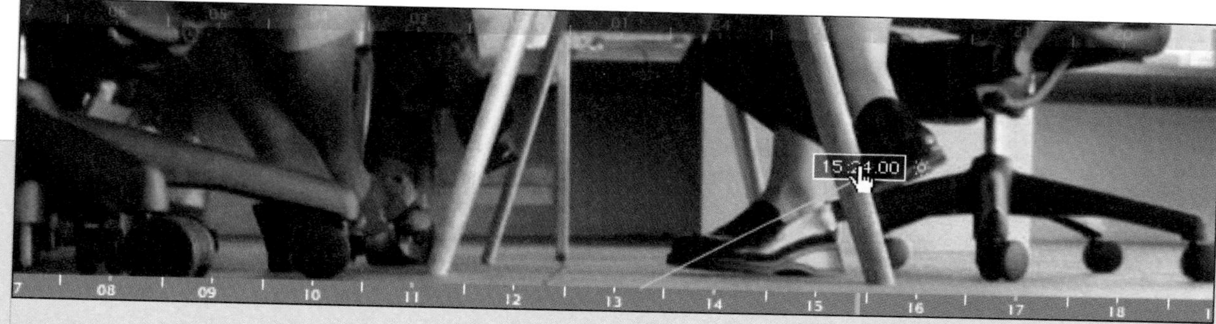

ClockWork ties pictures of the studio (taken every 15 minutes) to the hours of the day, creating a poetic vision of time as well as a fun interaction: You can grab the interactive "hand" to scroll through the day's scenes. Let it go, and it swings like a pendulum until it comes to a stop.

Running your pointer over a photo in PicFlip flips the squares of a hidden grid, uncovering the next photo, and the next, creating an interesting visual pattern as well as a sense of discovery. This version features photos of Tokyo.

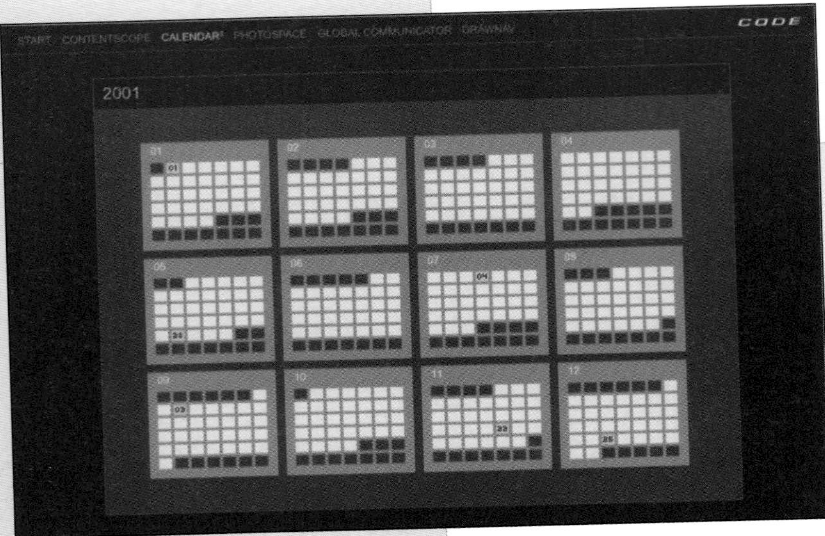

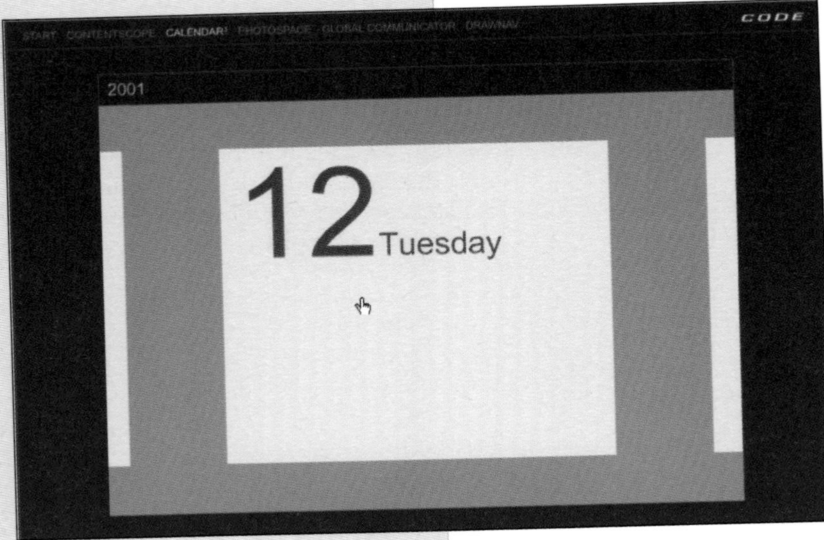

Calendar[3], featured in CODE, is an experiment that offers year, month, and day views in a single calendar. It features the simplest interaction possible. Clicking a date zooms in on it. Clicking outside a date zooms out a level.

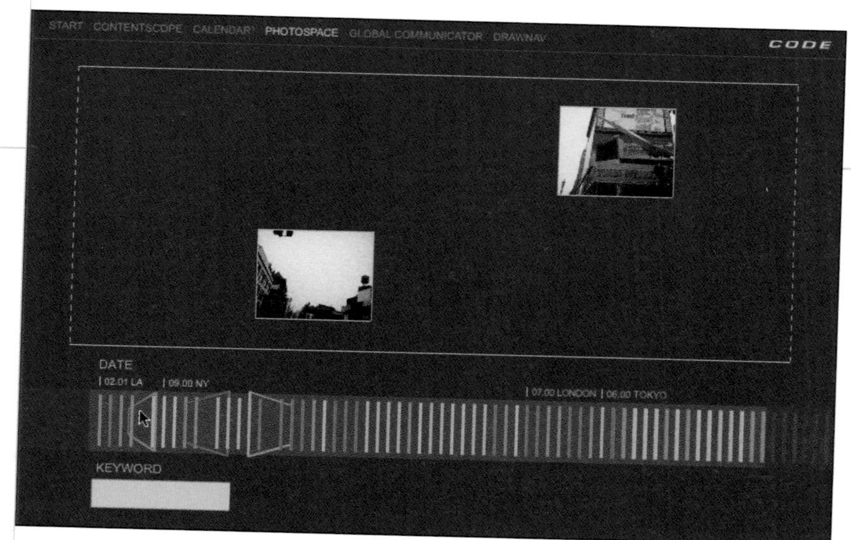

PhotoSpace, from CODE, displays filed photos as color-coded bars. Scrolling over the bars flips the photos into view. You can drag them up to the virtual light table for a better look (two are shown on the light table here), or search through the photos by keyword.

> Why Redesign?

When we spoke in spring 2002, Hello was getting ready to redesign its two-year-old site. After analyzing their current needs, though, the designers say they expect to make surprisingly few changes. The basic look and feel of the site will remain the same, Lai says, though the architecture will probably change somewhat: In 2002, the firm no longer feels the need to put recruiting (Careers) at the top level of its menu, as it did in the fast-growth days of the late 1990s. Now that Flash MX works so much better with databases than Flash 4 did, the designers can put a Flash interface on the database-driven Press Releases section of the site. They'll probably update the news and client list, and may show the case studies differently. All in all, though, changes will likely be few.

"We thought about redesigning the entire site, but we think the overall structure has worked really well for us," says Lai. The studio decided that change in and of itself—doing a complete makeover of the site just so that people will notice that it is new—isn't worth it. Lai acknowledges that design is an unpredictable process, and anything could happen once the redesign is underway, but, he says, "we don't want to do something new for new's sake. If it makes sense, people will just use it." ■

SPOTLIGHT
DESIGNING CONTROLS

One rule of usable interface design is to take advantage of standards: If people are used to seeing something work one way, don't reinvent a new way just because you can. Don't force your user to learn a new convention for your site if a workable convention for that action already exists.

The sites shown in this book, however, often break this rule. For example, no two scroll bars featured in these pages look the same. This is due in part to the lack of standard components for Flash. When programming for Windows or another operating system, you have access to a toolbox that includes code for standard scroll bars and other controls, ensuring a standard look and behavior for each. Until the release of Flash MX, however, no such toolbox existed for Flash. Now, Flash MX's components supply ready-made looks and behaviors for some standard controls, but designers are still free to add their own variations, bells, and whistles.

The video controls on the Riot Manhattan site are pared down to the minimum, with just enough detail to signal their use. The Play and Pause buttons are words that swap out depending on the current state of the video. Thin colored lines on each side of the bar act as a loading gauge.

The scroll bars for the PocketPC version of Beautiful Bay Area were designed with a stylus in mind. The arrows had to be large enough to be hit easily with the tip of a stylus. The designers opted for minimalism for the rest.

It's up to designers to make sure that even if their controls don't look exactly like another site's, they're still recognizable and work in a familiar way. "It's like inventing doorknobs," says David Lai of Hello Design. "There are many styles and kinds of doorknobs, but the interaction with that doorknob is pretty understood." Designers need to exert some self-control in their designs, says Lai. "You have to ask yourself, are you doing it like that to be gimmicky, or are you doing that to solve a problem? We're trying to make the content come to the foreground. If someone's trying to figure out how things work, you've shifted the focus from the content."

Lai sees an upside, though, to Flash's lack of cookie-cutter controls. "Sometimes it's good to put preconceived standards away," he says. "The idea is to put away what we think we know and go to a higher perspective—thinking, 'What might work here?' "

Hello Design's scroll bars are merely arrows pointing up or down, depending on where the extra content can be found. The only element these scroll bars really lack is the elevator box of a standard scroll bar. "Sliders are more useful for large amounts of information," says David Lai, Hello's CEO. "We didn't feel like we needed to add an extra interface component."

Quokka and IO Research developed a custom control to help users navigate the graphic display of the 2001 NCAA Basketball Championship site. Since no standard existed for the task, the firms created a control they called the Navigator, fine-tuned to meet their needs.

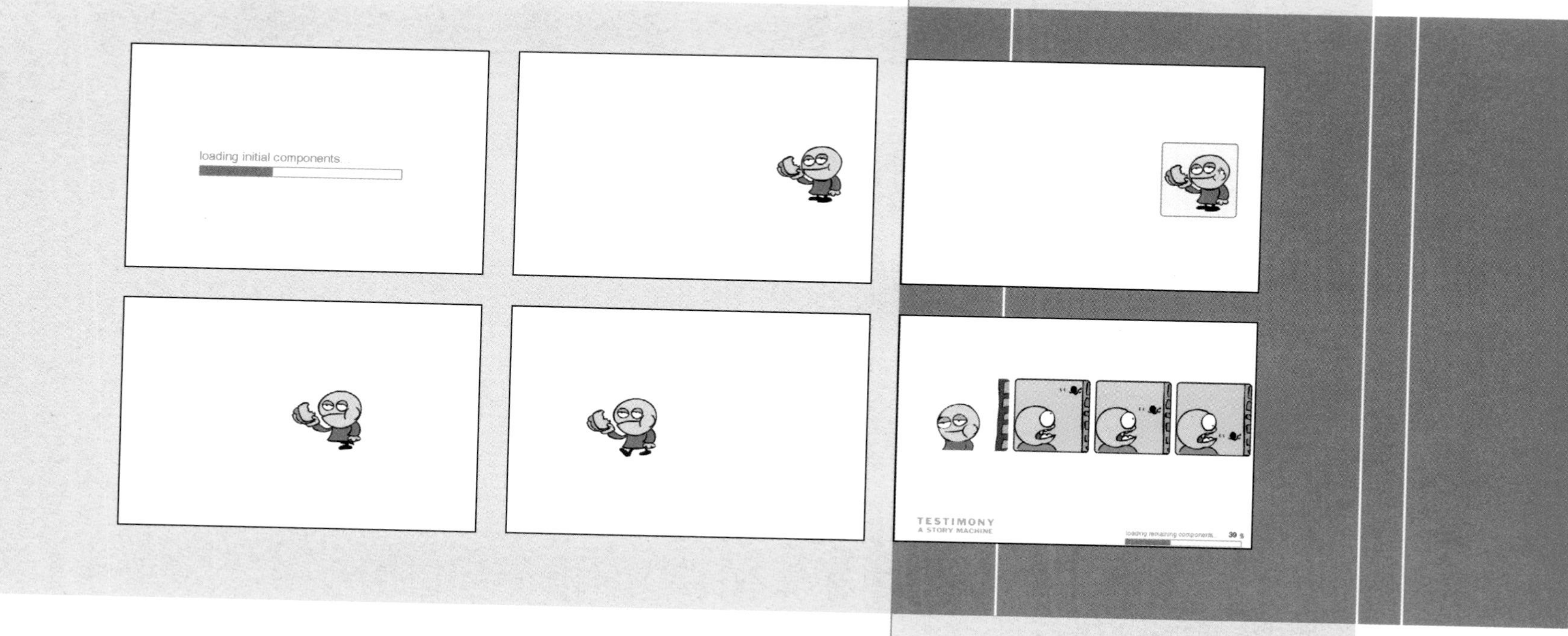

CHAPTER

TESTIMONY: A STORY MACHINE

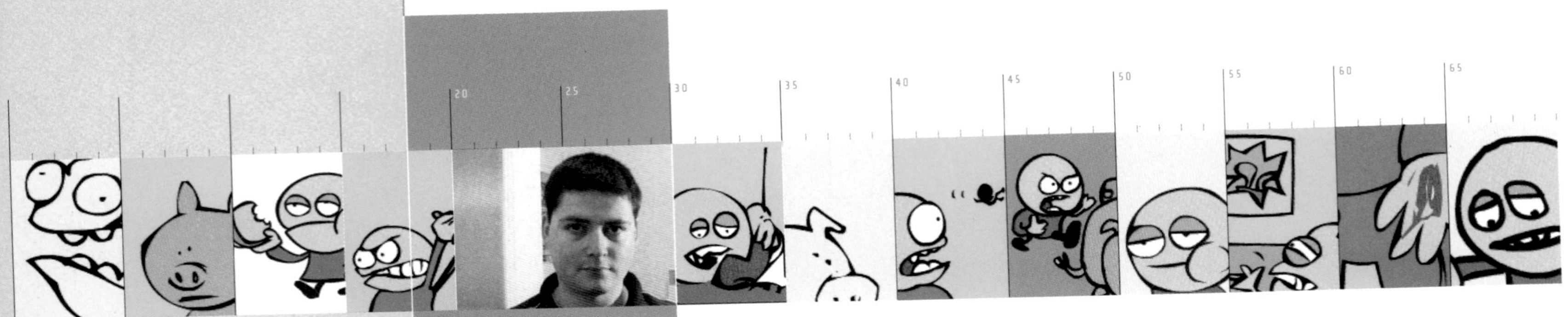

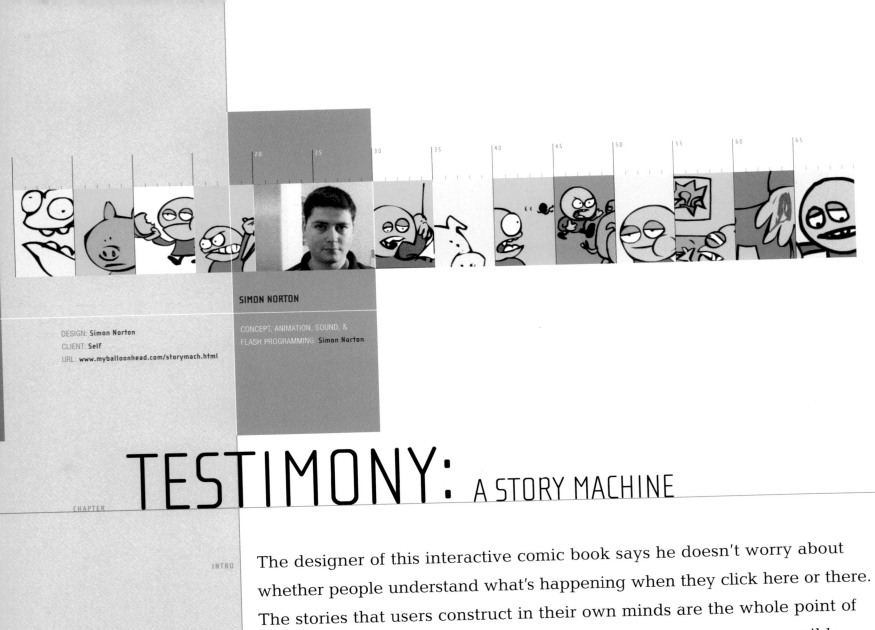

SIMON NORTON

DESIGN: **Simon Norton**
CLIENT: **Self**
URL: **www.myballoonhead.com/storymach.html**

CONCEPT, ANIMATION, SOUND, & FLASH PROGRAMMING: **Simon Norton**

CHAPTER

TESTIMONY: A STORY MACHINE

INTRO

The designer of this interactive comic book says he doesn't worry about whether people understand what's happening when they click here or there. The stories that users construct in their own minds are the whole point of this site. And it's only clever design that makes that ambiguity possible.

Pictured: Simon Norton

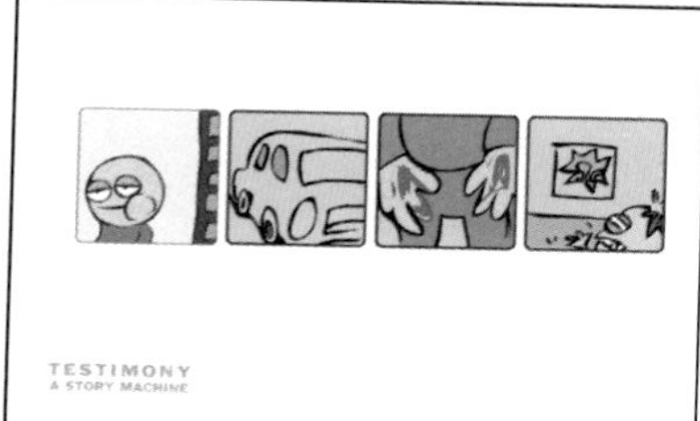

The first scenario always opens with the same scene: our protagonist witnessing a fall from a tall building. Clicking a story frame calls up a new image, drawn randomly from Norton's image library.

Simon Norton wasn't prepared for all the attention he got for his interactive comic book Testimony: A Story Machine. After all, he created the site as a school project (in pursuit of a degree in interactive media at Australia's Royal Melbourne Institute of Technology), and he characterizes it as "a first-time-out prototype."

The human propensity to construct stories from even the most random information is the engine driving Norton's Story Machine. As images and text combine and recombine in uncountable variations, visitors are led into an unfathomable world that they are somehow driven to make sense of. Norton's art lies in the ways he's found to both maximize and limit the information he presents to visitors to ensure that they bring their own imagination into play.

Clicking the orange-rimmed frame begins the transition to a new scenario. Our hero, in his frame, consumes the frames to the right as he crosses the screen. He then falls to a new position, where a pig chases a man (or is it the other way around?) in his thoughts. Clicking the orange frame once more moves you to Scenario 3, with our hero perched on a window ledge.

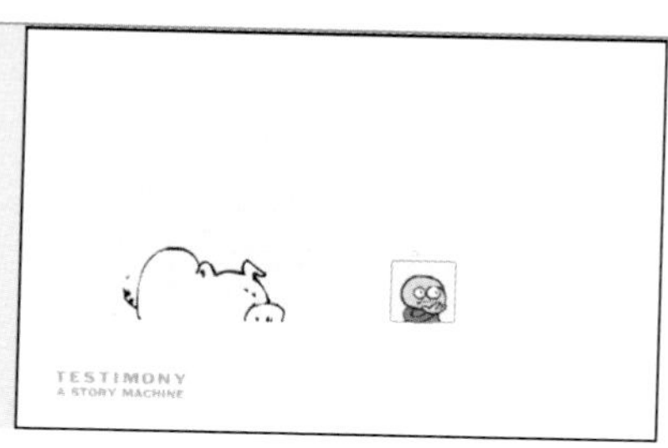

> Discovering the Rules

"There are no instructions, and that's deliberate," says Norton. "The user can't do anything 'wrong.'"

On entering the site (after the initial "loading" sequence), the user sees a little man munching on something (see page 55). When the user aims the pointer at the protagonist, an orange frame is drawn around him, providing a visual clue to click that frame. When the user does, the little man (still munching) marches across the window, then comes to a stop. Immediately, three frames open to his right, while a loading gauge tells visitors that more is to come. The fact that the pointer changes to a pointing finger when it's rolled over an image frame lets users know that they can start clicking even as the elements load.

As the visitor begins clicking, new images replace the original story frames. Norton says, "After a short time, it may become clear that clicking on a black-rimmed frame changes the image in that frame, while clicking on an orange-rimmed frame advances the character to a new scenario." Or it may not. "I've noticed this [rule] eludes a lot of people," says Norton. "But it's OK with me, too, if they just want to click all over the place and see what happens."

The user who masters the difference between these two types of clicks has mastered the site—though once in awhile, a click can still surprise.

Moving from the third to the fourth scenario, our protagonist leaps from a building—or was it all a dream?

> A Vaguely Defined Context

As author of this "nonlinear fiction" (as he calls it), Norton says his role is circumscribed. He describes it as providing "ingredients and limits"—images, animation, text, and sound as well as the rules the computer follows in serving them up. The computer does the rest of the authoring, serving the sequences of images that create the story variations. The readers complete the process by providing any meaning they choose.

Norton admits that the ingredients he has provided do have a theme: that of a murder mystery. In the site's initial design, images and text represented the testimony of witnesses at a murder trial (hence the site's title). Norton says he chose the murder-mystery theme because it included many of the elements he was seeking for the piece: "Witnesses often contradict each other, stories change over time, and what happened has to be pieced together by retrospective deduction."

The trial theme was more pronounced at the project's inception; however, the framing device was eventually discarded when users found it too distracting. "The shifting nature of the story was confusing enough for people, without adding the extra element of it being told by somebody in a specific context," says Norton.

Norton also believes the courtroom setting made people uneasy—a nervousness he thinks was caused by the contrast between users' confusion in this vaguely defined territory and their idea of the courtroom as an ordered place with clear rules and a final resolution. In contrast, the tabula rasa the story plays on now gives users carte blanche to do, and think, as they will. According to Norton, users "are quite happy to accept nonsense and vagueness on the plain white screen."

Beyond the idea of the murder, Norton had no particular narrative in mind. "The first images centered around someone falling from a building—perhaps jumping, perhaps pushed," he says. He arrived at the rest of the images "through free association on the themes of crime, surveillance, and so on." He also drew inspiration from movies, which he watched while he drew. In fact, he admits, "a few of them are shots from *Psycho*, with the characters replaced by balloonheads."

> The Right Amount of Detail

Norton realized that in order for the images to work together in many combinations, they would need to be almost iconic, without a lot of detail. The same held true for the characters in the story: Their lack of strongly defining features or personalities makes it easier for the site's users to project characteristics onto them.

"The tricky part is to find a balance where the characters don't seem too blank, but they're not too tied down in specific narrative roles, either," says Norton, who admits he probably could have done better on that count. "I think there's often too much ambiguity here," he admits.

Vague, threatening images appear in our hero's dream. Clicks do nothing here, but moving your pointer across the balloon multiplies the images as if you were using a cartoon paintbrush.

When you click the dreamer's frame, a mysterious figure (is that a Groucho mask?) appears and slaps him awake.

After that, our hero and the dad/psychiatrist/accomplice engage in a never-ending conversation. Random text and facial expressions for the hero are drawn from a database that includes more than 200 possibilities for each.

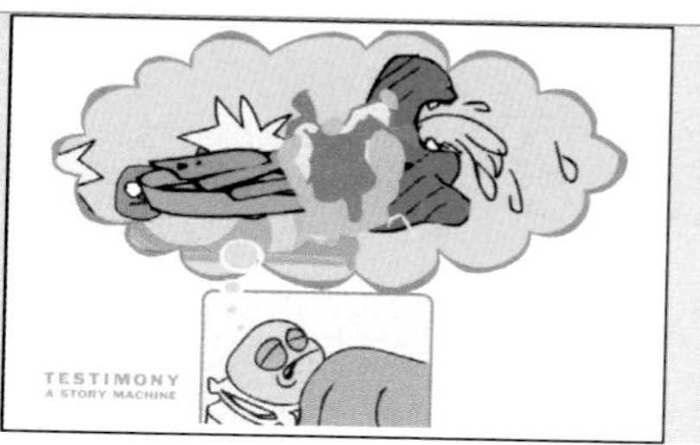

> Never the Same Story Twice

Story Machine's images and the text that fills the speech bubbles come from a library stored in movie clips, which Flash reaches into randomly at each click of a story frame (see "Random Sequencing," page 64. The core library includes about 250 different images, which are shared among most of the story sequences on the site. (Sequences that include animations or other special effects have their own image libraries.) If the story frame has a speech bubble, Flash pulls a random text from 200 possibilities, stored in another movie clip.

The math results in some high-magnitude numbers, but the story options reach virtually to infinity. Changing even one image in a sequence of frames changes the implied story. Each viewing adds new layers of meaning, as the user's experience of the site and the images viewed accumulate. And of course each user will have a unique interpretation of what he or she sees—even if by chance two viewers see the same sequence of scenes. I, for instance, saw a "dad" hitting our hero over the head with a frying pan in a transition sequence (see the facing page, middle). "Fascinating," remarks Norton. "Most people think he's a psychiatrist."

UNDER THE HOOD
RANDOM SEQUENCING

Figure 1

The `iconvchooser` movie clip has three frames, each of which holds a different conversation.

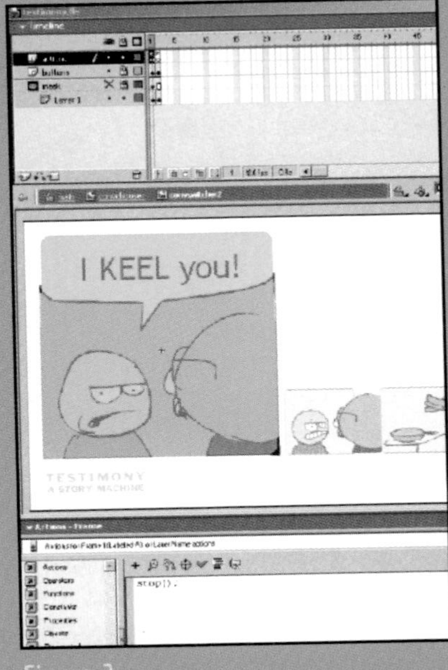

Figure 2

The `convswitcher` movie clip (inside `iconvchooser`) has two frames, one for each character. The actions layer holds a stop script that makes sure the movie moves to the next frame only when the button, which covers the image, is clicked.

In Scenario 4 (shown on page 62–63, bottom,) Norton creates a filmlike sequence featuring a conversation between two characters. The sequence looks storyboarded but, in fact, is purely random. The method, says Norton, "is embarrassingly simple, given all the attention it's gotten." A series of simple scripts draws random head images and random texts from movie clips, and combines them in hundreds of possible conversations.

To maximize the number of variations generated by this mixture of text and images, Norton created three different libraries of texts, called "conversations." (Since text takes up very little room, having multiple conversations makes for only a tiny increase in overall file size.) Each time the sequence plays, a script randomly picks one conversation from which it draws all of its content.

A movie clip called `convchooser` controls the action. In the main timeline, an instance of `convchooser`, named `iconvchooser`, sets up the starting animation:

```
tellTarget ("root.iconvchooser") [
     gotoAndStop (random(3)+1);
}
```

The script tells `iconvchooser` to randomly go to one of its three frames. Each frame inside `convchooser` (**Figure 1**) holds a different conversation movie clip—`convswitcher1` through `convswitcher3` —all identical except for their text libraries. (The movie clip `convswitcher3` has more text options, making for a greater number of possible conversations.) These movie clips are the source of the over-the-shoulder images.

Figure 3

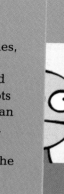

The *Ax* movie clip (inside `convswitcher`) holds shots of our hero. (*Bx* holds shots of the Groucho-masked man). A script controls the choice of random speech texts and head images.

Figure 4

The speech movie clip holds the texts that fill the speech balloons. (The heads movie clip holds the drawings.)

These movie clips, too, are quite simple: Each has two frames, one for each character (**Figure 2**), as well as a layer, named `Ax&Bx` (`A1&B1` for `convswitcher1`, `A2&B2` for `convswitcher2`, and so on), that holds the images and text for each character. Shots of our hero are in Frame 1; shots of the Groucho-masked man are in Frame 2. An invisible button covers the image: When clicked, it simply goes to the other frame in the clip, so that the shots will alternate between characters. (Stop scripts in the actions layer ensure that the shots alternate only when the button is clicked.)

Frame 1 of `convswitcher` holds another movie clip, called `A1` (or `A2` or `A3`) (**Figure 3**). In `Ax`, a speech layer has a movie clip (with the instance name `ispeech`) that holds the texts (40 for `A1` and `A2`, 160 for `A3`). The heads layer has a movie clip (with the instance name `iheads`) that holds the head drawings—40 of them, each with a different facial expression. In the actions layer, a script tells both `ispeech` and `iheads` to go to a random frame. In the actions layer of both movie clips is a stop script (**Figure 4**).

The technique is simple. The surprise is that when the script runs, it creates a running conversation that Norton says surprises even him sometimes with its crazy sense.

The over-the-shoulder conversation always ends the same way—with the hero bonked over the head with a frying pan.

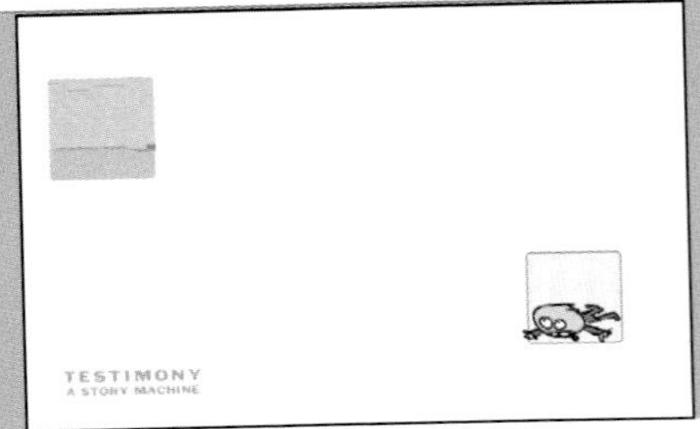

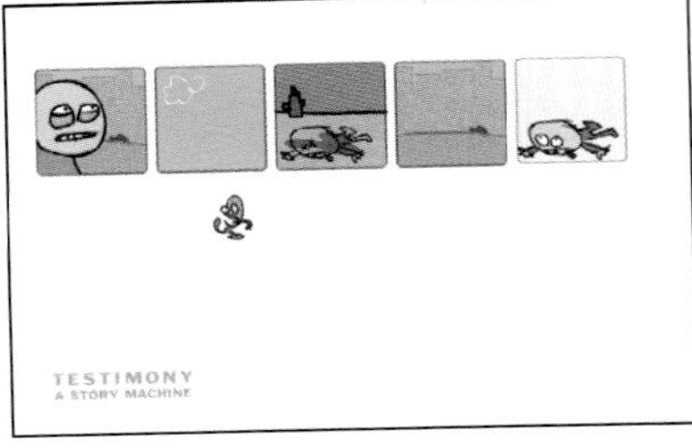

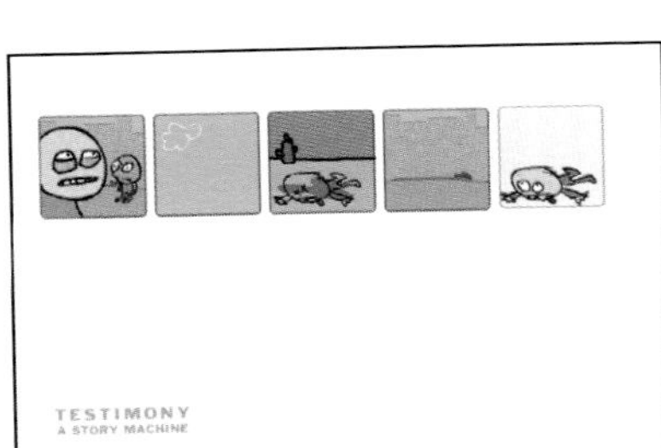

Then our smashed hero becomes part of the next scenario. Here, the images don't swap out from the main image library. Instead, the characters move between frames to create new situations.

> Moving the Story Forward

For this first iteration of the site, Norton designed seven "scenarios," or situations in which we see our hero. (It's these scenarios that change when the user clicks an orange-bordered frame.)

The transitions between scenarios are amusements in themselves. Our hero falls from a ledge into a bed, he tosses the frames from the screen, or the frames create a train that tunnels into his head.

As the scenarios change, so does the use of Story Machine's screen real estate. Each scenario takes place in a different part of the rectangle.

Scenarios can also differ in the way that users interact with them. While each scenario uses the simple click-to-change-images action, the effect of a click can vary subtly or not so subtly in different scenes. In one scene, our hero ponders a memory of a pig chasing a man (or the man chasing a pig, depending on your interpretation). Clicking the empty thought balloon between the characters' appearances triggers a sound file that makes it clear that one of them has caught the other, and it wouldn't be a pretty sight, if you could see it.

In the next scenario, the action takes place in our hero's dreams. Here, it's not clicks that change the images, but simple mouse movements. Your pointer seems to paint new images across the dream canvas.

In another sequence, you need to click the characters in the frames to see the programmed action. The characters animate and move into position in neighboring frames, changing the images and the story line in a whole new way.

> Subtle Sound

Story Machine's sound is as important as its images in creating the site's mood.

The sounds, which Norton pulled from old movies and sound-effects CDs, include running water, traffic, chants, and unidentifiable vocalizations, all of which play quietly in the background (except in the last scenario, which is silent). During transitions, appropriate sound effects accompany the action—footsteps, a slap, the sound of the freight train.

"I was aiming to keep the sound from being very manipulative or hip," says Norton. "I wanted it to be a sort of background noise that smooths over gaps and transitions."

Given the playful nature of the graphics, the sound is unexpectedly subdued. For the most part, it sets a spooky, rather than comic, tone, though it uses nothing so obvious as creaking doors or screams. At times almost Zen-like, the sound lends a seriousness to the site that, I think, somehow prods users to slow down and consider the scenes more carefully than they would in a silent or more manically scored context.

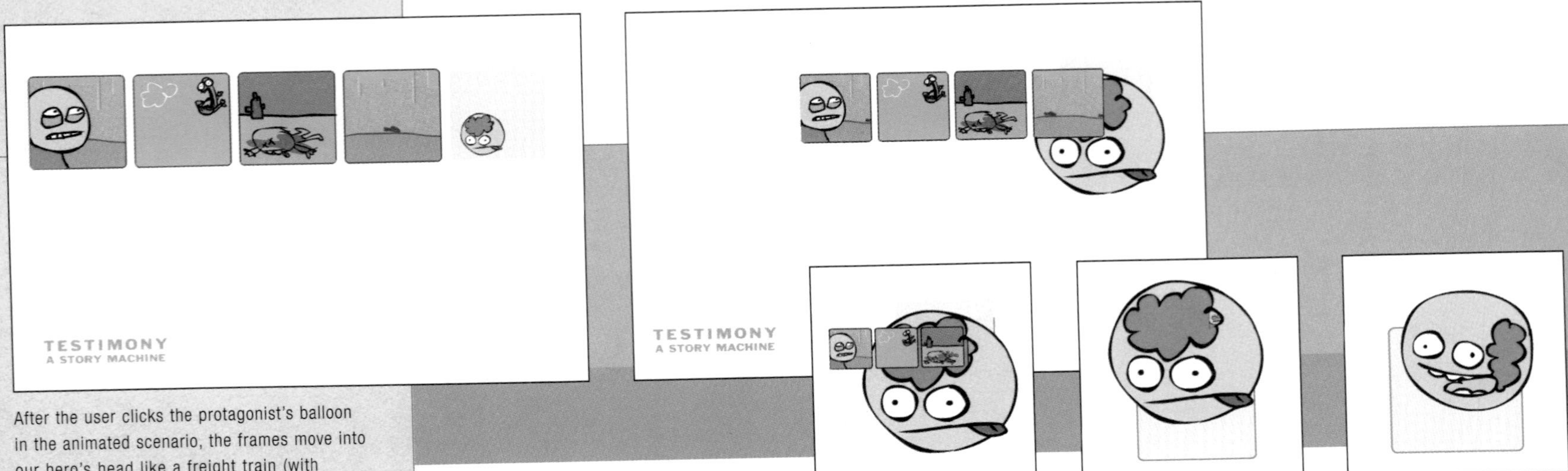

After the user clicks the protagonist's balloon in the animated scenario, the frames move into our hero's head like a freight train (with appropriate sound effects). He then drops into another frame and spits out another series of frames, which not only swap out images and frames, but change the frame shapes for added texts, but change the frame shapes for added interest. When you're ready to move on, our hero throws away the old frames and, voilà, we're back at the beginning, where it all starts again.

> Complexities to Come

At first, users may assume that Testimony is more complex than it is. I, for one, assumed that when the story progressed to a new scenario, the new action would vary depending on the sequence of images in the frames. I was disappointed when I realized story development wasn't that complex. "People assume the computer is 'tracking' their choices and responding to them. It isn't; it's just random," Norton says. He points out, though, that the current version of the site was only created as an experiment in storytelling. "The next one I make, I would like to have it tracking user choices," he says ruefully, "but my scripting skills aren't up to that yet!" ■

TESTIMONY
A STORY MACHINE

So when do you...
You do it.
TESTIMONY
A STORY MACHINE

So when do you...
You do it.
TESTIMONY
A STORY MACHINE

TESTIMONY
A STORY MACHINE

SPOTLIGHT
TESTING FOR FLASH

On any Flash site, one of the first actions you'll want to take is to sort out visitors who have a Flash plug-in from those who don't. It sounds straightforward, but how you handle this task makes an important first impression on your users.

Basically, you can tackle the situation in one of two ways (and either approach is reasonable). The first is to present a screen that tells users your site requires a certain version of Flash. If they have it, they can go ahead and click in to the site. If they don't have it, they can link to a site to download the plug-in, or click over to an HTML version of the site (if one exists).

The second way to handle the situation is to automate it. A simple JavaScript sniffer on your site's home page can test for the correct version of the plug-in on the user's system and then automatically send any user who has it to the Flash version of the site.

Some usability experts suggest that you should always follow the first option, arguing that it assigns control where it properly belongs: with the user. Others (including me) prefer the second. I think users who have the Flash plug-in are probably willing to accept Flash content (provided, of course, that you've followed good Flash practice in componentizing, preloading, and using whatever other methods you need to, to make your

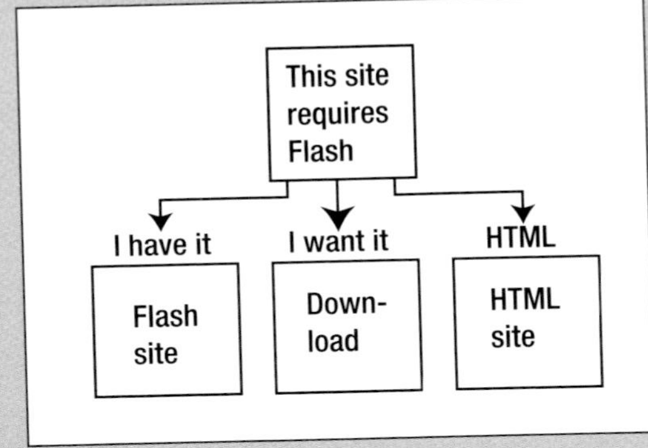

The simplest route is to ask users to select their own paths: to the Flash site, to download the Flash plug-in, or to the HTML version (if one exists).

Flash site load quickly). Having to read a page and make a decision is not the first experience that users are probably hoping for when they visit your site. And many users who aren't familiar with the contents of their systems, or who don't know much about the difference between Flash and HTML, won't know what you're talking about, anyway.

If you're doing a plug-in test, make sure you also pay attention to what happens next. You have two paths to choose from: shunt users without a plug-in to an alternate HTML version of the site (if one exists), or send them to a page that lets them download the plug-in. On the face of it, the first way seems best. If someone doesn't have the Flash plug-in, you can probably assume that getting it is not their first priority—so just get them to the content, already. However, the second option has its uses, too. Flash Player 6 was released while I was writing this book, and after I installed the new plug-in, almost every Flash site turned me away; they were checking for Flash 5, not 6. Some were impossible to get into at all, even though I knew I had the right software. I was peeved. So if you think people might be coming specifically to see your Flash content, I say use the warning page—with an important added feature: Add a link that lets users click into the Flash site if they think they have the right plug-in.

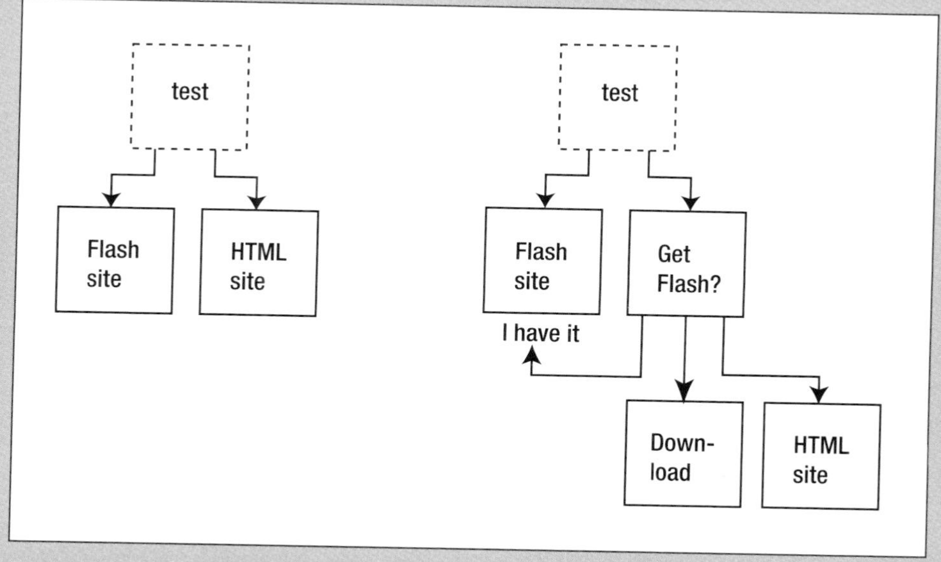

"Sniffing" for the plug-in with a simple server-side script automates the sorting—making it easier on the user, but providing an opening for a problem if your script fails in its duty. Offering the user the ability to click into the Flash site (the path on the right) covers that eventuality.

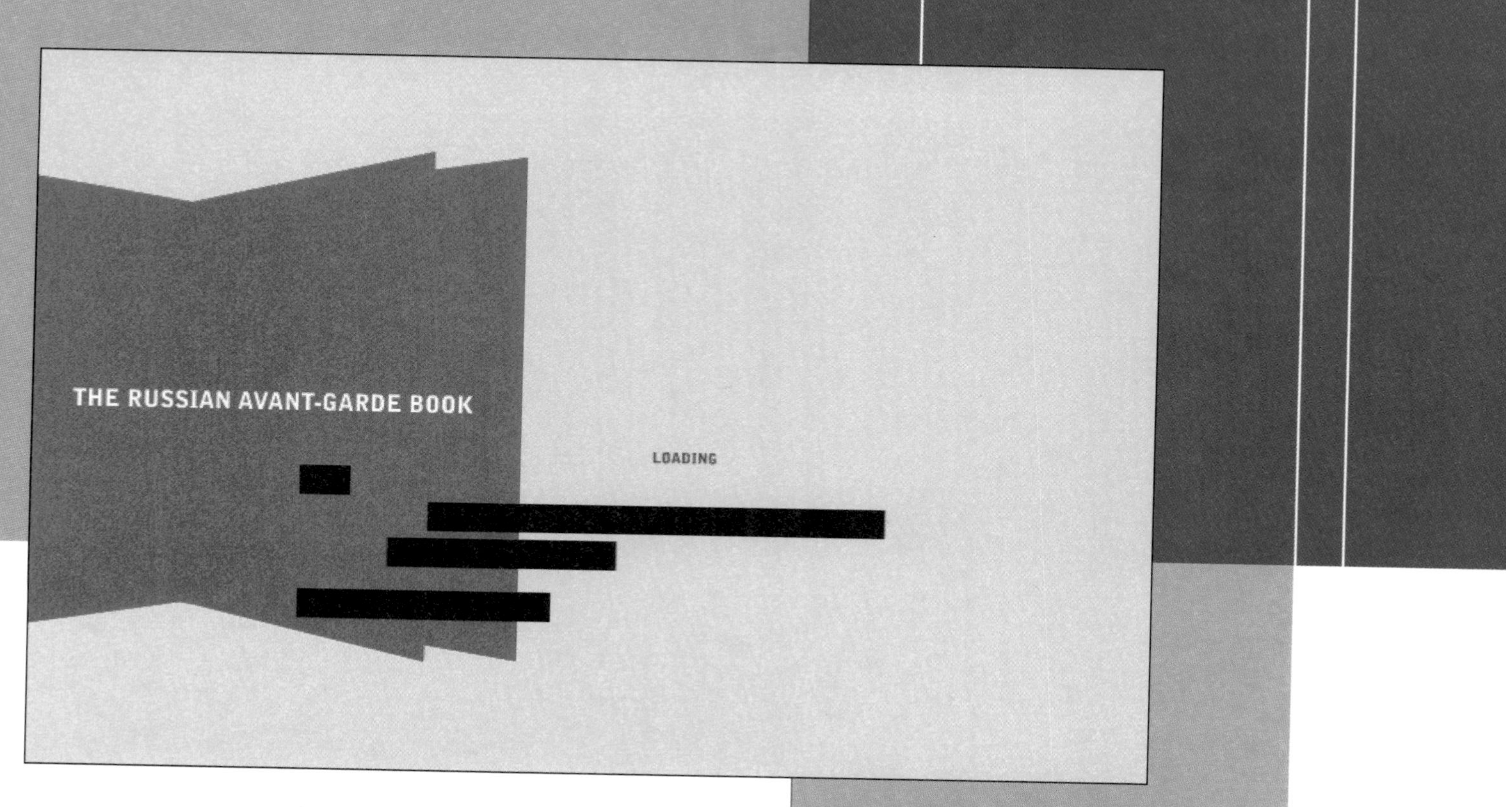

CHAPTER

MOMA: THE RUSSIAN AVANT-GARDE BOOK 1910–1934

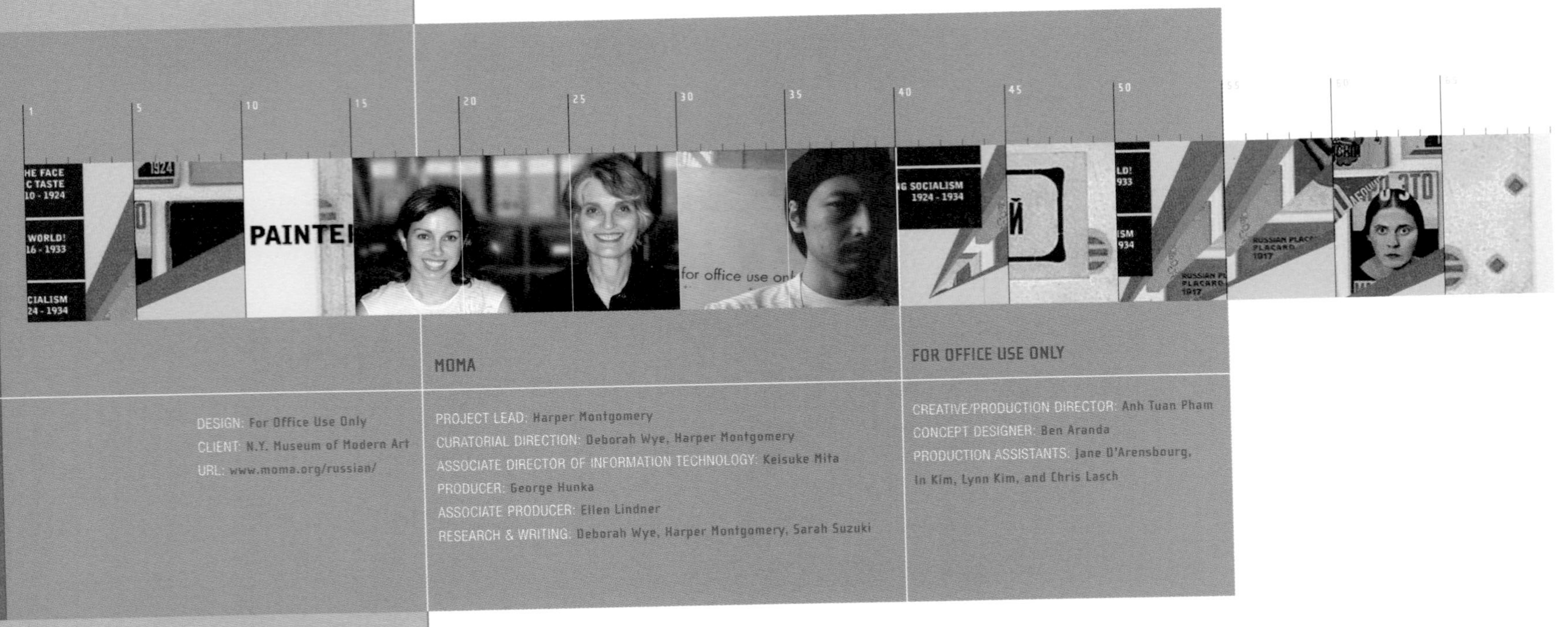

MOMA
FOR OFFICE USE ONLY
DESIGN: For Office Use Only
CLIENT: N.Y. Museum of Modern Art
URL: www.moma.org/russian/
PROJECT LEAD: Harper Montgomery
CURATORIAL DIRECTION: Deborah Wye, Harper Montgomery
ASSOCIATE DIRECTOR OF INFORMATION TECHNOLOGY: Keisuke Mita
PRODUCER: George Hunka
ASSOCIATE PRODUCER: Ellen Lindner
RESEARCH & WRITING: Deborah Wye, Harper Montgomery, Sarah Suzuki
CREATIVE/PRODUCTION DIRECTOR: Anh Tuan Pham
CONCEPT DESIGNER: Ben Aranda
PRODUCTION ASSISTANTS: Jane D'Arensbourg, In Kim, Lynn Kim, and Chris Lasch
PAINTE
for office use on

CHAPTER

MOMA: THE RUSSIAN AVANT-GARDE BOOK 1910–1934

INTRO

A Flash site shows off a collection of rare books in ways the accompanying museum exhibition, catalog, and touchscreen kiosks can't.

Pictured: [from left] Harper Montgomery, Deborah Wye, Anh Tuan Pham

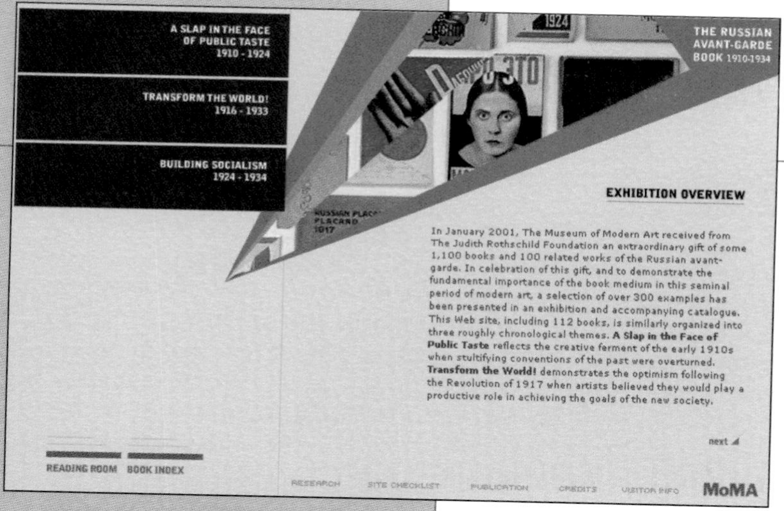

An exhibition overview dominates the home page. It describes the collection as well as the three main sections of the site.

In 2001, New York's Museum of Modern Art (MOMA) received a valuable gift from the Judith Rothschild Foundation: 1,100 rare illustrated books created in early 20th-century Russia by artists such as El Lissitzky, Aleksandr Rodchenko, and Vladimir Mayakovsky.

As museum staff members registered, cataloged, and conserved the books, they set about devising ways to make the collection available to public view. The books can always be viewed privately, in the museum's Study Center, but to make them even more accessible, the museum provided four other ways to get to know these important works of art: An exhibition, on view at MOMA from March 26 through May 21, 2002, presented 300 of the books to the public. A 304-page catalog offers a longer-lasting document of the same selection. Touchscreen kiosks available at the show let visitors page electronically through five of the most significant books. And finally, a Flash-based Web site—created with New York design firm For Office Use Only and launched along with the exhibition—provided a variety of ways to experience the books, both at the museum and beyond.

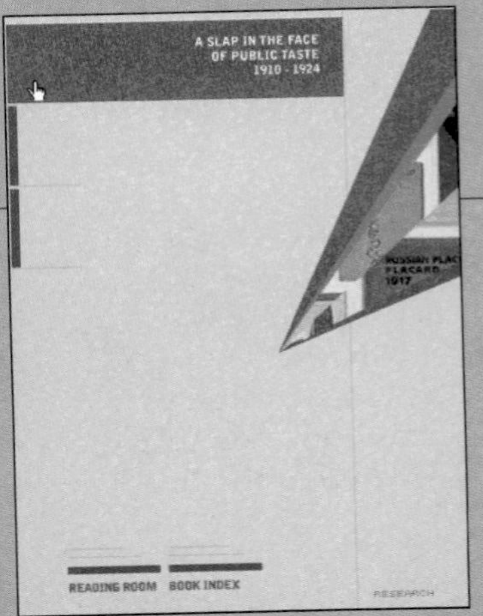
A SLAP IN THE FACE
OF PUBLIC TASTE
1910 - 1924
READING ROOM
BOOK INDEX

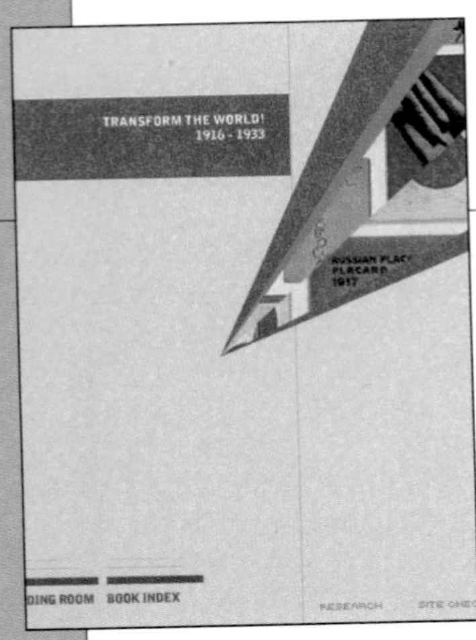
TRANSFORM THE WORLD!
1916 - 1933
BOOK INDEX

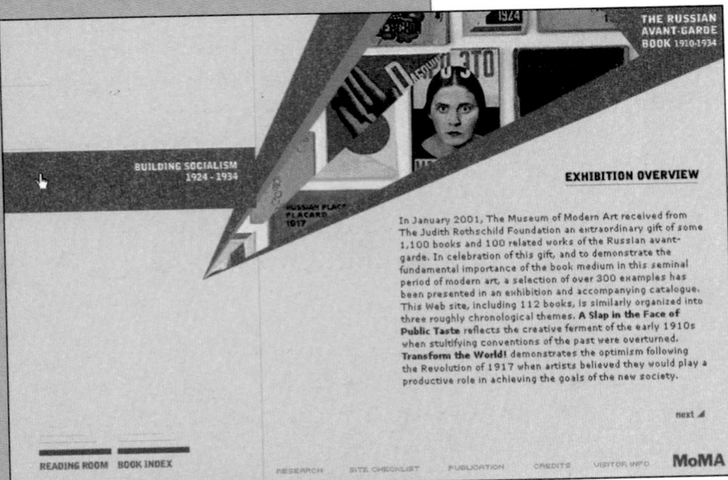
THE RUSSIAN
AVANT-GARDE
BOOK 1910-1934
BUILDING SOCIALISM
1924 - 1934
EXHIBITION OVERVIEW
In January 2001, The Museum of Modern Art received from The Judith Rothschild Foundation an extraordinary gift of some 1,100 books and 100 related works of the Russian avant-garde. In celebration of this gift, and to demonstrate the fundamental importance of the book medium in this seminal period of modern art, a selection of over 300 examples has been presented in an exhibition and accompanying catalogue. This Web site, including 112 books, is similarly organized into three roughly chronological themes. A Slap in the Face of Public Taste reflects the creative ferment of the early 1910s when stultifying conventions of the past were overturned. Transform the World! demonstrates the optimism following the Revolution of 1917 when artists believed they would play a productive role in achieving the goals of the new society.
next
READING ROOM
BOOK INDEX
MoMA

The main navigation unfurls as the site is loading, but each red bar curls into a narrow gray bar as soon as it is rolled over. After that, the bar opens again—ready for clicking—each time a pointer rolls over the area near it.

> A Virtual Exhibition

The museum's curators were careful to exploit the strengths of each of the venues. Only the exhibition could present the books in all their physical glory, but because the books were displayed in glass cases and couldn't be handled, the experience was necessarily limited, even for people who made it to New York for the show. The touchscreen kiosks mitigated that problem by letting museum visitors see multiple pages of five of the books. And the printed catalog made it possible for viewers to see more pages of more books (in high-quality reproductions), along with comprehensive essays by the curators explaining the importance of individual books and the collection.

The Web site extends the experience of the books still further, and to a much broader audience. "The exhibition is only up for two months, and we wanted people to be able to see it for a longer time, and to see it outside of New York," says Deborah Wye, chief curator of the Department of Prints and Illustrated Books at MOMA. "And we realized right away that the Web site could offer new kinds of information not in the exhibition and not in the catalog."

Like the catalog, the site can present multiple pages of each book. Unlike the catalog, though, the site, with Flash, can provide an experience more like the one offered by the museum's Study Center, by letting visitors interact, through animation, with the three-dimensional qualities of the book, as well as with an interactive Book Index, which lets them view the books by year, artist/author, or publisher. The site also offers educational enhancements, such as pop-up definitions of terms.

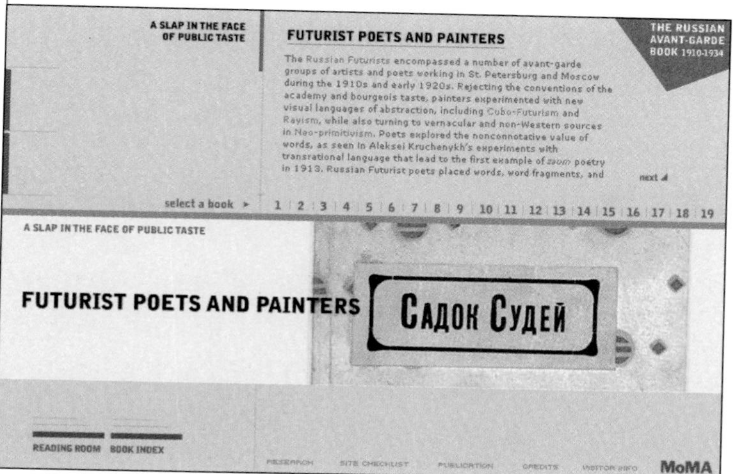

Each main theme has subthemes, which are displayed in the navigation block when a user has chosen a main theme (top). Choosing a subtheme (bottom) delivers an introductory essay and a menu of books that illustrate the topic.

> A Conceptual Model

Anh Tuan Pham, creative director of For Office Use Only, says that an important tool in developing this Web site was the brainstorming period that the design firm uses to research and develop concepts for all of its projects. "The result isn't to present working interfaces, but just to establish a mood or form that will inform the site's structure and its look and feel," he says. For this site, a number of concepts brewed during the two-week research period.

As his team read the essays Wye and others had written for the catalog, Pham says he was struck by the importance of turning pages to the experience of the books. The artists who made these books used their pages the way a filmmaker might have used different frames in the early cinema that influenced them. "The book would tell a story through time when you turned pages from one page to the next," Pham says. Another idea the team worked with was the concept of the Web site as a library, "a space where you experience books in different ways," Pham says. Just as a library has display tables, stacks, and a reading room, the Web site could have different places for different experiences as well.

Last was the concept of a book itself, and how it's used. "The site is more or less linear, but there are lots of opportunities to flip back and forward," Pham says. "We felt that people should go through the site like they'd go through a book."

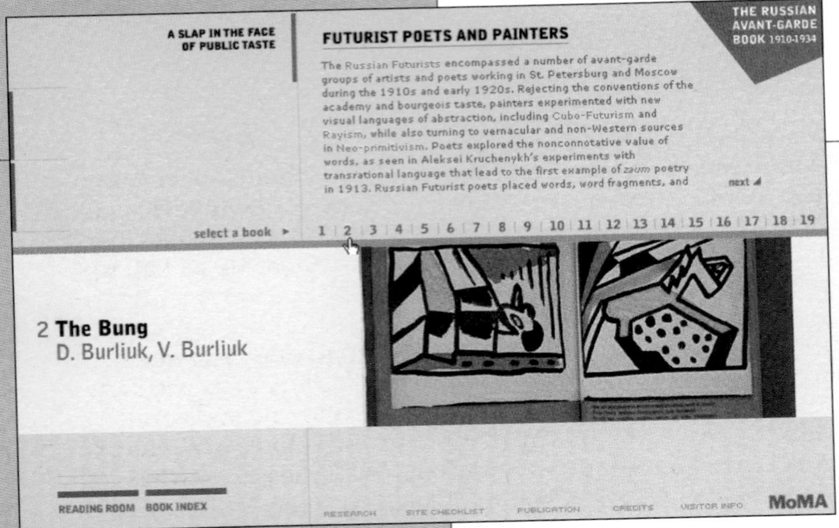

As the user delves deeper into the book information, the viewing window (reminiscent of a wide-screen movie, says Pham) and the book image grow, representing the act of going "deeper" into a book.

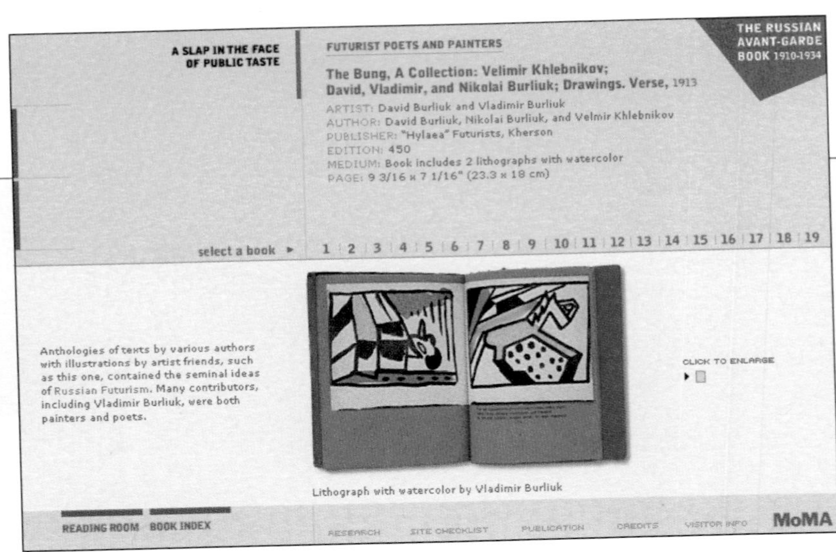

All of these ideas percolated through the site's design, but Pham emphasizes that none of them was meant to define the site completely. In fact, their influence on the design could be very subtle. "The underlying structure should all be in line with some guiding direction, but no concept should be used too rigidly," he says. "We don't want to say, 'This site is a library,' and then make it literally a library."

> A Bookish Site

Perhaps the concept that most influenced the look and feel of the site was the idea of a book, and how one interacts with it.

For instance, Pham says, "there is a cover, a visual element that introduces you to the site." And both the site's structure and its interaction reflect those of a book. Pham says the team tried to create an experience that would be like turning pages. "It's not like you jump from one place to another," he explains. "Instead,

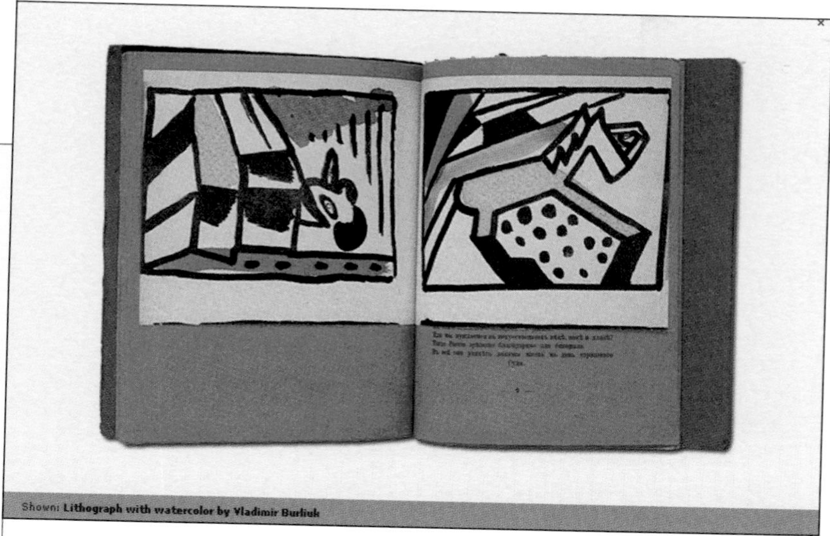
Shown: **Lithograph with watercolor by Vladimir Burliuk**

you go deep, and then go back out." Pham used size to interpret that feeling: A window that holds the book images starts out small, with close-cropped views of the book. However, as you click deeper into that book's information, the size of the viewing area grows subtly, until finally it fills the whole page. It's a psychological, rather than literal, interpretation of the act of delving into a book.

The "bookness" of the site can be seen in other ways as well. The animations that play while a new area of the site is loading are Pham's interpretations of the fanning pages of a book. However, Pham doesn't mind if people don't realize his intent as they watch it. "We wanted to abstract it so that people won't even recognize it as a book till the second or third time they see it," he says, adding that he hopes the mere visual effect is enough to justify it for those who don't make the connection. "For the people who don't see it, I hope they still see something that's in line with the rest of the site."

> Inspiration from the Printed Page

During the research phase, Pham and Ben Aranda, the concept designer for the project, had the privilege of going backstage with Wye and her team to view the books. Pham says that much of the site's visual design developed from ideas he picked up from the books during that visit.

"A lot of the design that came out of that period is almost perfectly suited for Flash," Pham notes. "The artists used lots of geometric shapes and flat colors, and they played with motion." Pham compares what the Constructivist designers of the early Soviet Union were doing in book design to what Flash users do with animation. "The first thing you learn to do in Flash is how to tween a square into a circle. That's what a lot of these designers were doing—making these abstract shapes dynamic," he explains.

Pham says he drew both individual details and general concepts from the books he saw that day. He sketched out those ideas during his tour and applied them later to the site's design. One example: the black bars that show the progress of the site's initial load, and that stand in for the main site navigation when the section titles are hidden. Pham drew his inspiration for these not only from graphic elements used in the books, but from another instance he found interesting. "A lot of these books were handmade, one by one, and the artist would make mistakes," he explains. In one, the artist hid mistakes in the text with black bars, Pham says, which worked in the design because the design itself was so geometric.

The bright red blocks and contrasting black used throughout the site are clearly inspired by the Russian designers' aesthetic.

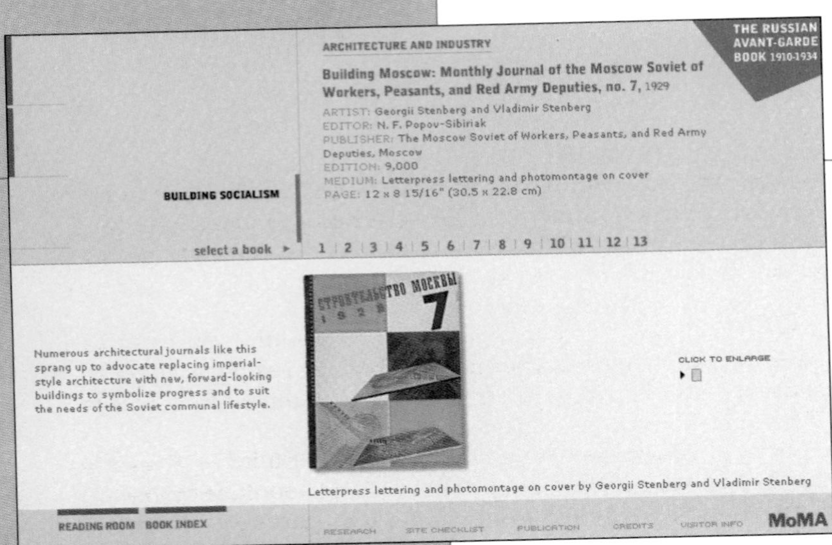

Two types of information are offered for each book: bibliographic information in the text area, above the viewing window, and a short blurb about the book's significance, to the left of the book image itself. Credits for the page or cover shown are below the book image.

> Images That Draw You In

MOMA and For Office Use Only immediately agreed that visual information should take precedence over text on the site.

Harper Montgomery, MOMA's project lead and co-curator for the site, says, "We wanted to foreground the images of the books themselves. We wanted to entice people with the beauty of the books." People don't generally think of books as art objects, she notes, and the team wanted that association to be their first impression as they viewed the site.

As the designers at For Office Use Only sketched out design proposals for the different site pages, they showed the number of lines of text available on each. The MOMA staff then set about fine-tuning the text to fit the space. "At one point, the texts were much longer than they are now," says Wye. "We just made the essays shorter and shorter, until we had the right amount of information." Pham calls this process "optimizing the content," akin to optimizing images to suit the Web.

On its side, the MOMA team was also very conscious of keeping things short. "The text wasn't our main focus," says Wye. "We wanted the text explanation for people who might be interested, but we didn't want them to get bogged down in it. We were very conscious of the length of time people would want to spend reading."

The team carefully chose what types of information to include and where to place it onscreen. Short contextual essays introduce each section. And each book page includes three short sections of text. One, which Wye calls "a nugget for readers to take away," offers some facts about what makes the book important or interesting, and is positioned in the viewing window to the left of the book

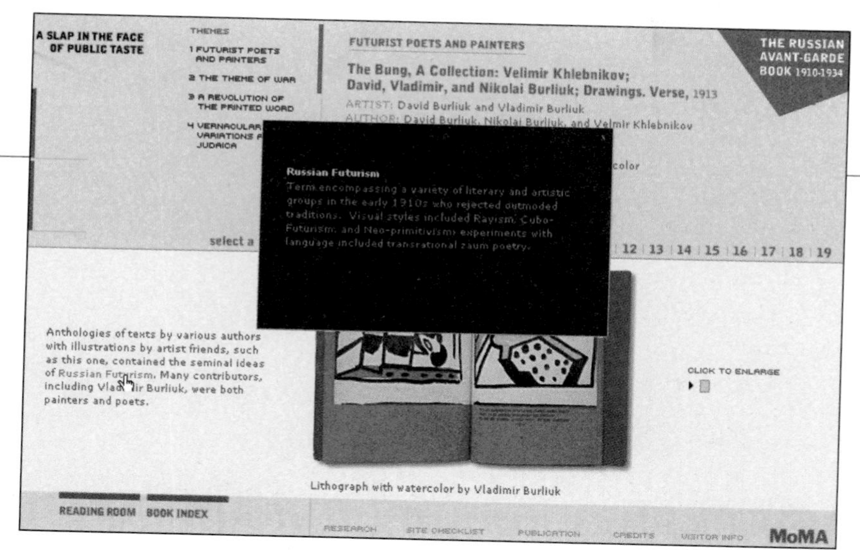

Definitions of key terms pop up in a new window. This type of information appears only on the Web site.

image. Another, with bibliographic information, is above the viewing window, in the blue-tinted area used elsewhere for introductory essays. The third, below the book, adds specific attributions for the page or cover shown.

Wye says that the positions of the two main information blocks were reversed in an earlier design, but the resulting page seemed "too stiff." The team's goal was to highlight the "nugget."

"I was thinking that if the reader took only 1 minute, their eye might go to the left first," says Wye. "For people who spent more time or wanted to know more, it requires a little more effort to go to the top for it." The highlighting of the white background and its proximity to the book image does indeed make this "nugget" information more likely to catch your eye than the facts up top.

Visitors can obtain other types of information about the books elsewhere on the site. Terms specific to the era or art form are highlighted in red within the text; clicking them pops up a window containing a definition. Information about the artists, authors, and publishers is centralized in the Book Index. And complete documentation from the catalog is available through the Research link in the footer.

"What we produced was about restraint in terms of the content," says Pham. He contrasts the experience with MOMA to his usual conversations with clients about onscreen text. "MOMA really realized that we couldn't just copy and paste the content from the catalog to the Web site and have it work in both mediums," says Pham. "People read less onscreen

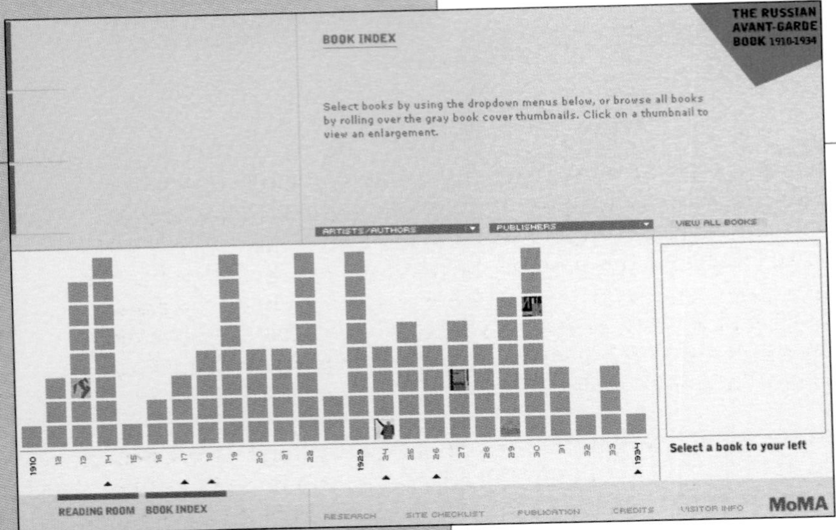

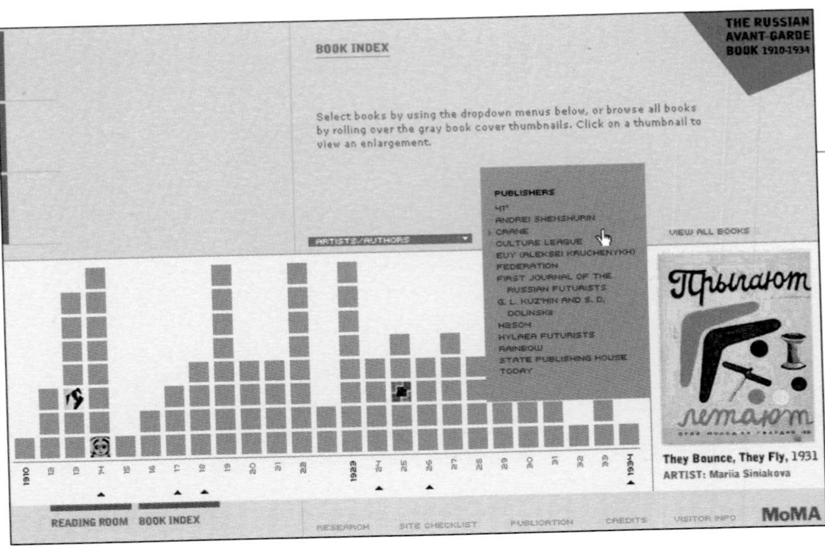

The Book Index presents the books by the year they were created, showing, at a glance, the relative activity during different years. When the Index is first opened, random books are highlighted, hinting to users that rolling over the squares will reveal more information (left).

Drop-down menus let users view the books by a certain artist/author or publisher (right). Once a user selects an item from the menu, only that entity's books are highlighted in the grid.

than from the printed page. Usually, that's something I have to fight clients for. They feel that every piece of screen real estate should be devoted to content. But my argument is that if you want people to read the content, it should be focused and shorter."

Size considerations extended to the total number of books shown on the site as well. The site presents 112 books, compared with the catalog's 300. Part of the paring down had to do with budget, says Wye. But mostly, the team felt that cutting down the number of books made for "the right experience," she says. "If one section had been twice as long, people wouldn't go to the second section and the third section."

> The Book Index

In addition to the "browsing table" of the theme sections, users will find two of the site's other "rooms" at the bottom-left corner of the window—the Reading Room and the Book Index.

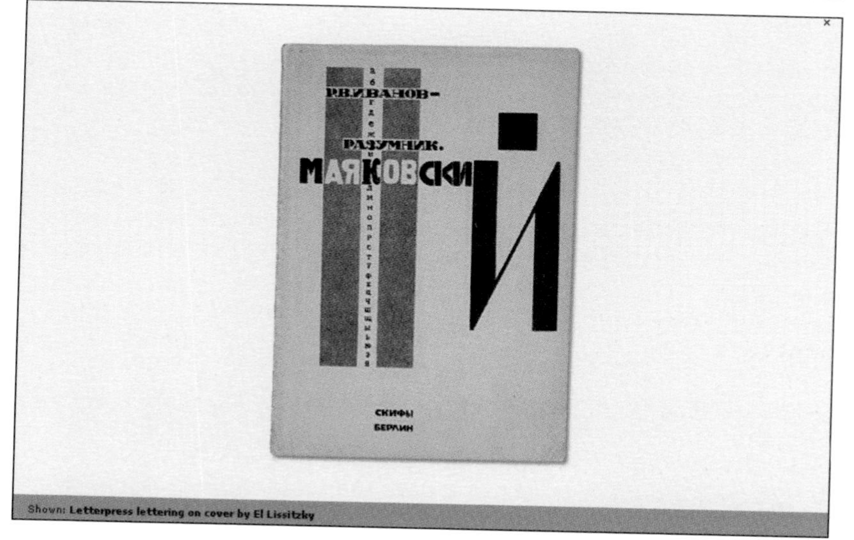

When the square for a book in the grid is rolled over, the book appears in an area at the far right (top). Clicking it reveals the full-size image (bottom).

The Book Index might be thought of as a particularly sophisticated card catalog. Clicking the Book Index button reveals a timeline that covers the era under discussion—1910 to 1934. For each year, gray boxes represent books published that year. Randomly, the gray boxes become book covers for a second or so, disclosing their role as stand-ins for books and enticing you to roll over the boxes to view more information about the books they represent.

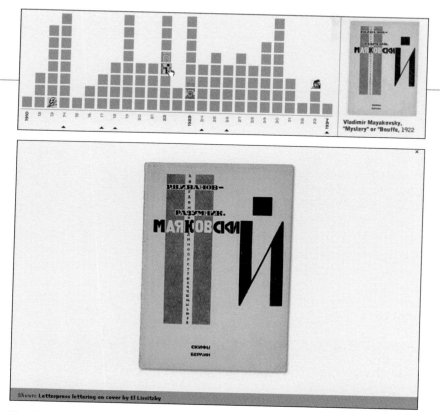

When your pointer rolls over a book box, information about it appears in an area at the far right—first the image and then, a second later, a transparent layer of text that holds bibliographic information. When you click the box, the entire window opens like an eyelid to show an enlarged image of the book (like the one you'd see from its book page in the theme interface).

Drop-down menus above the timeline let the user select an author/artist or a publisher. Selecting one highlights the books that person or publisher has produced. (It's a somewhat odd interface: You cancel your choices in the drop-down menus by clicking the View All Books button to their right.) This is a case in which the interface is the information. Before you touch any controls, the timeline presents a new understanding of the scope of the site and of the artists' productivity.

Viewing the timeline by artist is even more interesting. Suddenly, you have all of the site's information in the palm of your hand. The master works of such design stars as Rodchenko and El Lissitzky are served up in easily grasped handfuls. The index grew out of conversations about a search feature

UNDER THE HOOD
CALLING THE RIGHT ASSETS

BookList_final.xls [Read-Only]

	#	ID	title	log	image file	artist	author	year	publisher
2	1. SLAP IN THE FACE OF PUBLIC TASTE 1910-1924								
3	1A. Futurist Poets and Painters: 1910-1916								
	94	3A_02	Building Moscow, no 2	622	3A_02_01.eps			1930	
100	90	3A_03	Building Moscow, no 7	625	3A_03_01.eps			1929	
101	104	3A_04	Architectural Fantasies: 101 Compositions in Color, 101 Architectural Miniatures	841	3A_04_01.eps	Iakov Chernikhov	Iakov Chernikhov	1933	Mezhdunarodnaia kniga (International Book), Leningrad
102	101	3A_05	The Construction of Architectural and Machine Forms	617	3A_05_01.eps	Iakov Chernikhov	Iakov Chernikhov	1931	Leningradskoe obshchestvo arkhitektorov (Leningrad Society of Architects),
103	76	3A_06	CA. Contemporary Architecture, nos 2-3	629 633 630	3A_06_01.eps 3A_06_02.eps	Aleksei Gan	Moisei Ginzburg and Aleksandr Vesnin, eds.	1926	Gosudarstvennoe izdatel'stvo (State Publishing House), Moscow
104	95	3A_07	CA. Contemporary Architecture, no.6	629 633 630	3A_07_01.eps	Aleksei Gan	Moisei Ginzburg and Aleksandr Vesnin, eds.	1930	Gosudarstvennoe izdatel'stvo (State Publishing House), Moscow
105	96	3A_08	Russia. The Reconstruction of Architecture in the Soviet Union (New Ways of Building in the World	627	3A_08_01.eps	El Lissitzky	El Lissitzky	1930	Anton Schroll & Co., Vienna
106	97	3A_09	America. The Development of Style in New Buildings in the United States (New Ways of Building in the World	628	3A_09_01.eps	El Lissitzky	Richard Neutra	1930	
107	98	3A_10	France. The Development of New Ideas of Construction and Form (New Ways of Building in the World	626	3A_10_01.eps	El Lissitzky	Roger Ginburger.	1930	
108	79	3A_11	All-Union Printing Trades Exhibition: Guidebook	694 693	3A_11_01.eps 3A_11_02.eps	El Lissitzky Solomon Telingater	M. O. Shenderovich, ed.	1927	Komitet poligraficheskoi vystavki (Committee for Polygraphic Exhibitions), Moscow
109	84	3A_12	The Complete Annotated Guide to Books Published from 1922-1928 by Moskovskii Rabochii [The Moscow Worker Publishing House	640 641	3A_12_01.eps 3A_12_02.eps	L. Shteiner Solomon Telingater		1928	Moskovskii rabochii (The Moscow Worker), Moscow-Leningrad

Checklist of images / Sheet1

Figure 1

An Excel spreadsheet was used to keep track of the codes associated with each book, artist/author, and publisher.

Creating the Book Index was as much a job for Microsoft Excel as it was for Flash, says For Office Use Only developer Anh Tuan Pham. Each of the 107 books in the index was assigned a number that identified every piece of information representing it (thumbnail, enlarged thumbnail, enlarged image, and publishing information) throughout the index. Likewise for every publisher and author represented by the books. Pham used Excel to keep all of this information straight (**Figure 1**).

With the naming system defined, Pham created movie clips to manage the actions common to every book. The most important of these, a clip named `thumbsContainer` (**Figure 2**), controls all of the gray boxes' actions on rollover—fading the books' images in and out, and placing the proper enlarged view and book information in the right-hand box. This movie clip also controls the opening, random animation that plays after the movie has loaded.

Pham then placed 107 instances of `thumbsContainer` on the timeline. "Since they are all instances of the same movie clip, arranging them is pretty easy—just making sure the right number of thumbnails are lined up for each year, and making sure everything is aligned," Pham says. He then named each with a book identifier: `t1` through `t107`.

Inside the `thumbsContainer` movie clip is another movie clip, called `thumbsMC`, which holds the thumbnail images, each in a different frame (**Figure 3**). The first frame of `thumbsContainer` tells Flash to get the name of the current instance:

```
myName = getProperty("",_name);
stop ();
```

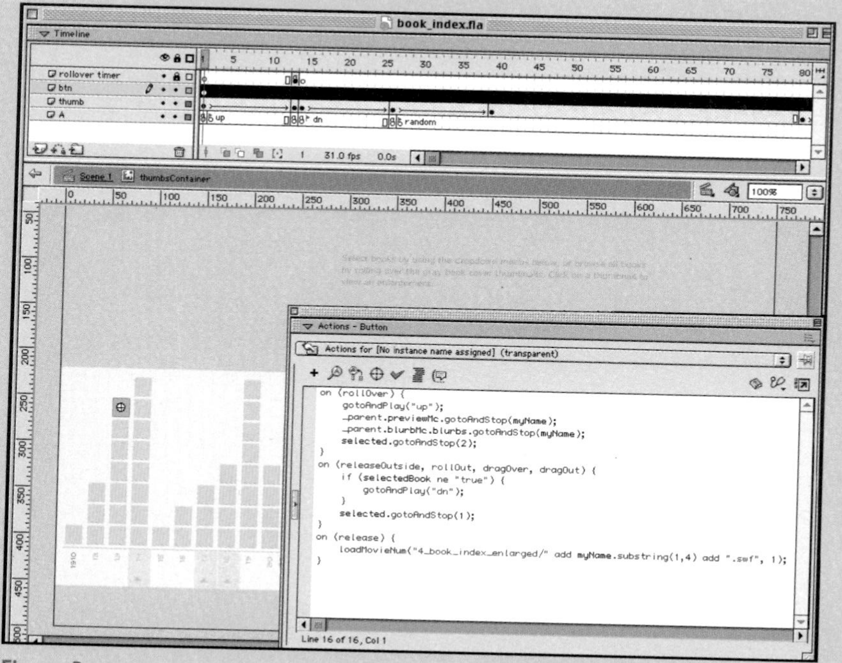

Figure 2

The thumbsContainer movie clip was instantiated 107 times—once for each gray box representing a book in the timeline. This script controls what happens when the user interacts with the clip. Since all images associated with a book have the same identifiers, the script can use the myName variable to call the matching images for each instance of the clip.

After this, Flash can just refer to the myName variable to find all the matching images. For instance, an onClipEvent(load) action finds the matching thumbnail:

```
onClipEvent(load)
      gotoAndStop (_parent.myName);
}
```

The same naming system was used to identify the enlarged thumbnails and book descriptions displayed to the right of the timeline. Called previewMC and blurbMC, those clips were saved on the root level of the movie. As with the thumbnail images, each of the 107 enlarged thumbnail images and book descriptions was placed in a separate frame, and each frame was labeled with its identifier (t1, t2, and so on). After playing the up animation, the rollover script in thumbsContainerMC uses the same technique to find the correct movie clip to play.

Each artist/author and publisher represented in the timeline is identified using a similar numbering system: Each artist/author is coded a1 through ax, and each publisher is coded p1 through px. Each instance of thumbsContainer has an onClipEvent(load) action that associates it with the right entities, for use when the user selects those settings from the drop-down menus:

```
onClipEvent (load) {
      author = "a3";
      author1 = "a5";
      pub = "p8";
}
```

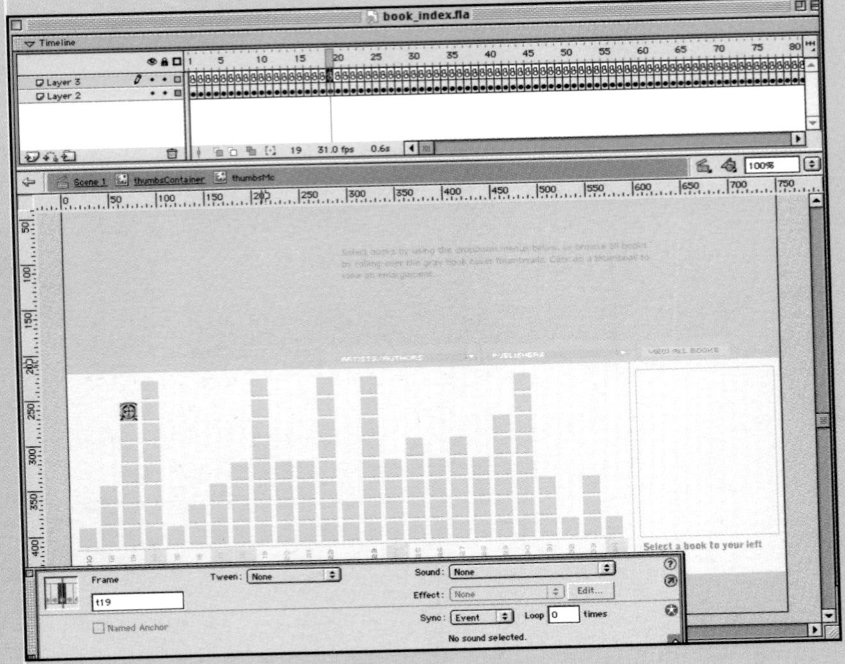

Figure 3

The thumbsMC movie clip holds every thumbnail image. Each image is labeled with the identifier of the book it's associated with. Pham created similar movie clips to hold every enlarged thumbnail, book blurb, artist/author bio, and piece of publisher information.

The book-description text and the author/publisher information at the top of the screen use the same codes. The system for calling the information works just like the system for calling the book description. One movie clip holds every artist/author bio, and another holds the information about every publisher. Then a script like the one used to call up the thumbnails determines which items to bring up, depending on which author/artist or publisher is selected from the menus.

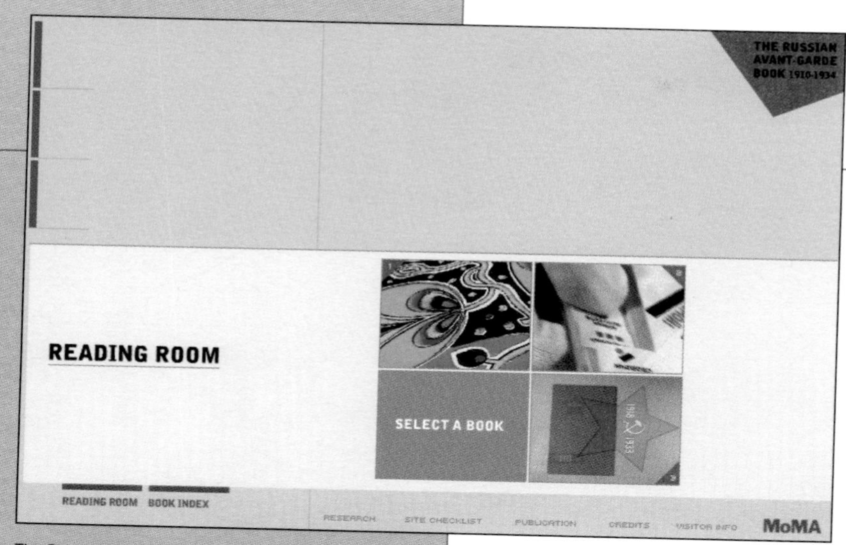

The Reading Room opener presents an animated menu of three books.

Rolling over one of the quadrants reveals the book's title and more of its cover.

for the site, says Pham. The chronological organization grew out of team meetings in which, he says, the team sat down and said, "Here's a framework, here's the information. How do we convey this?"

Users may draw an interesting lesson—and maybe some confusion—from the fact that the dates on the timeline have no relation to the start and end dates defining the three themes. I, for one, expected to see the beginning and end dates of each theme noted somehow, to help me see how each theme related to the overall time period. It made me take a closer look at the three periods, to learn that they overlapped significantly. The timeline draws attention to 1923 (the only year, other than the beginning and end years, written out in full) simply because it represents the middle of the time span, says Pham.

> The Reading Room

The companion link to the Book Index is the Reading Room—the place in the library where a reader begins to dig in. The Reading Room is designed to offer the kind of experience that can only be realized by turning a book's pages to view the artist-created sequence and by examining the workmanship of the printing, binding, and other features. Or rather, to come as close to that experience as you can without actually having the book in hand.

As in other sections of the site, the action of the Reading Room takes place in the white viewing window. In this section, a custom menu appears in that space: a rectangle split into quadrants, showing animations of three books. The words "Select a Book" appear in the fourth corner.

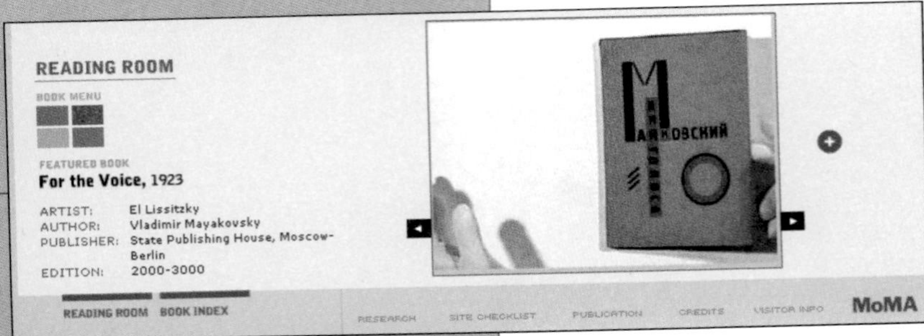

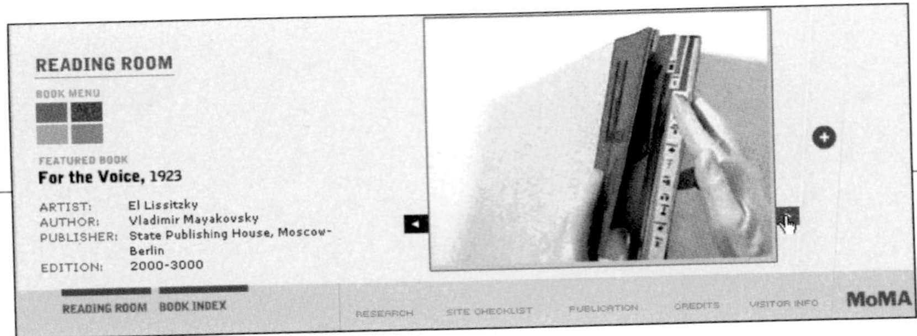

Clicking a book opens an interactive animation. With each click of the forward arrow, gloved hands turn one page of the book.

When you click a book choice, the viewing window changes to contain a clever animation. Gloved hands hold the book. When you click the forward arrow, the hands turn one page for you. Showing hands holding the book gives an idea of its scale, explains Montgomery. Not incidentally, it also provides a small but appreciated kick for the user, who gets to control the hands with mouse clicks. Information about the book and an iconic but functional version of the menu appear to the left. A plus sign appears to the right.

The plus sign is a mystery until you click it. Then, a second animation window opens. This view is unexpected, showing an impressionistic montage of the book at many angles and openings. You can close this second window at any time (by clicking what is now the minus sign). Play and stop buttons beneath each window show that they can be separately controlled. You can stop one window to enhance your focus on the other, or play both simultaneously to maximize the animation.

To create the section, Pham and Aranda videotaped Montgomery as she showed them three of the most spectacular books. The original idea was to show just the first animation—the hands paging through the book. When the For Office Use Only team viewed the video footage to be used, however, they realized they had other, even more interesting views. As Montgomery handled the books to show

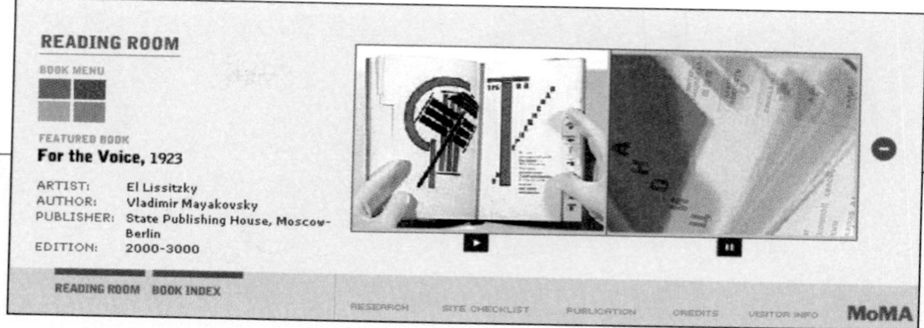

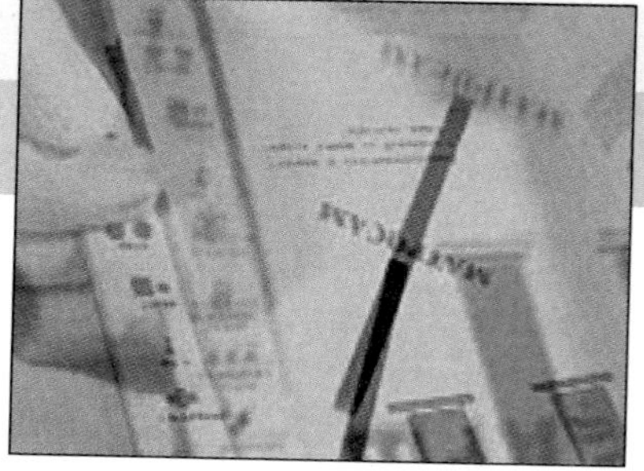

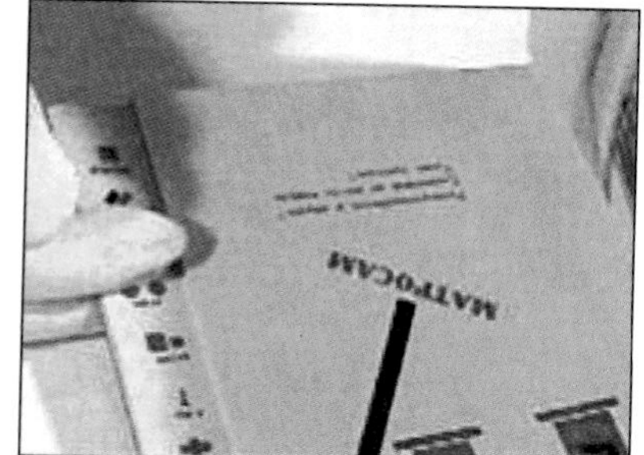

Clicking the plus sign to the right of the animation window opens a second animation, a montage that shows different aspects of the book. Each animation can be stopped or played separately. Clicking the minus sign closes the second window.

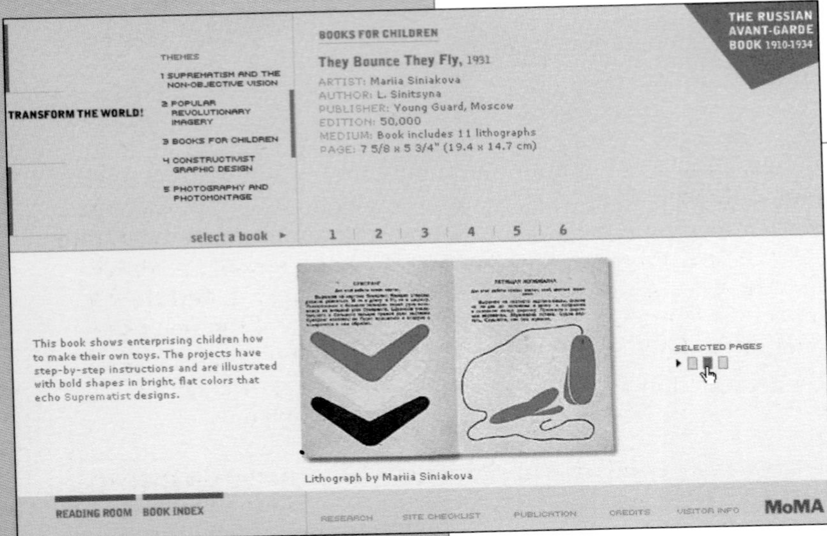

The complex system for navigating the themes is made clearer by the placement of its layers. The theme and subthemes are shown in the theme menus at the upper left. The next level, book selection, is above the viewing window. Navigating between pages of the book takes place next to the book image.

the designers their bindings and idiosyncrasies, the designers captured images that could only come from interacting with the book in an unscripted, natural way. Pham and Aranda turned that footage into impressionistic montages. "They show that the books aren't just layouts on a page," says Pham. "They have all these unique physical aspects, like the binding, or unusual materials, like wallpaper. You get to see the pages bending and the spine opening out."

> Complex Structure, Hidden Navigation

In addition to the three themes and their subthemes (and the multiple views of multiple books under each), the Book Index, and the Reading Room, the site offers footer navigation, which presents users with six more choices: Research (essays and full documentation from the catalog), Site Checklist (bibliographic information for all the featured books), Publication (a link to MOMA's store for purchasing the print catalog), Credits (a list of those responsible for the exhibition and site), Visitor Info (the museum's location and hours), and MOMA (a link to MOMA's main site).

The plethora of choices can be confusing at first. The three-part theme navigation is clearly paramount—a fact made clear not only by its placement and size but also by clever use of animation as the site first loads. After the angular red title graphic loads, the three themes unscroll one at a time. Then the buttons for the Reading Room and Book Index appear, and finally the footer, drawing your attention to each in turn.

The structure of the three main themes is itself complex. Each theme is subdivided into as many as five subthemes, which are divided in turn into as many as 19 books, which may have several

Shown: Letterpress lettering and photomontages on covers by Aleksandr Rodchenko

When the visual image—the book as art—is the focus, the site navigation disappears altogether.

pages, shown in two different views. The complexity of navigating these many layers, though, is mitigated by the placement of the navigation tools. Themes and subthemes are chosen from the theme menus. The next layer, choosing a book, is above the viewing window in which the book is shown, and finally, tools for navigating between different views of the book are next to the book image itself. Not only are the options clearly marked, but the placement of the controls makes clear what area of the page will be affected by your choice.

The main navigation—the theme menu—actually disappears as soon as you touch it with your mouse, rolling away into placeholder bars at the far left of the site window, and thereafter appearing only when it's rolled over. "The three-part structure is so simple that it doesn't need to be in your face," Pham says. The initial unfurling of the theme menus (and the unfurling again whenever the mouse hits that area) lets you know it's there.

"I thought the best way to design the site was for the interface to come in when it was needed and to disappear when it doesn't have to be there," says Pham. In enlarged book views, the site navigation disappears completely. The cursor turns into a pointing hand, though, and a click anywhere returns you to the previous view. A tiny x representing a close box sits at the upper-right corner, for those looking for it. "There are parts of the site when you need the interface to exist and other parts when it should just be about the image," says Pham.

As each book loads, a low-resolution image of it is displayed in the viewing window, using the loading time to give the user a preview of the books that illustrate the theme.

> Making the Wait Count

With more than 1,000 images (comprising multiple views of multiple pages for the 100-plus books), Pham had to be clever about how he managed load times. And he was.

To take up the (sometimes significant) time used for loading a subtheme and its accompanying phalanx of book images and information, Pham offers an edifying preview of the content you're waiting to see. As the book information loads, an image of that book grows in the viewing window. By the time the entire list is loaded, the user has already had a preview of the books to be seen —and something interesting to look at during the entire loading sequence. In this way, the loading sequence itself becomes an important part of the information presentation.

The result is both effective and simple. "I'm not the world's premier ActionScripter," says Pham. "I make things as easy as they have to be." More important, he thinks, is the simple art of timing. "I worked on the flow—when things happen. That's not ActionScripting. It's looking and tweaking and putting an extra frame here or there."

Pham says he first tried tying the rate of the image's growth in the window to the percentage completed of that book's information, but found that the pace didn't work. "I wanted to create this flow of pages turning," he says. "With the percentage script, the rhythm wasn't right." In the end, he just used simple tweened animation (with the first image in Frame 1, the second in Frame 2, and so on), with the playhead moving to the next frame only when the previous book's information was loaded. The same effect is used while the program loads a main theme's subthemes, or when you click a book choice, as a book's page images download.

In other places, such as while animations load in the Reading Room, the wait can be long and lightened only by the type of looping animation used by so many Flash sites to mark loading times. The designers did what they could to minimize file sizes and wait times, but in the end, they say, everyone agreed that the most important thing was that the site be visually compelling. So Pham and his team used techniques like the one just mentioned to make download wait times as painless as possible. "The right techniques can override page specifications, like a maximum page size, as long as you present information so that no one feels they're being stalled," says Pham.

> At the Show

In addition to its extended life on the Web, the Flash site also had a place in the exhibition—in a small room at the end, where four stations running Flash shared space with the exhibition catalogs.

The curators kept the terminals somewhat separate from the show on purpose. "At MOMA, we feel that our primary responsibility is bringing people together with the art," says Wye. "There was a balance in the amount of technology we wanted to have in the exhibition proper." In addition, she says that in other exhibitions, the staff had noticed that young people often rush to the workstations—a medium they're familiar with—rather than interact with the physical objects on display, which they aren't immediately sure how to relate to. Wye is very happy with what the site has accomplished and thrilled with what the Web can do for the department. But, she adds, "we want them to look at the real art when they're at the show." ■

SPOTLIGHT

THE PROBLEM OF THE BACK BUTTON

One of the dangers of Flash, say usability specialists, is that it breaks the rules of browser navigation. The browser's Back and Forward buttons, for instance, don't work for Flash sites. A user who clicks the Back button to return to a previous state of a Flash site will often be confused when that causes the Flash movie to reload from the beginning.

One way to mitigate this problem is to organize your Flash site so that different sections are on different HTML pages. That way, clicking the Back button will load the previous section, at least providing a logical, and perhaps understandable, result—even if it's not exactly the one the user was expecting. This technique is used to good effect in Bud Greenspan's Ten Greatest Winter Olympians, which is separated into three HTML pages: prologue, introduction, and shell. The user consciously clicks a control to move from one page to the next, establishing an explicit separation so that the Back button—if used—takes the user to a logical previous point.

Who would you select as the 10 Greatest Winter Olympians?
At February's 2002 Olympic Winter Games, renowned sports documentarian and historian Bud Greenspan will reveal his Top Ten list for the very first time!
Bud Greenspan, in partnership with General Motors, invites you to join this historic effort. Cast your ballot and enter to win a trip to see the 2004 US Olympic Team compete in Athens.
SALT LAKE 2002
GM
I have been privileged to witness thousands of great athletes
YOU COULD SEE THE US TEAM COMPETE IN ATHENS! ENTER
Bud Greenspan's 10 Greatest Winter Olympians
ATHLETES
Alberto Tomba
ITALY
ALPINE SKIING
VOTE FOR YOUR TOP 10 ATHLETES
SUBMIT VOTE
BUD GREENSPAN
FOR 50 YEARS, BUD HAS CAPTURED THE GREATEST MOMENTS IN SPORTS HISTORY.
VIEW BUD'S TOP 10 | VIEW CURRENT STANDINGS | REPLAY INTRO

Bud Greenspan's Ten Greatest Winter Olympians is organized onto three pages. If users click the Back button, they'll be taken to a recognizable and logical previous state.

Other designers do away with the problem by loading their sites into new Flash windows, minus the navigational chrome. That way, users don't have access to the Back button, and so can't be confused by its action.

Of course, simply taking away functionality may not be the best answer to a problem. If the browser buttons are missing, many designers feel responsible for providing their own Back and Forward functionality that works for the site. Euro RSCG Circle went to great lengths to build a Back button–type functionality into the MINI USA site (see "Under the Hood: Deep-Linking in Flash" on page 14). While the Back button on that site doesn't work exactly like the Back button in the browser, it does take users smoothly back and forth to previously visited pages—a useful functionality. And the effort of providing that functionality paid off in other ways, too. The same engineering gave the site's publishers the ability to link directly to content within the movie from emails and other marketing communications.

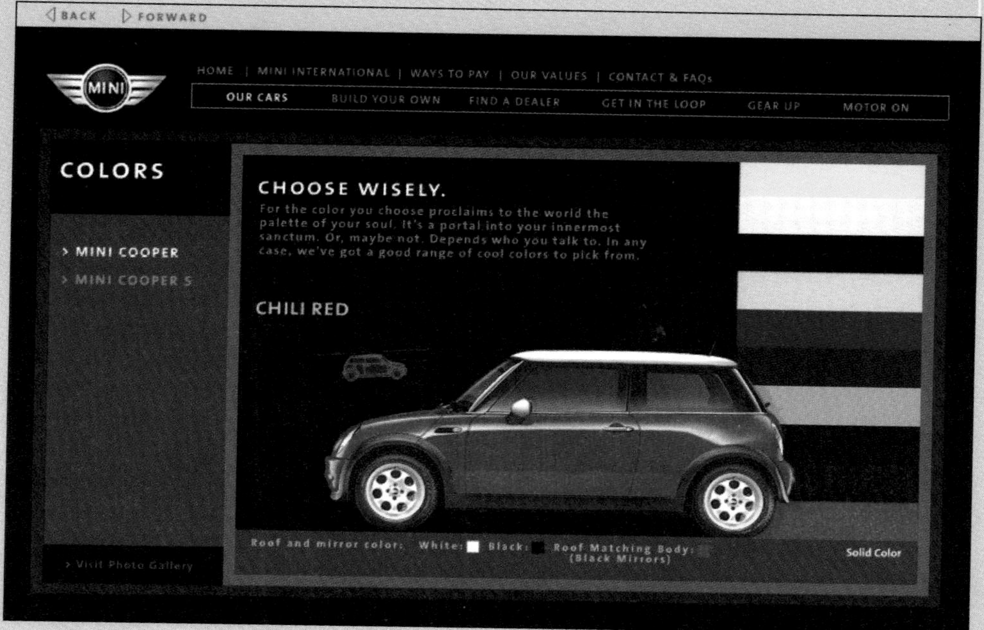

On MINI USA, the browser's Back button isn't available, and Back and Forward button functionality is built into the movie.

TCUP THE COLLECTIVE UNCONSCIOUSNESS PROJECT

→

1. CREATE A DREAMER ACCOUNT.
2. LOG A DREAM.
3. EXPLORE THE COLLECTIVE.

CHAPTER

TCUP THE COLLECTIVE UNCONSCIOUSNESS PROJECT

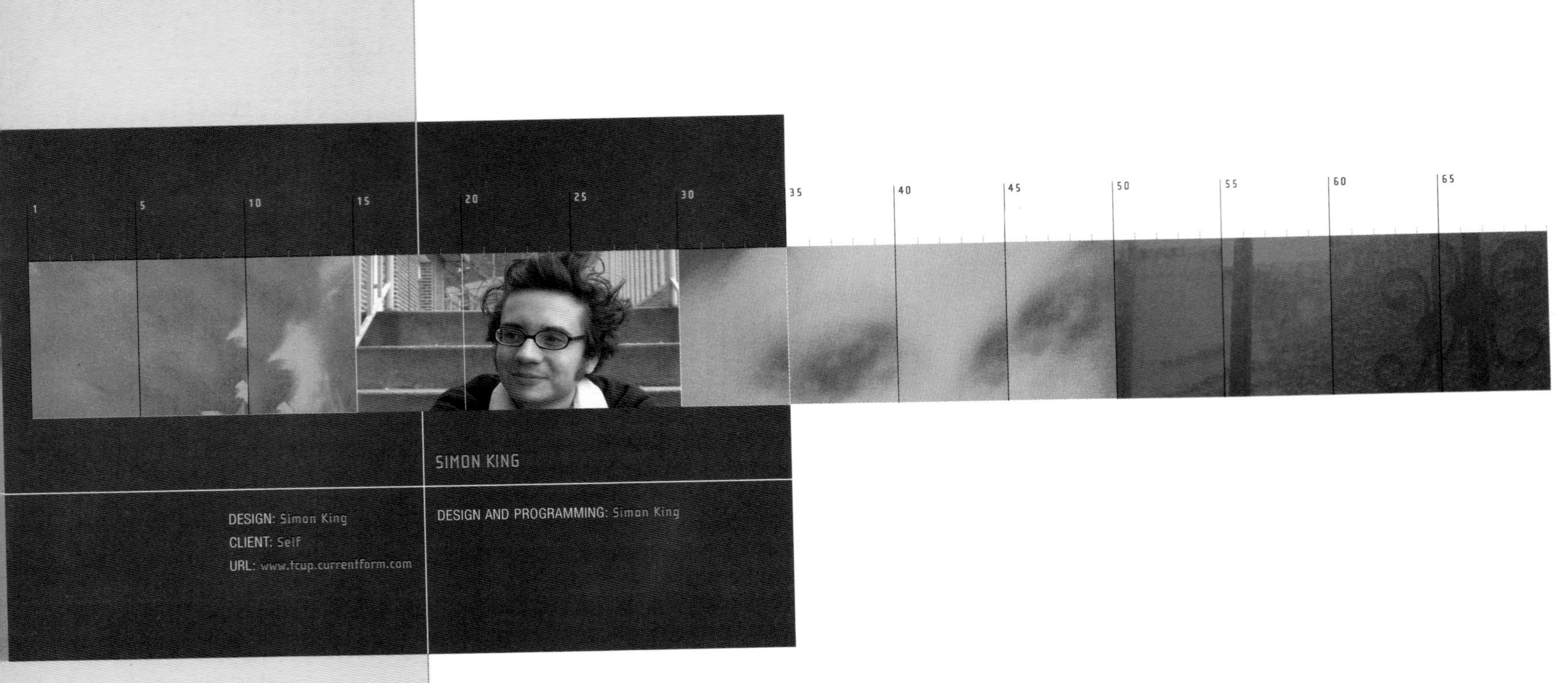

SIMON KING

DESIGN: Simon King
CLIENT: Self
URL: www.tcup.currentform.com

DESIGN AND PROGRAMMING: Simon King

CHAPTER

TCUP THE COLLECTIVE UNCONSCIOUSNESS PROJECT

INTRO

What do dreams look like as a Flash interface? An art student uses random motion, half-glimpsed images, and vibrant but murky colors to carry users through a remarkable database of the unconscious.

Pictured: Simon King

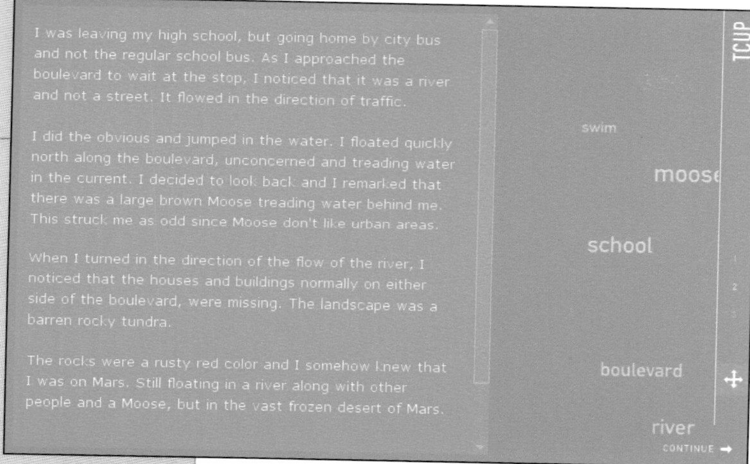

I was leaving my high school, but going home by city bus and not the regular school bus. As I approached the boulevard to wait at the stop, I noticed that it was a river and not a street. It flowed in the direction of traffic.
I did the obvious and jumped in the water. I floated quickly north along the boulevard, unconcerned and treading water in the current. I decided to look back and I remarked that there was a large brown Moose treading water behind me. This struck me as odd since Moose don't like urban areas.
When I turned in the direction of the flow of the river, I noticed that the houses and buildings normally on either side of the boulevard, were missing. The landscape was a barren rocky tundra.
The rocks were a rusty red color and I somehow knew that I was on Mars. Still floating in a river along with other people and a Moose, but in the vast frozen desert of Mars.
TCUP
swim
moose
school
boulevard
river
CONTINUE

Dreams logged in TCUP are displayed simply, with unadorned text taking up the left part of the page, and the keywords that describe it and the dream-viewing controls on the right.

Art student Simon King's friend Josh Dahl came up with the idea of a Web site that would find connections between people's dreams. Dahl doesn't build Web sites, but King does, and he soon started thinking about how he might make Dahl's vision a reality. Still in college, King proposed the idea as an independent study for his graphic design degree at Western Michigan University and went about creating The Collective Unconsciousness Project (TCUP). The site, launched in March 2001, now holds more than 1,200 dreams, contributed by hundreds of different visitors.

King has no special expertise in dreams and their meanings, but he didn't need it. "What I wanted wasn't something that would provide interpretations, but something more subtle, where visitors could make connections themselves by going from dream to dream," he says. The subtlety works. The interface creates an evocative atmosphere where visitors can speak—and draw conclusions, or not—for themselves.

TCUP THE COLLECTIVE UNCONSCIOUSNESS PROJECT
Log a dream
* = required field
Logging your dream adds it to the database for use in the explore section.
Along with contributing to the collective you can use this to keep a record of your dreams for personal use.
If you are logging your dream anonymously, please skip the first two form fields.
Username (email):
Password:
Title:
Only shown in the dream log area. Useful for finding a particular dream.
Dream: *
All HTML tags will be stripped from the dream, so use straight text please. Also, please let your lines wrap at the end of the textbox, instead of pressing enter.
Spell Check

List some keywords * from your dream, in order of importance, that stand out as main themes:
Try to use the singular version (i.e. cat not cats). This will help when finding matches with other people's dreams.
The more you list, the greater the chance of finding a connection between dreams in the explore section.
Does a particular emotion seem to define your dream?:
List of Emotions
Don't see your emotion here? Please email simon about adding it.
Would you associate a color with this dream?
Re-occurring?:
Lucid?:
Submit Dream
You can also submit dreams with your Palm Pilot by subscribing to the TCUP AvantGo channel.
Questions? Email Simon.
home | create | log | explore | view | about

The dream-logging page (above, left and right) provides a simple structure for describing a dream, including fields (such as spaces for keywords and colors) that will later be used to sort and display the dreams from the database.

> The Collective Mind

There's something undeniably fascinating about dreams. Poetic, surreal, uncensored—they're all the things real life isn't. Do they mean anything, really? Experts disagree. But their emotional charge, their humor, and their mystery make for good stories. And when the same images come up over and over, in your own dreams or in others', it's hard not to believe they have some significance.

The trick to finding the connections among these common images is collecting a lot of dreams from all types of people. And if you can get them on a computer, in a database that can automatically sort them by their important images, all the better. It's the kind of thing that can really only be done on the Web.

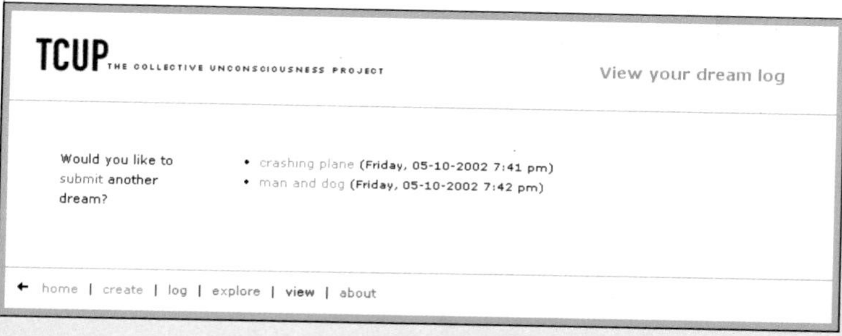

A View function gives you access to all the dreams you've logged, with an identifying title and date.

> Gathering Dreams

To make the site work, King had to first figure out how to get people to participate—to build up the database that makes exploring the site interesting. King asked himself, "Why would people log a dream online? How can I get people to do it, and do it consistently?" His answer: Provide a personal dream log, where visitors can create a searchable record of their dreams.

It worked. The site was up for about two months with just the dream-logging functions (and no way to explore the collection), and netted 250 dreams—enough of a database to get started. To help draw serious users, King posted to the alt.dreams newsgroup and listed the site in Yahoo's dream-logging area.

The dream-logging area of the TCUP site is a simple HTML form. The first part lets users record their dreams. The second lets them categorize them, using keywords, colors, emotions, and other characteristics.

King feels that in some ways the interface for the logging portion of the site is as important as the Explore section, where you view the database of dreams. "If people find the logging process interesting, it gives more fuel to the exploring," he says. Since the function of the logging section is pretty basic, the most important consideration was to make logging and viewing dreams as easy as possible. King accomplished this with straightforward forms. Although it can seem cumbersome to log in each time you want to view your dream log, it does add an extra feeling of security. That way, no one else can just click the Back button to read your unconscious.

King says that he hasn't been completely successful in getting people to use the site regularly. Most users log five or six dreams when they first discover the site, then move on to other things. King has found, however, that he can increase his return rate by inviting infrequent visitors back via the site's mailing list.

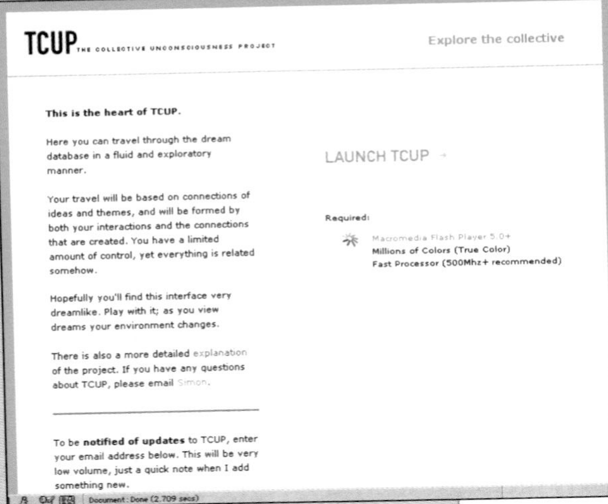

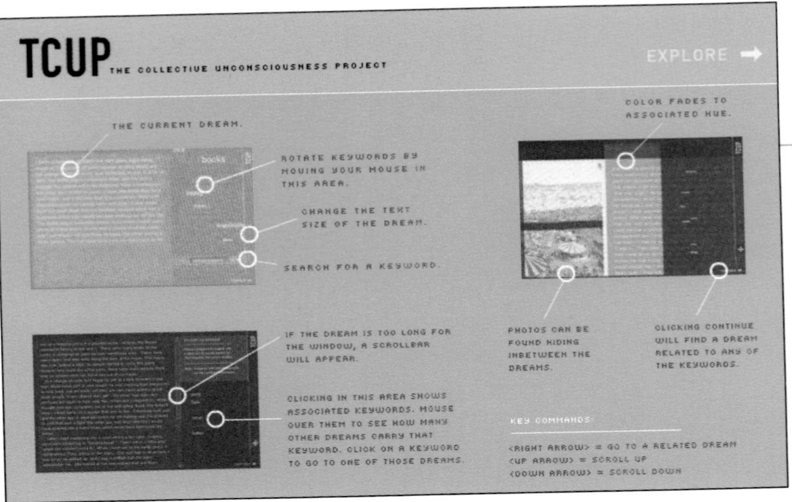

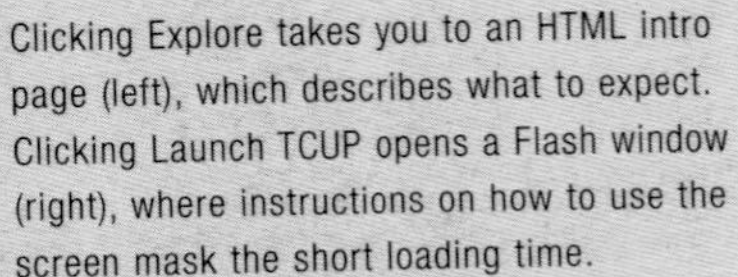

Clicking Explore takes you to an HTML intro page (left), which describes what to expect. Clicking Launch TCUP opens a Flash window (right), where instructions on how to use the screen mask the short loading time.

> So Far, All HTML

The introduction and dream-logging sections of the site are all built in straight HTML. Says King: "You can create experiences with Flash that would be impossible to create without it, but I also think that XHTML, CSS, and JavaScript have things that they do exceptionally well." One thing that HTML did better—at least at the time King was building the site—was forms. "To custom-code all the interactions that you expect with forms would have been a lot of work that HTML had already taken care of for me," he says. Plus, he adds, in Flash 5, which he used to build the site, "it was also a lot easier to integrate data from a database into an HTML page than to create custom functions and custom form elements."

King says he's considering doing the next version of the site entirely in Flash MX, since its components make it much easier to create custom form elements and hook databases up to them. "I can imagine some nice integration happening between the Explore and the Log sections once they are both accessible through the same interface," he says.

> A Site That Builds Itself

King exerts very little control over the site's content. He does review each submitted dream before allowing it to be viewed in the Explore function section (the dreams still appear in the user's personal log). It's not a matter of censorship, however, but of data integrity. He disallows entries that don't add to the overall value of the database, such as "two-liners that say something like, 'I can't remember my dream last night.' " Other entries that don't make it into the public site are random characters. And sometimes, he says, people misunderstand the purpose of the site and write about their aspirations for the future: the wrong kind of "dreams."

Aside from this approval pass, the site runs itself. Visitors' dreams and accompanying keywords are automatically filed in a MySQL database. King wrote PHP scripts to query the database and format the responses in XML, which is sent to Flash for display.

The logging function is missing some features that might seem like obvious additions, such as the ability to delete or edit dreams you've entered. "I want the initial conception of the dream," King explains. "Dreams fade quickly, and then they kind of change in your mind." King says he wants the dream stories in TCUP to have the urgency of the first telling, not the polish of an edited version. He will delete dreams at a user's request, but the person has to ask. "I don't want the deletion to be impulsive," he says.

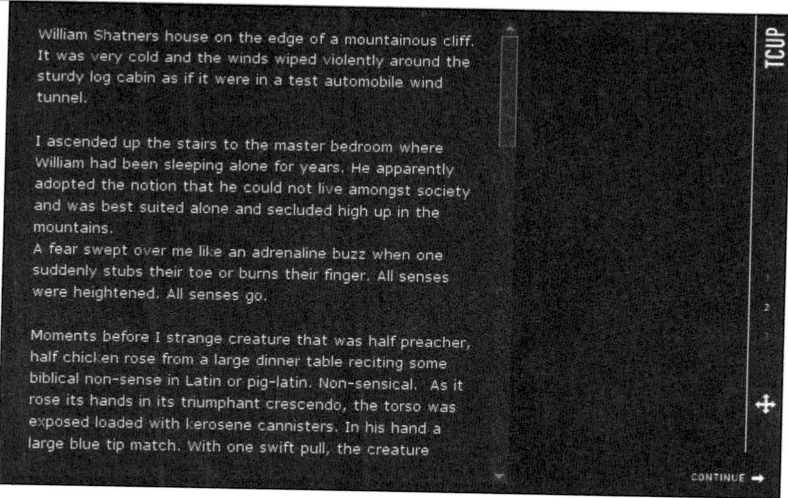

William Shatners house on the edge of a mountainous cliff. It was very cold and the winds wiped violently around the sturdy log cabin as if it were in a test automobile wind tunnel.
I ascended up the stairs to the master bedroom where William had been sleeping alone for years. He apparently adopted the notion that he could not live amongst society and was best suited alone and secluded high up in the mountains.
A fear swept over me like an adrenaline buzz when one suddenly stubs their toe or burns their finger. All senses were heightened. All senses go.
Moments before I strange creature that was half preacher, half chicken rose from a large dinner table reciting some biblical non-sense in Latin or pig-latin. Non-sensical. As it rose its hands in its triumphant crescendo, the torso was exposed loaded with kerosene cannisters. In his hand a large blue tip match. With one swift pull, the creature
TCUP
2
CONTINUE

The first view of a dream has only text, an open space, and some rather mysterious controls at the right. The only clear action is Continue.

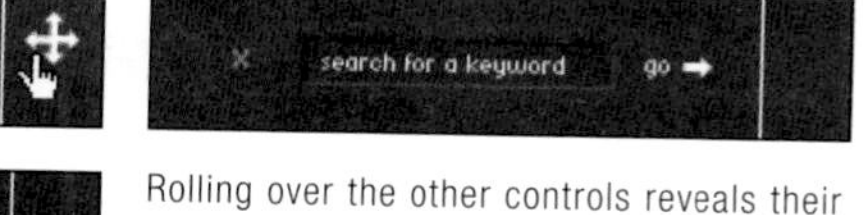

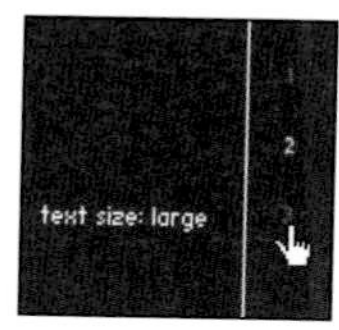

Rolling over the other controls reveals their uses: searching for a specific keyword or changing the text size of the dream display.

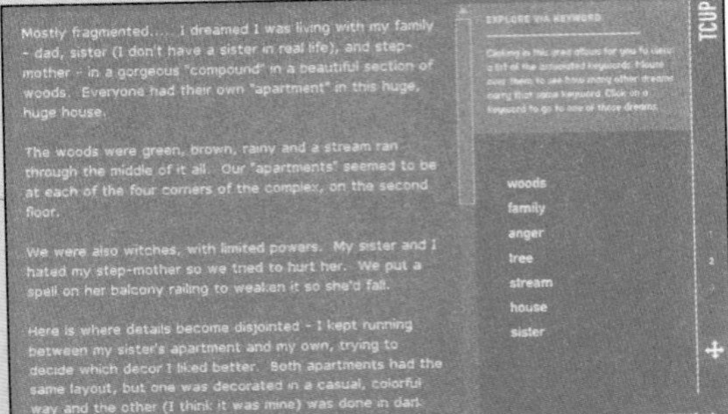
Mostly fragmented..... I dreamed I was living with my family - dad, sister (I don't have a sister in real life), and step-mother - in a gorgeous "compound" in a beautiful section of woods. Everyone had their own "apartment" in this huge, huge house.
The woods were green, brown, rainy and a stream ran through the middle of it all. Our "apartments" seemed to be at each of the four corners of the complex, on the second floor.
We were also witches, with limited powers. My sister and I hated my step-mother so we tried to hurt her. We put a spell on her balcony railing to weaken it so she'd fall.
Here is where details become disjointed - I kept running between my sister's apartment and my own, trying to decide which decor I liked better. Both apartments had the same layout, but one was decorated in a casual, colorful way and the other (I think it was mine) was done in dark
EXPLORE VIA KEYWORD
woods
family
anger
tree
stream
house
sister
TCUP
CONTINUE

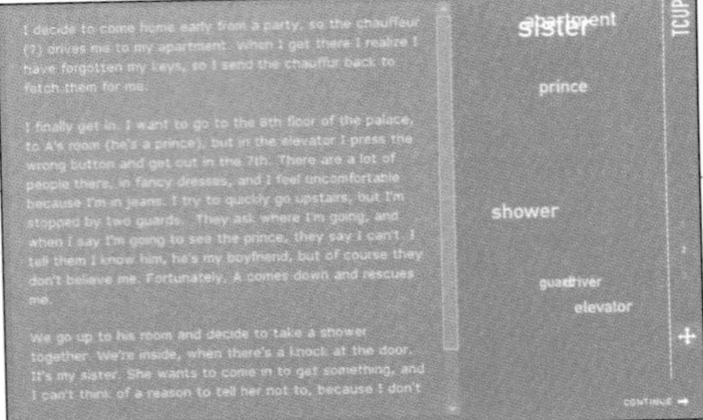
I decide to come home early from a party, so the chauffeur (?) drives me to my apartment. When I get there I realize I have forgotten my keys, so I send the chauffur back to fetch them for me.
I finally get in. I want to go to the 8th floor of the palace, to A's room (he's a prince), but in the elevator I press the wrong button and get out in the 7th. There are a lot of people there, in fancy dresses, and I feel uncomfortable because I'm in jeans. I try to quickly go upstairs, but I'm stopped by two guards. They ask where I'm going, and when I say I'm going to see the prince, they say I can't. I tell them I know him, he's my boyfriend, but of course they don't believe me. Fortunately, A comes down and rescues me.
We go up to his room and decide to take a shower together. We're inside, when there's a knock at the door. It's my sister. She wants to come in to get something, and I can't think of a reason to tell her not to, because I don't
apartment
sister
prince
shower
guard
driver
elevator
TCUP
CONTINUE

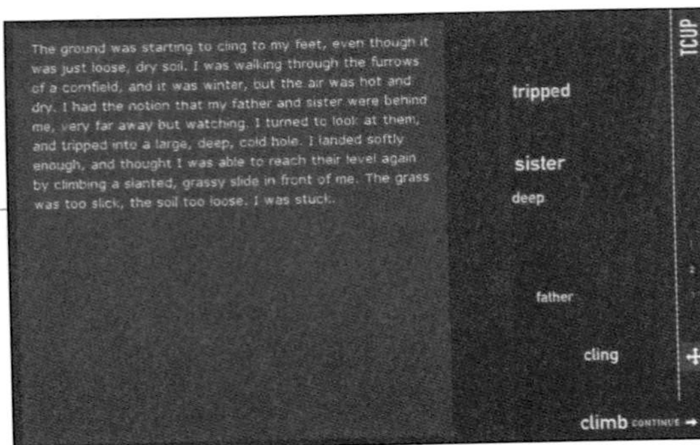
The ground was starting to cling to my feet, even though it was just loose, dry soil. I was walking through the furrows of a cornfield, and it was winter, but the air was hot and dry. I had the notion that my father and sister were behind me, very far away but watching. I turned to look at them, and tripped into a large, deep, cold hole. I landed softly enough, and thought I was able to reach their level again by climbing a slanted, grassy slide in front of me. The grass was too slick, the soil too loose. I was stuck.
tripped
sister
deep
father
cling
climb
TCUP
CONTINUE

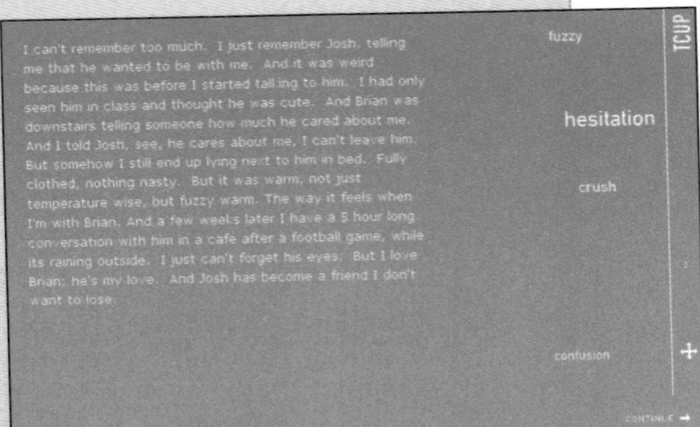
I can't remember too much. I just remember Josh, telling me that he wanted to be with me. And it was weird because this was before I started talking to him. I had only seen him in class and thought he was cute. And Brian was downstairs telling someone how much he cared about me. And I told Josh, see, he cares about me, I can't leave him. But somehow I still end up lying next to him in bed. Fully clothed, nothing nasty. But it was warm, not just temperature wise, but fuzzy warm. The way it feels when I'm with Brian. And a few weeks later I have a 5 hour long conversation with him in a cafe after a football game, while its raining outside. I just can't forget his eyes. But I love Brian; he's my love. And Josh has become a friend I don't want to lose.
fuzzy
hesitation
crush
confusion
TCUP
CONTINUE

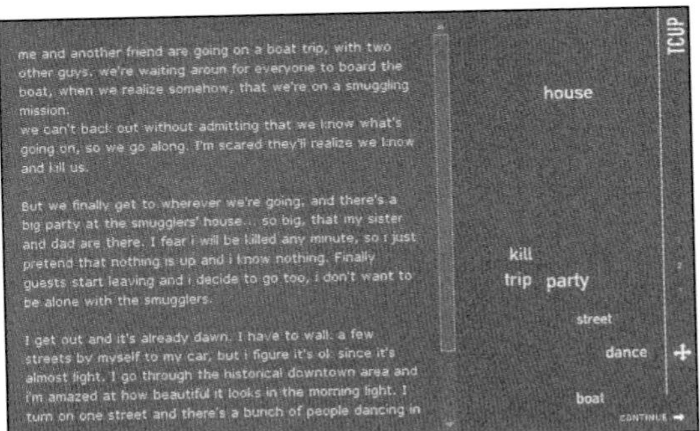
me and another friend are going on a boat trip, with two other guys. we're waiting aroun for everyone to board the boat, when we realize somehow, that we're on a smuggling mission.
we can't back out without admitting that we know what's going on, so we go along. I'm scared they'll realize we know and kill us.
But we finally get to wherever we're going, and there's a big party at the smugglers' house... so big, that my sister and dad are there. I fear i will be killed any minute, so i just pretend that nothing is up and i know nothing. Finally guests start leaving and i decide to go too, i don't want to be alone with the smugglers.
I get out and it's already dawn. I have to walk a few streets by myself to my car, but i figure it's ok since it's almost light. I go through the historical downtown area and i'm amazed at how beautiful it looks in the morning light. I turn on one street and there's a bunch of people dancing in
house
kill
trip
party
street
dance
boat
TCUP
CONTINUE

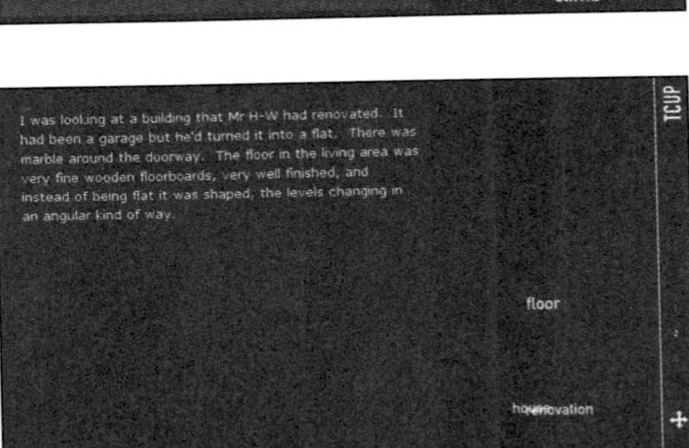
I was looking at a building that Mr H-W had renovated. It had been a garage but he'd turned it into a flat. There was marble around the doorway. The floor in the living area was very fine wooden floorboards, very well finished, and instead of being flat it was shaped, the levels changing in an angular kind of way.
floor
renovation
TCUP
CONTINUE

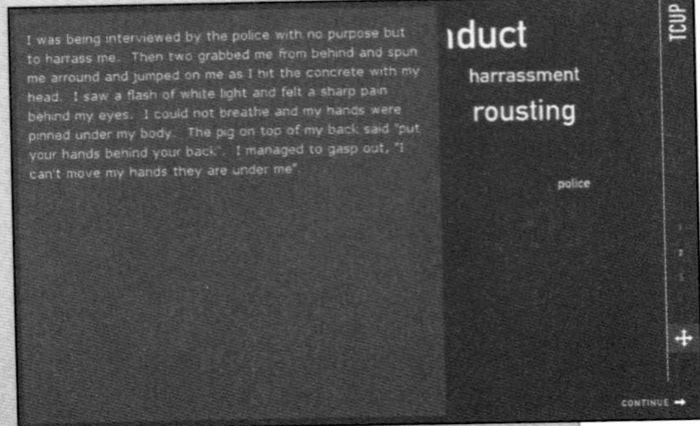
I was being interviewed by the police with no purpose but to harrass me. Then two grabbed me from behind and spun me arround and jumped on me as I hit the concrete with my head. I saw a flash of white light and felt a sharp pain behind my eyes. I could not breathe and my hands were pinned under my body. The pig on top of my back said "put your hands behind your back". I managed to gasp out, "I can't move my hands they are under me".
duct
harrassment
rousting
police
TCUP
CONTINUE

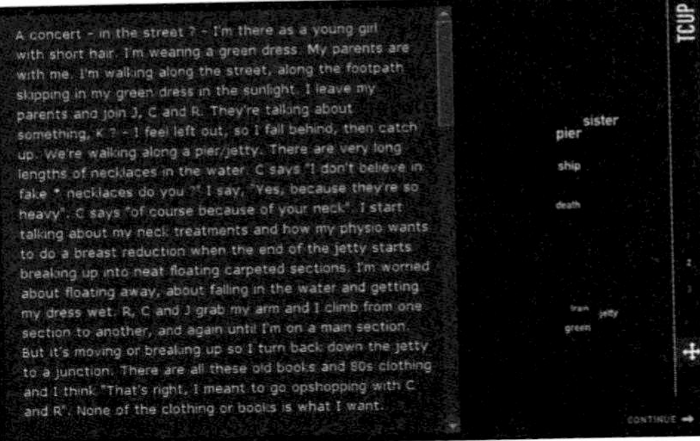
A concert - in the street ? - I'm there as a young girl with short hair. I'm wearing a green dress. My parents are with me. I'm walking along the street, along the footpath skipping in my green dress in the sunlight. I leave my parents and join J, C and R. They're talking about something, K ? - I feel left out, so I fall behind, then catch up. We're walking along a pier/jetty. There are very long lengths of necklaces in the water. C says "I don't believe in fake * necklaces do you ?" I say, "Yes, because they're so heavy". C says "of course because of your neck". I start talking about my neck treatments and how my physio wants to do a breast reduction when the end of the jetty starts breaking up into neat floating carpeted sections. I'm worried about floating away, about falling in the water and getting my dress wet. R, C and J grab my arm and I climb from one section to another, and again until I'm on a main section. But it's moving or breaking up so I turn back down the jetty to a junction. There are all these old books and 80s clothing and I think "That's right, I meant to go opshopping with C and R". None of the clothing or books is what I want.
sister
pier
ship
jetty
green
TCUP
CONTINUE

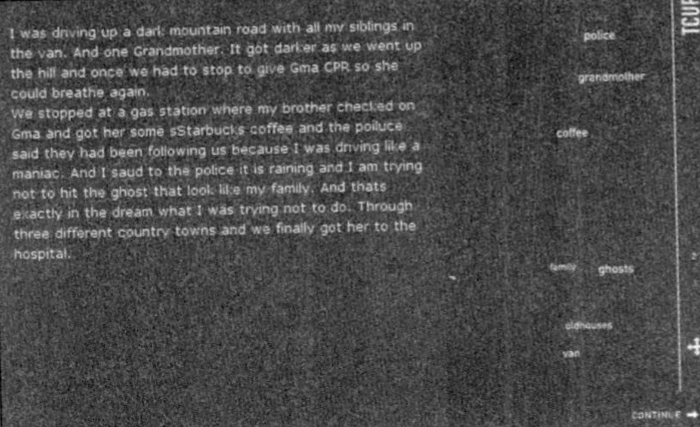
I was driving up a dark mountain road with all my siblings in the van. And one Grandmother. It got darker as we went up the hill and once we had to stop to give Gma CPR so she could breathe again.
We stopped at a gas station where my brother checked on Gma and got her some sStarbucks coffee and the poliuce said they had been following us because I was driving like a maniac. And I saud to the police it is raining and I am trying not to hit the ghost that look like my family. And thats exactly in the dream what I was trying not to do. Through three different country towns and we finally got her to the hospital.
police
grandmother
coffee
family
ghosts
oldhouses
van
TCUP
CONTINUE

When logging a dream, users select a color they might associate with it. That color is then used to display the dream in the Explore function. King characterizes the palette as "mellow." Dark colors were required to set off the white text, but King also thought dark colors would be more dreamlike. Bright or neon colors, he felt, seemed too "awake."

> Explore—But First ...

The Explore section is the heart of TCUP; the other sections exist only to feed it and make it richer. However, it takes a few clicks to get to the section. It would be interesting to know whether users could launch TCUP and then figure out its economical interface without explanation. King felt they needed some help. That's why when you click Explore the Collective from the site's first page, you go through two pages of explanation before you get to the dreams.

After viewing an HTML page introducing the concept, you click Launch TCUP, and a Flash window opens. Here, the first thing you see is a page of instructions for how to use the Explore interface. The page also fills the time while the dreamscape loads, according to King. My guess is that most people simply click through that page without close reading, since the page seems dauntingly complex. To me, the interface seems discoverable enough without the instructions.

The first dream loads, sliding in from somewhere offscreen. All you see is the text of a dream. Across a blank area are a few controls and one clear button: Continue.

"There are very few interface elements," says King. "I wanted everything to focus on the dream, not the interface elements." Color is the design's primary graphic element.

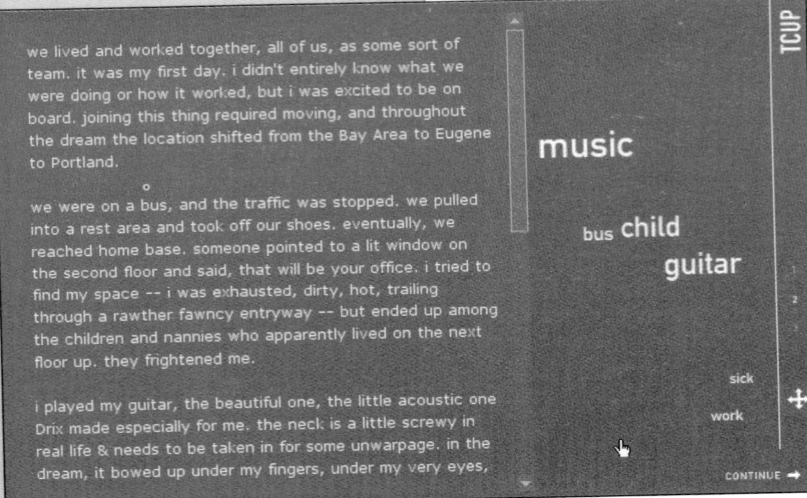

we lived and worked together, all of us, as some sort of team. it was my first day. i didn't entirely know what we were doing or how it worked, but i was excited to be on board. joining this thing required moving, and throughout the dream the location shifted from the Bay Area to Eugene to Portland.
o
we were on a bus, and the traffic was stopped. we pulled into a rest area and took off our shoes. eventually, we reached home base. someone pointed to a lit window on the second floor and said, that will be your office. i tried to find my space -- i was exhausted, dirty, hot, trailing through a rawther fawncy entryway -- but ended up among the children and nannies who apparently lived on the next floor up. they frightened me.
i played my guitar, the beautiful one, the little acoustic one Drix made especially for me. the neck is a little screwy in real life & needs to be taken in for some unwarpage. in the dream, it bowed up under my fingers, under my very eyes,
music
bus child
guitar
sick
work
TCUP
CONTINUE

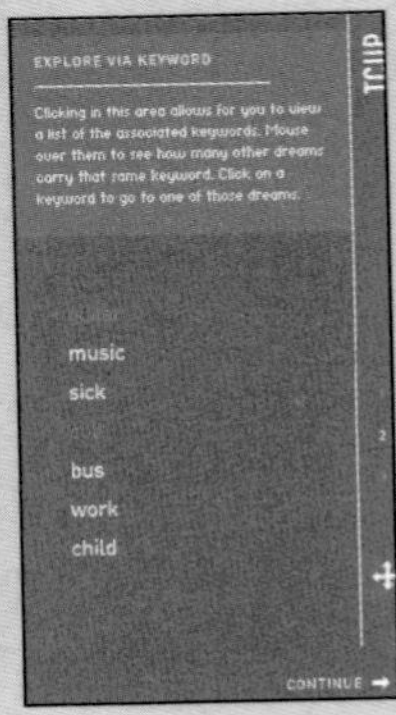

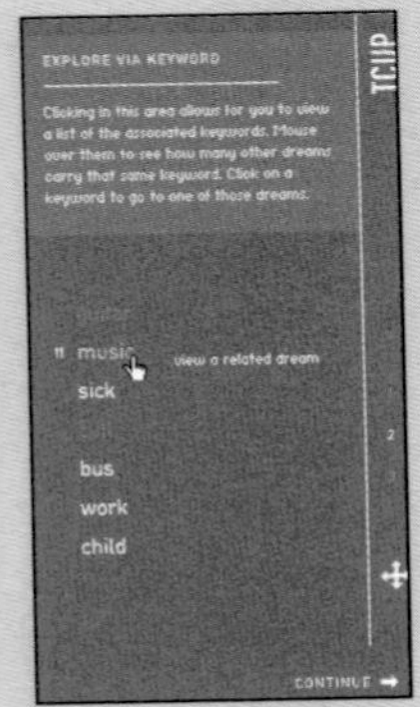

Rolling over the blank area calls up keywords that move randomly, changing size as they swim in and out of view (top). Clicking anywhere in that area aligns the keywords into a list and adds a box of instructions that tells you how to use them (bottom left). Rolling over a keyword shows how many other dreams that you haven't seen are associated with it (bottom right). Clicking a keyword calls up a related dream.

> Navigating the Unconscious

The rest of the interface becomes apparent almost by accident. Rolling over the controls in the right margin calls up a description of their use: changing the text size of the dream display or searching for a dream by a specific keyword.

As you roll over the blank area (almost impossible to avoid as you move your pointer to the controls at the right margin of the page), words swim into view. These are the keywords the writer supplied when logging the dream. Again, the dream is the focus. King explains the hidden interface: "I wanted the keywords to be there but not be in your face as you're viewing the dream."

Instructions also appear, explaining that you can roll over the keywords to see how many unviewed dreams are associated with each, and you can click a keyword to see one of those dreams.

This method of interacting with the keywords is a recent addition, added at users' request. The first version included the swimming keywords but no option for picking the one you wanted to follow. The only way to move to the next dream was via the Continue button. "I thought that the fact that the keywords were moving would make them seem not clickable," says King. Visitors, however, tried it anyway. The new interface assumes that users *will* click the moving words; the list and instructions don't appear until they do.

If users are feeling laissez-faire, the Continue button will choose a keyword and a dream for them—the first dream listed, if there is more than one associated with the keyword. This action offers a more passive, dreamlike path: just reading and clicking, going where the dream machine takes you.

> Creative Disorientation

The site enters deeper into a dreamworld when you click to continue. The window begins to deconstruct itself, seeming to pan across a vast canvas of dreams, colors, and dreamlike photographs before reassembling itself in the monochromatic, single-dream view.

Intermixed with the dream texts are 48 photographic images by Lucas Shuman. "I wanted photos that are nonspecific as to place and time, that can be read into. You glimpse the story as you go past," says King. Occasionally there are coincidental matches between the photos and the dreams you've viewed. A photograph of the World Trade Center was on the site pre-September 11; now many posters are submitting dreams about it.

The effect looks complex, but it was surprisingly simple to create (see "A Dream Landscape," page 110). The seemingly endless landscape of text and image that the window appears to pan across is really a 5-by-5 square grid. The first dream to load is chosen randomly from the database. Each time the user clicks a keyword or the Continue button, the database draws on a related dream and photo, loads them into one of the 25 squares, chosen at random, and moves the view to the new dream text. "It moves over gray space on its way to the second dream. On the way to the third, you may move past the first one, or you may not," explains King. When all 25 squares are filled, the program begins writing over the first texts and photos.

All the loading takes place offscreen; the window doesn't move to the new dream until loading is finished. For the user, this creates the effect of an endless landscape containing every dream. King says, "I wanted to create something where you felt like you were going from dream to dream, but not losing the past ones as you move. The feeling is that they're behind you, and you could find them again." Interestingly, though, you can't. As part of a general strategy of keeping things uncontrolled enough to seem dreamlike, there's no easy way to find a dream you've seen before. "On your way to the next dream, you might encounter the ones you've already viewed, but you can't stop on [them]," King says.

The patchwork of colors is also surprisingly complex, seeming to use more than the palette offered in the logging page. King explains that when a new dream is loaded, the page turns the color associated with that dream (the one selected by the writer, or if none was chosen, a color chosen randomly from the palette). The alpha level, though, is set to 20 percent, gradually fading up to 100 percent as the window moves to the new position. The mixing of the colors in different percentages as the alpha level changes creates the complex coloration.

As one dream exits the screen and another enters, the window seems to pan across a vast canvas containing other dreams and dreamlike images.

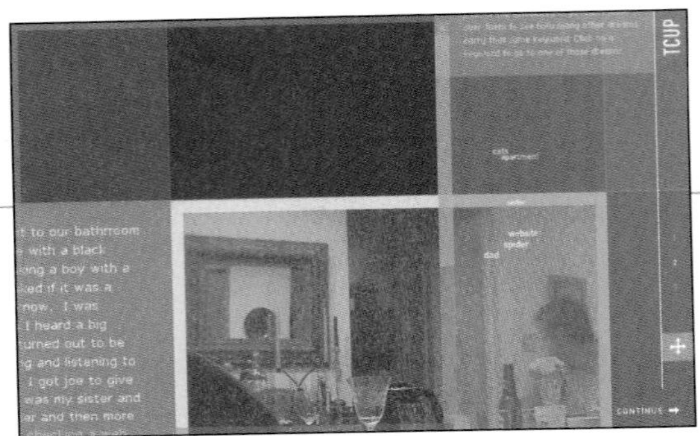

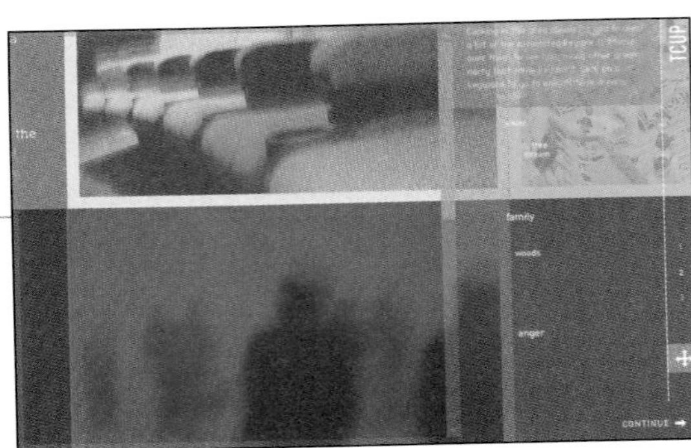

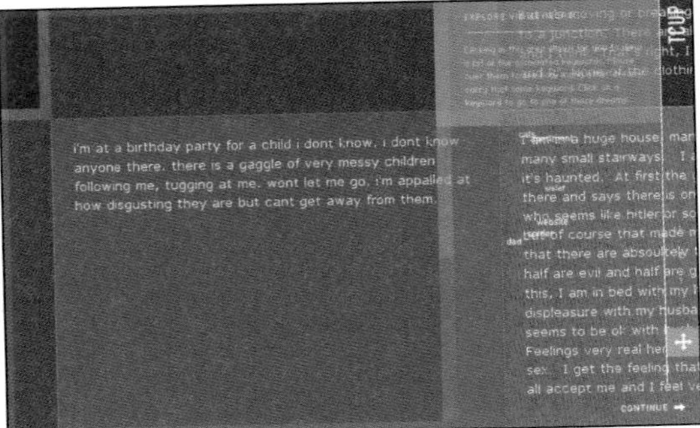

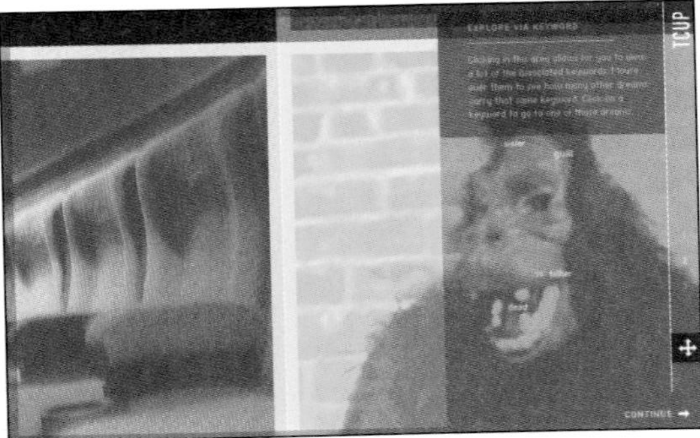

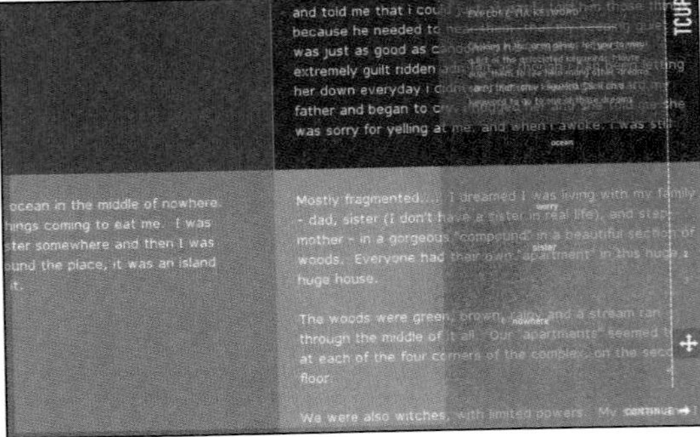

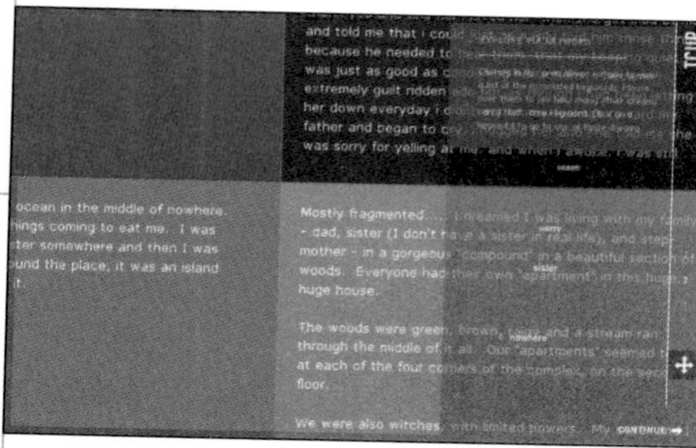
TCUP
and told me that i could
because he needed to
was just as good as
extremely guilt ridden
her down everyday i
father and began to cry
was sorry for yelling at me, and when i awoke, i was still
ocean in the middle of nowhere.
Mostly fragmented
- dad, sister (I don't have a sister in real life), and step-
mother - in a gorgeous "compound" in a beautiful section of
woods. Everyone had their own "apartment" in this huge,
huge house.
The woods were green, brown,
through the middle of it all.
at each of the four corners of the complex, on the sec
floor.
We were also witches, with limited powers. My
CONTINUE

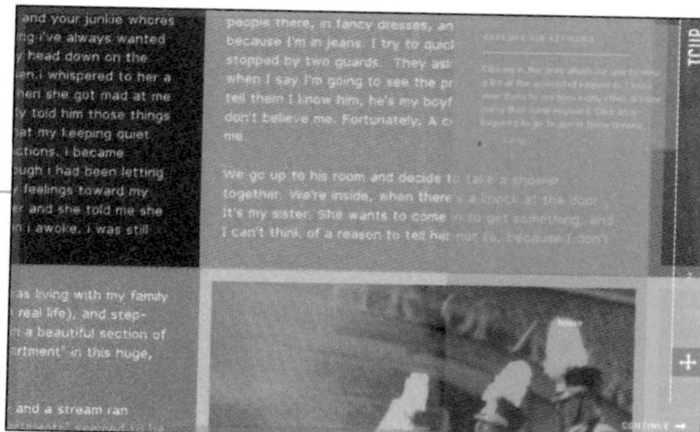
TCUP
and your junkie whores
ng i've always wanted
y head down on the
hen she got mad at me
ly told him those things
at my keeping quiet
ctions. i became
ugh i had been letting
y feelings toward my
r and she told me she
n i awoke, i was still
people there, in fancy dresses, an
because I'm in jeans. I try to quic
stopped by two guards. They as
when I say I'm going to see the pr
tell them I know him, he's my boyf
don't believe me. Fortunately, A c
me.
We go up to his room and decide to take a shower
together. We're inside, when there's a knock at the door
It's my sister. She wants to come in to get something, and
I can't think of a reason to tell her not to, because I don't
as living with my family
real life), and step-
a beautiful section of
rtment" in this huge,
and a stream ran
CONTINUE

TCUP
ted in a casual, colorful
mine) was done in dark
apartment
prince
sister
shower
CONTINUE

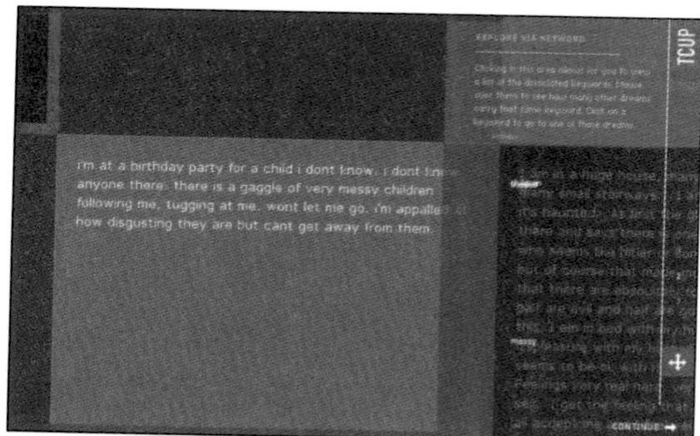
TCUP
EXPLORE VIA KEYWORD
i'm at a birthday party for a child i dont know. i dont know
anyone there. there is a gaggle of very messy children
following me, tugging at me. wont let me go. i'm appalled at
how disgusting they are but cant get away from them.
shower
messy
CONTINUE

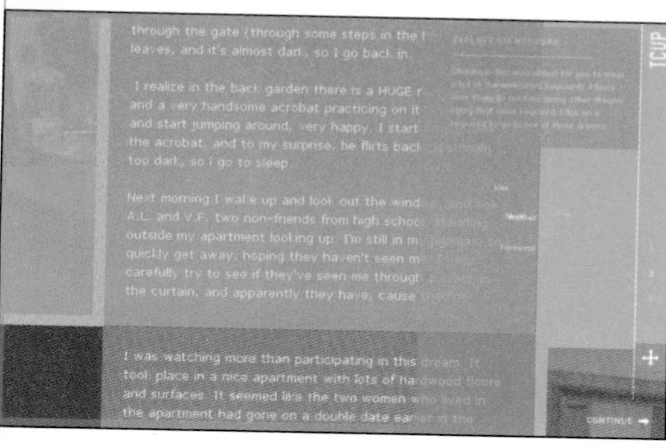
TCUP
EXPLORE VIA KEYWORD
through the gate (through some steps in the
leaves, and it's almost dark, so I go back in.
I realize in the back garden there is a HUGE
and a very handsome acrobat practicing on it
and start jumping around, very happy. I start
the acrobat, and to my surprise, he flirts back
too dark, so I go to sleep.
Next morning I wake up and look out the wind
A.L. and V.F. two non-friends from high school
outside my apartment looking up. I'm still in m
quickly get away, hoping they haven't seen m
carefully try to see if they've seen me through
the curtain, and apparently they have, cause
I was watching more than participating in this dream. It
took place in a nice apartment with lots of hardwood floors
and surfaces. It seemed like the two women who lived in
the apartment had gone on a double date earlier this
CONTINUE

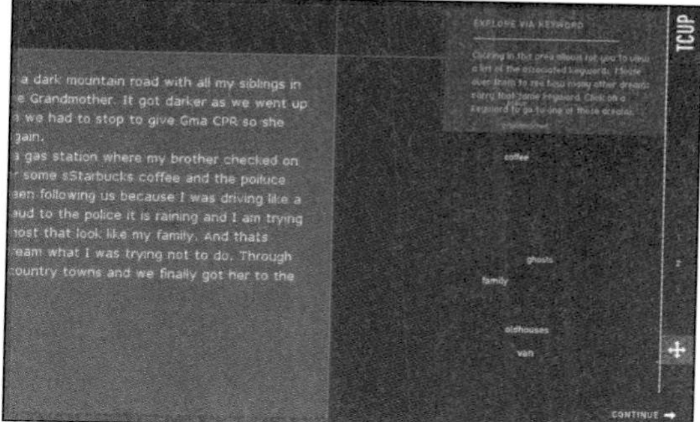
TCUP
EXPLORE VIA KEYWORD
a dark mountain road with all my siblings in
e Grandmother. It got darker as we went up
we had to stop to give Gma CPR so she
gain.
a gas station where my brother checked on
some sStarbucks coffee and the poiluce
een following us because I was driving like a
ud to the police it is raining and I am trying
lost that look like my family. And thats
eam what I was trying not to do. Through
ountry towns and we finally got her to the
coffee
ghosts
family
oldhouses
van
CONTINUE

UNDER THE HOOD
A DREAM LANDSCAPE

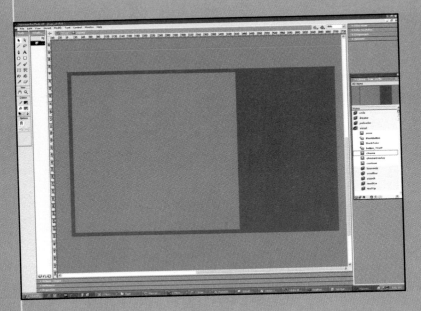

Figure 1
The chrome movie clip is a simple box that frames the keywords interface and the current dream. (Another movie clip, chromeOverlay, fits inside the chrome movie clip to hold the keywords and navigation tools.) The color of chrome changes with each dream it holds, as assigned by the XML.onLoad method (see Figure 5).

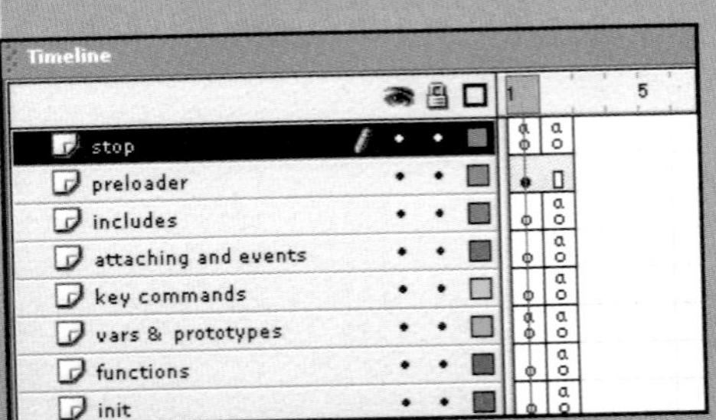

Figure 2
The gGotoLink function manages links from inside the movie (as opposed to calls that go through the server). The gCompareLink function is used by gHistory (see Figure 6).

TCUP creates the illusion of a never-ending landscape of dreams and photos with a 5-by-5-box grid, created from 25 instances of a single movie clip. Another movie clip, chrome (**Figure 1**), forms a frame around the currently viewed area. When the user clicks a keyword or the Continue button to move to the next dream, a new dream is loaded into one of those boxes, randomly chosen, and the grid moves to position the new dream within the frame.

King organized his movie into two frames. The first holds all of the preloaded elements, while the second contains all of the code (**Figure 2**). A movie clip called dreamHolder (**Figure 3**) holds the 25 instances of the dreamBox movie clip. The dreamHolder clip is instantiated by an initialization function that runs as TCUP loads. As the site loads, another function, findMovePos, picks a random number between 1 and 25, and correlates it to the grid coordinates within dreamHolder. (That randomly selected number will be used later to target the container for loading movies.) Finally, the initialization function defines and runs a setupBoxes function, which sets up the dreamBox instances and sets properties for each, including location and assigned number. Each dreamBox is 450 pixels square—small enough to allow room for the keyword interface as well as the dream within the chrome frame.

When the user clicks a keyword or the Continue button, an onRelease function calls a changeDream function, passing it a random number between 1 and 25 (excluding the number of

```
attachMovie("dreamHolder", "dreamHolder", 1);
// call a custom function (findMovePos) that correlates a number
// to that container's grid coordinates. this is so we can start at
// a random location on the grid
var holderPos = findMovePos(Math.getRandom(1, 25));
// position the dream holder based on the coordinates we found
dreamHolder._x = holderPos.x;
dreamHolder._y = holderPos.y;
// create an onLoad event that will load all our dream boxes

dreamHolder.setupBoxes = function() {
        // loop through the grid structure and create all of the
        // dream boxes, setting their location and default properties
        var n = 1;
        for (var i = 0; i<5; ++i) {
                for (var j = 0; j<5; ++j) {
                        this.attachMovie("dreamBox", "dreamBox"+n, (i-1)*5+j);
                        // assign ourselves some variables to use later
                        this["dreamBox"+n].location = i+"_"+j;
                        this["dreamBox"+n].num = n;
                        // set the location of this dreambox
                        // each one of them are 450px square
                        this["dreamBox"+n]._x = j*450;
                        this["dreamBox"+n]._y = i*450;
                        n++;
                }
        }
};
// call the function we've just created to set up our dreamBoxes
dreamHolder.setupBoxes();
```

Figure 3

An initialization routine attaches the `dreamHolder` movie clip from the library, sets up a numbering system for the 25 `dreamBox` positions within it, and defines and calls the `setupBoxes` function to place 25 instances of `dreamBox` within the holder.

```
/*
 *   Method: changeDream ()
 *   Desc: Performs preliminary work before loading dream.
 *   Parameters:
 *     dreamBox       The dreamBox to load the dream into.
 *     keyword        An optional keyword to find a dream based on.
*/
_global.changeDream = function(dreamBox,keyword) {
        // get our keyword ready to be a part of a URL
        var keyword = escape(keyword);
        // change our tool tip to let people know the dream is loading
        // this is calling a custom tool tip handling function
        tooltip.set("        loading...");
        // save the last box we were at -- useful when loading images,
        // and for when a search result goes bad
        _global.lastlastDreamBox = _global.lastDreamBox;
        _global.lastDreamBox = _global.currentDreamBox;
        // note our current dreamBox for use in other functions
        _global.currentDreamBox = dreamBox;
        // inside of every dreamBox there is a MovieClip called photoHolder
        // in case there is a photo in our box, get rid of it
        _root.dreamHolder["dreamBox" + currentDreamBox].photoHolder.unloadMovie();
        // call loadDream, the next step in our dream loading process
        loadDream(keyword);
};
```

Figure 4

The `changeDream` function is called when you click a keyword or the Continue button. It sets up variables and prepares the `dreamBox` for loading a dream.

```
/*
 *   Method: loadDream ()
 *   Desc: Loads XML, parses the dream and sets everything else into motion.
 *   Parameters:
 *     singleKeyword      An optional keyword to base the dream lookup on.
 *                        If not specified, it will use all keywords in the dream.
*/
_global.loadDream = function(singleKeyword) {
    dreamXML = new XML();
    dreamXML.ignoreWhite = true;
    // create a function that defines what to do when it's loaded
    dreamXML.onLoad = function() {
        // our XML structure is known, so we can hardcode these variables
        var dream = this.firstChild;
        var nodeList = this.firstChild.childNodes;
        var color = dream.attributes.color;
        var rand = dream.attributes.random;
        var keywords = new Array();

        // loop through to get at the info we need
        for(var i=0; i<nodeList.length; i++) {
            if(nodeList[i].nodeName == "text") {
                // define our text var
                var text = nodeList[i].firstChild.nodeValue;
            }else if(nodeList[i].nodeName == "keywords") {
                keywordList = nodeList[i].childNodes;
                for(var j=0; j<keywordList.length; j++) {
                    if(keywordList[j].nodeName == "keyword") {
                        // fill our keywords array
                        currentKeyword = new Object();
                        currentKeyword.word = keywordList[j].firstChild.nodeValue;
                        currentKeyword.matches = keywordList[j].attributes.matches;
                        keywords.push(currentKeyword);


                    }
                }
            }
        }
```

Figure 5

Now that the environment is prepped, `loadDream` loads the XML dream file, saving the dream's attributes for use by the XML `onLoad` function, which will update the environment with the proper color and keywords and then move `dreamHolder` into position to show the new dream.

```
        // pass our dream information on to our current dreamBox
        var thisDream = eval("_root.dreamHolder.dreamBox" + currentDreamBox);
        thisDream.plainText = text;
        thisDream.color = color;
        thisDream.rand = rand;

        // the following are all custom methods that set up
        // some aspect of the interface now that the dream is loaded

        _global.keywordList = keywords;
        _global.numKeywords = keywords.length;
        updateKeywords();
        changeTextSize(fontSize);
        changeColor(thisDream, color);
        // now that everything is loaded, move to our next dream
        moveDream(rand);
        // since we have some free bandwidth now, load an image in the background
        loadImage();
        // update our tool tip, we're done loading now
        tooltip.clear();
    };

    // Here is where the actual XML loading begins
    // set up our query string to feed the select page our keywords
    var xmlfile = "select.php?random=" + Math.random();
    // make sure that singleKeyword is a usable string
    if(singleKeyword.length > 0) {
        // if we are looking for a particularly keyword, we only create
        // a query string with that one keyword
        xmlfile += "&keywords=" + singleKeyword + "&search=1";
    }else{
        // otherwise we loop through all the keywords in the current
        // dream and build a query string with all of them
        xmlfile += "&keywords="
        for(var h=0;h<numKeywords;h++) {
            xmlfile += _global.keywordList[h].word + ",";
        }
    }

    dreamXML.load(xmlfile); // Load our xml file
};
```

the current dreamBox) for the next dream to load into. The changeDream function (**Figure 4**) sets up variables and prepares the dreamBox into which a dream will be loaded. The function then calls loadDream (**Figure 5**), which loads an XML-formatted dream (**Figure 6**), updates the new dream's colors and keywords, calls moveDream to move the new dream into view, and (finally) calls loadImage to load an image into another random frame. The XML file is created by a PHP script that loads the data from a MySQL database.

King designed the environment so that low-bandwidth information (the dreams) comes in quickly and behind the scenes, and high-bandwidth information (the images) is loaded in a way that makes its loading time unimportant—if the image isn't loaded when its dreamBox passes under the chrome frame, the user won't notice.

Throughout TCUP, King used the Flash API, created by DoubleYou (www.doubleyou.com/flashAPI), to automate repetitive tasks such as fading or moving movie clips.

```
<?xml version="1.0" encoding="iso-8859-1" ?>
<dream reoccuring="0" lucid="0" random="1" color="00A0A0">
        <text>There were two speed boats on the ocean, not far from the
shore. I was in one of them and friends of mine were in the other. We
wanted to dock the boats next to each other so that we could go from boat
to boat and hang out with each other without going to shore.<br><br>Every
time that either one of us started to head toward the other the boat would
go uncontrollably fast and the driver would have to quickly steer away so
as not to hit the boat. We couldn&#8217;t go slowly for some
reason.<br><br>We developed the idea to start going in the wrong
direction, thinking that it would speed up and then we could just turn
around and glide near the other boat. Instead, the boat went haywire and
started turning in circles violently. It then pointed itself toward the
other boat and rammed it at full speed.</text>
        <keywords>
                <keyword matches="11">friends</keyword>
                <keyword matches="7">boat</keyword>
                <keyword matches="4">speed</keyword>
                <keyword matches="5">control</keyword>
                <keyword matches="42">water</keyword>
                <keyword matches="0">direction</keyword>
                <keyword matches="0">glide</keyword>
        <keywords>
</dream>
```

Figure 6

The XML dream file, created by a PHP script from a MySQL database, includes the text of the dream as well as the author's choices for keywords, color, and other settings.

As soon as the system knows what dream it's going to display next, it changes the screen to that dream's color—but at a 20 percent transparency, which slowly fades up to 100 percent as the new dream slides into view. The effect creates an interesting palette far in excess of the ten basic tones.

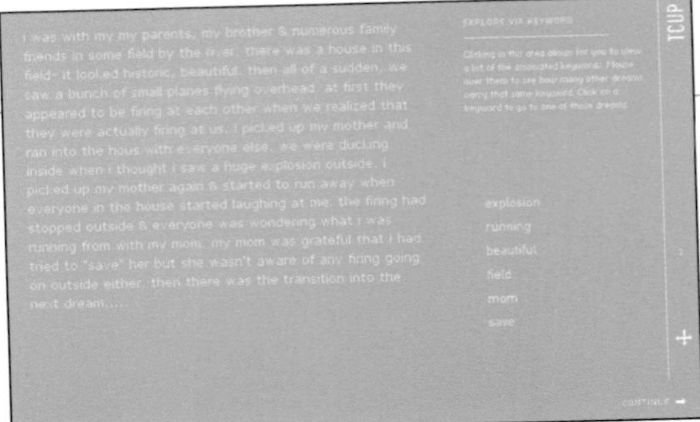

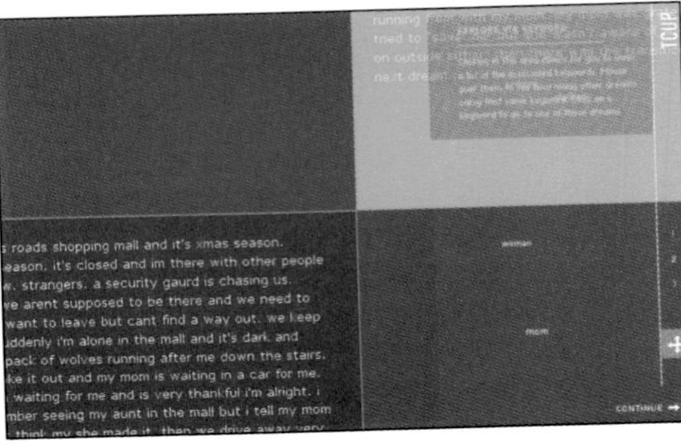

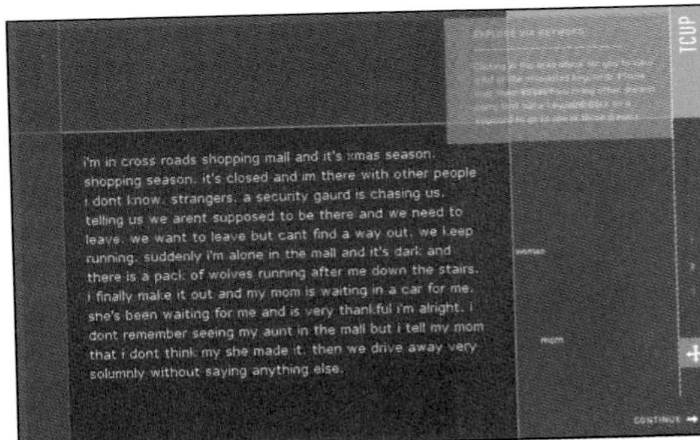

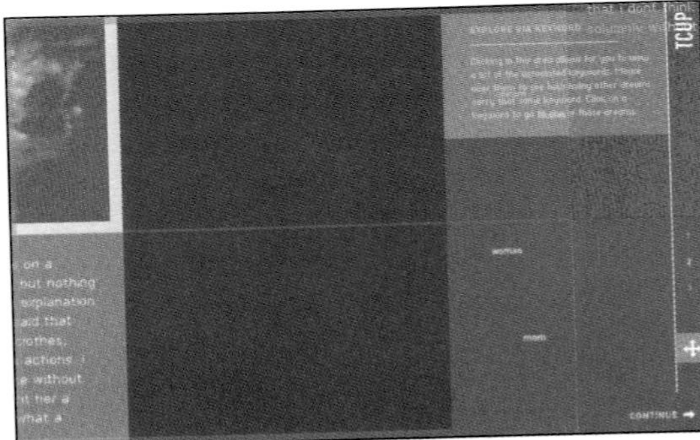

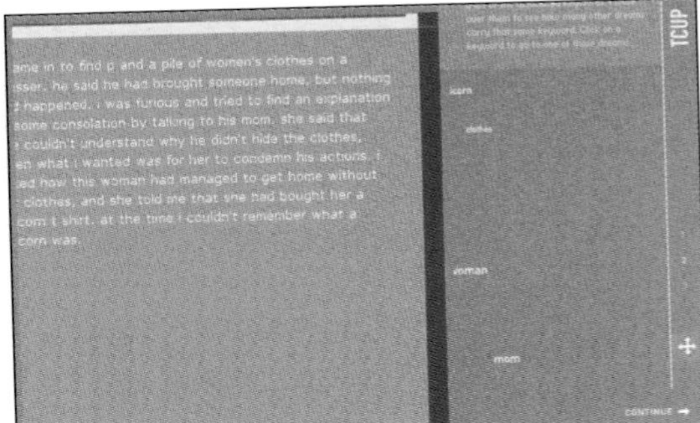

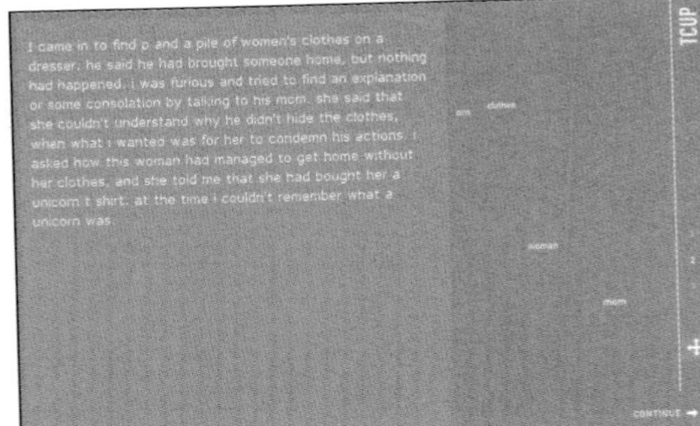

King was worried that all the randomness involved in the interface could become monotonous. "Sometimes randomness feels like a cop-out. It gets boring," he says. "You need a certain amount of reason to be interesting, a balance between randomness and reason." The randomness here is balanced by the connection between the dreams created by the keywords. To keep things interesting, he also added code to vary the speed of the movement.

> Less Is More

King has limited his site to the simple functionality described here: entering your dreams and viewing the dreams of others. Visitors have asked for more features, but King has resisted. "I wanted the site to have one simple thing that it does—I don't want it to lose focus," he says.

King has a special interest in community-oriented Web sites, where people can share thoughts or just pass the time with others. Another project of his, MopedArmy.com, is a site where moped enthusiasts can share stories and advice. At first, a dream-sharing site seems a perfect place for interacting with other users, but King decided against including that feature because dreams are so personal, and so emotionally charged. "When you have a database of information like TCUP has, it's tempting to add all sorts of features to it," he says. "I thought about rankings, and 'Email this dream,' and all sorts of silly things that don't really belong on this site."

But what about features that might enhance the core idea—like allowing people to add their own interpretations of other people's dreams? King says he decided against offering the ability to post any kind of comments, again due to the oddly private nature of this particular public forum. "I thought people would be much more likely to post if they didn't have to worry about people making fun of their dream or posting immature nonsense about the dream into a comments system," he says. Similarly, he decided against hosting discussion groups, worried, he says, that the tone might degrade into something "unserious."

It's a paradox. Only through tight control—over the features of the site and the workings of the code—can King create TCUP's sense of a dreamlike world that's beyond conscious control. ■

SPOTLIGHT
LAUNCHING NEW WINDOWS

Lots of Flash sites launch in their own windows—a practice designers debate the wisdom of. Flash designers need to consider both the pluses and the minuses of this practice when deciding whether to launch their movies in new windows (using the JavaScript `window.open` function) or load them into the current browser window.

Hello Design's site, for one, stays in the current window. "I didn't see a need for a pop-up window," says David Lai, Hello's CEO. "I've seen a ton of pop-up window sites, even before Flash, and it really feels disconnected to me."

Many Flash designers, however, feel that launching a new window helps with usability. The new window is typically launched minus the navigational "chrome" of a default browser window—removing access to the Back, Forward, and other buttons whose actions can confuse users within a Flash movie (see "Spotlight: The Problem of the Back Button" on page 94).

Others feel it's an aesthetic choice. Anh Tuan Pham, the designer of MOMA's Russian Avant-Garde Books site, says that he needed every extra pixel to get the design to work in the 800-by-600-pixel space he was designing

Hello Design loads its site into the current browser window. CEO David Lai feels that the disconnection caused by launching a new window doesn't pay off.

for. "We all agreed that the design required a good amount of negative, or empty, space to allow for the type of content and interactivity that we were producing. Putting the site in a pop-up without the toolbar allowed us those extra vertical pixels to work with."

The Flash section of the Collective Unconsciousness Project launches in a new window for entirely different reasons. "I imagined people might just leave this window up on their screen, as they did other things," says its creator, Simon King. (If you do, the site will navigate itself, loading new dreams every several seconds.) The downside, he acknowledges, is that you can't bookmark the dream browser in the new window.

The Web has one well-established convention for launching new windows. When clicking a link will take the user to a different site, it's common to open the new site in a different window. From a user's point of view, that clearly signals a break. It also has advantages for the site publishers: Launching a new window ensures that users will return to the original site—when they close the new window, the original site is still there, waiting underneath.

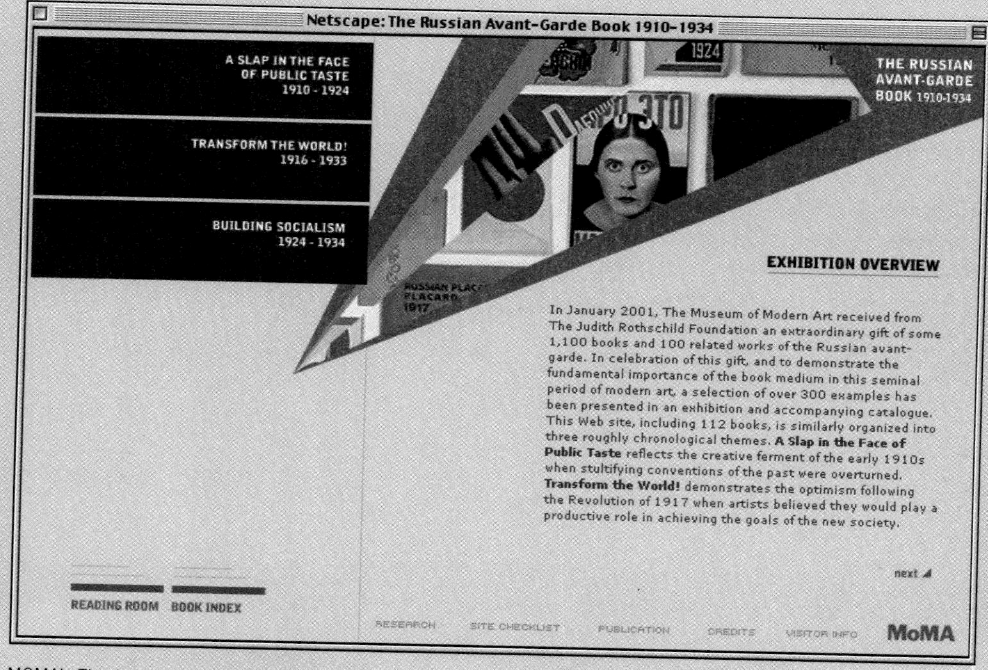
Netscape: The Russian Avant-Garde Book 1910–1934
A SLAP IN THE FACE OF PUBLIC TASTE 1910 - 1924
TRANSFORM THE WORLD! 1916 - 1933
BUILDING SOCIALISM 1924 - 1934
THE RUSSIAN AVANT-GARDE BOOK 1910-1934
EXHIBITION OVERVIEW
In January 2001, The Museum of Modern Art received from The Judith Rothschild Foundation an extraordinary gift of some 1,100 books and 100 related works of the Russian avant-garde. In celebration of this gift, and to demonstrate the fundamental importance of the book medium in this seminal period of modern art, a selection of over 300 examples has been presented in an exhibition and accompanying catalogue. This Web site, including 112 books, is similarly organized into three roughly chronological themes. A Slap in the Face of Public Taste reflects the creative ferment of the early 1910s when stultifying conventions of the past were overturned. Transform the World! demonstrates the optimism following the Revolution of 1917 when artists believed they would play a productive role in achieving the goals of the new society.
next
READING ROOM
BOOK INDEX
RESEARCH
SITE CHECKLIST
PUBLICATION
CREDITS
VISITOR INFO
MoMA

MOMA's The Avant-Garde Russian Book 1910–1934 site used a pop-up window without the navigational tools to create extra space for the design.

CHAPTER

SLEEPING GIANTS

KODAK eMAGAZINE
SECOND STORY INTERACTIVE STUDIOS
DESIGN: Second Story Interactive Studios
CLIENT: Kodak eMagazine
URL: www.kodak.com/US/en/corp/features/sleepingGiants/
EDITOR: David Kassnoff
CREATIVE DIRECTOR: Brad Johnson
STUDIO DIRECTOR: Julie Beeler
PRODUCER: Aleen Adams
DESIGNERS: Gabe Kean, Martin Linde
PROGRAMMERS: Seb Chevrel, Sam Ward
DESIGN TECHNOLOGIST: Sam Ward
ANIMATOR: Martin Linde
MUSIC COMPOSER: Brad Purkey

CHAPTER

SLEEPING GIANTS

INTRO

The job was to tell the story of AMARC, the Aerospace Maintenance and Regeneration Center, a sort of field hospital for military aircraft. Second Story Interactive Studios turned still photographs and voice-over narration into an engaging documentary that stirs emotions as it streams smoothly over 56 K modems.

Pictured: (from left, front row) Brad Johnson, Julie Beeler; (back row) Aleen Adams, Gabe Kean, Sam Ward, Seb Chevrel, Martin Linde

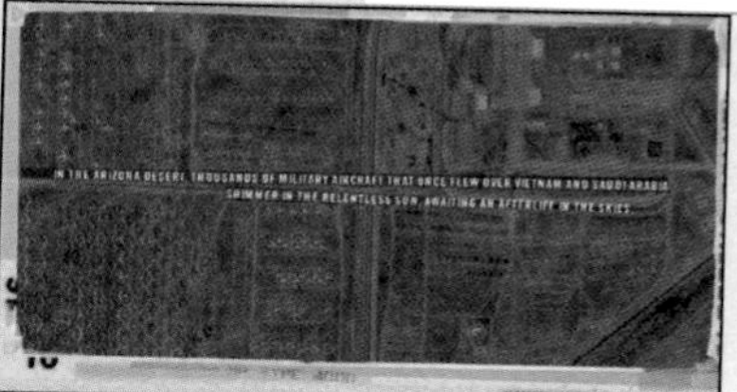

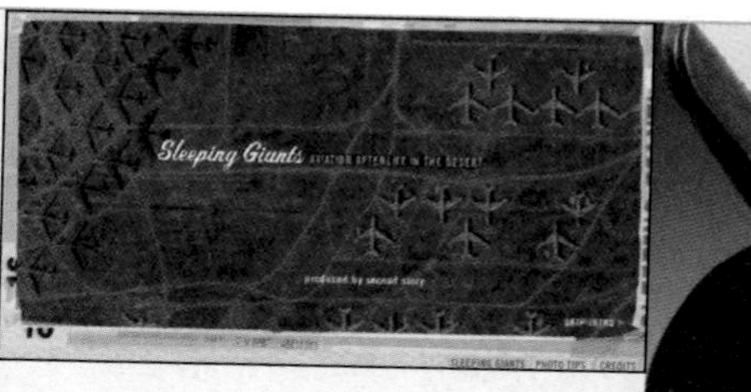

The Sleeping Giants site begins with a carefully paced intro sequence. The first photo, an overhead shot of the field, is zoomed into slowly. In the second frame, the Ry Cooder–ish soundtrack starts. In the third frame, the narration is layered over the guitar. The three elements—the photo and evocative typography, the Paris, Texas–like soundtrack, and the folksy comments of the narrator (a worker at AMARC)—combine to create a surprising poignancy.

Kodak's eMagazine speaks to the company's customers—professional and amateur photographers—with visual essays that celebrate the beauty of still photography and aim to inspire practitioners of the art. Second Story Interactive Studios, a Portland, Oregon–based Web development company that specializes in online storytelling, is one of several interactive development companies that work with the magazine's editor, David Kassnoff, to develop the stories. In 2001, Kassnoff approached Second Story with the idea for a story about AMARC, the Aerospace Maintenance and Regeneration Center.

"One thing we like to do with our stories is take people places they can't ordinarily go," says Kassnoff. For example, tourists can normally see AMARC only through the tinted windows of a tour bus. To take people behind the scenes at AMARC, Kassnoff got permission to take a personal tour, and came back to Second Story with two CDs of photos and a DAT tape holding an hour and a half of interviews with AMARC employees.

After spending hours poring through the photos, listening to the stories, and brainstorming ideas, Second Story decided that the best way to present the story would be as a straight documentary. Unlike most of the projects the company has produced, this one would be light on interactivity and more like a film, washing over relatively passive viewers. The trick would be getting the material to engage those relatively passive viewers.

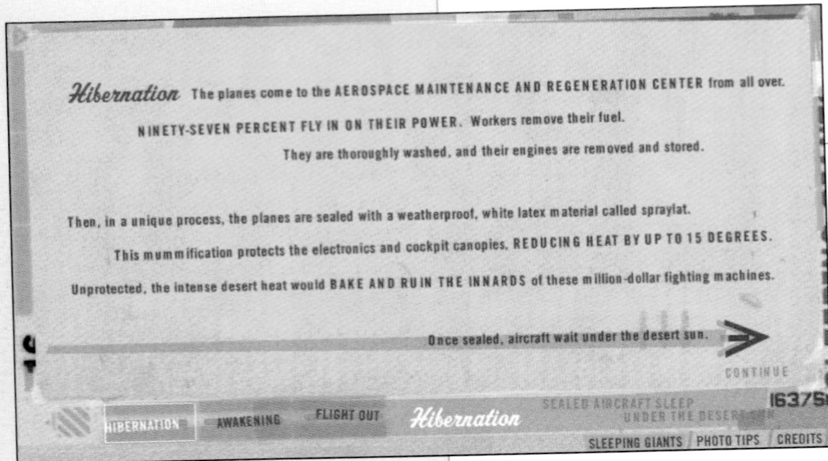

The intro sequence (previous page) fades directly into the first section of the site: Hibernation. Another text-based intro, overlaid by the lonely guitar, holds the viewer's attention as the movie loads. The continue arrow appears when the movie has streamed in enough to support a smooth playback at 56 K.

> Lessons from the Masters

Julie Beeler, Second Story's studio director, says that both the process for creating Sleeping Giants and the product itself are very different from the studio's typical work. "Usually, we get 50 million different things, and the client wants a million different options," she says. "This time, we got some pictures and some audio, and had to turn that into a Web site."

The team spent about a month with the materials, collaborating on ideas for how to use them, before the design really came together. "We knew we had to do some kind of documentary," Beeler says, which prodded the designers to look at different kinds of documentary treatments. The style that struck them as most interesting and relevant to their project was that of Errol Morris. Director of *The Thin Blue Line, A Brief History of Time*, and *Mr. Death*, Morris creates fascinating pieces by letting the quirky, real characters tell the story themselves. The team looked especially at Morris's *Fast, Cheap, and Out of Control*, a film in which four people passionately describe their unusual professions. Similarly, the team found that it was the employees' dedication and character that brought the AMARC facility to life for them.

Beeler says that what struck the design team most was the AMARC employees' passion for their work: "Each of these planes is like their baby, and they really care for them. They were there to save them. It was their mission." In the end, the character of the interviews determined the character of the site. When asked how a documentary about planes in the desert manages to evoke the poignancy it does here, Beeler says. "The simplicity and emotion comes from the interviews."

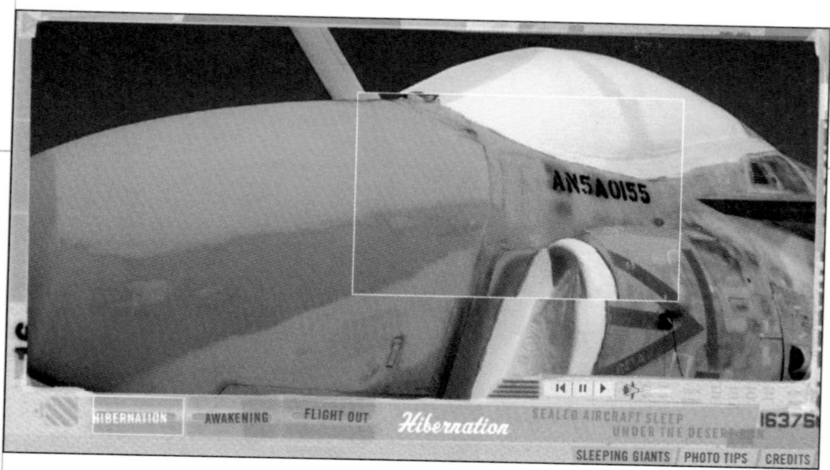

Kassnoff's still photos of AMARC create a backdrop for the action of Sleeping Giants. The graphic elements surrounding the photos combine elements from the stories (for example, the white spray lacquer that protects the planes in storage), military-style typography, and a playfulness that reflects the quirkiness of the characters providing the narration.

> Sound in the Foreground

Interestingly, sound turns out to be the primary medium of the Sleeping Giants site. "The pictures play a significant role, but they're really sort of secondary," says Beeler. The workers' narrated stories, layered over with evocative music, provide the main path through the material.

The inspiration for the music track also clearly owes something to documentarian Morris, who is known for the haunting, minimalist music that magically heightens the emotion of his films. Second Story also credits another film, Wim Wenders's *Paris, Texas*, for inspiration. In that movie, Ry Cooder's guitar score is practically a lead character, giving much of the personality to the film's lonely desert setting. Second Story borrowed the technique here for a similar effect.

"Brad [Johnson, Second Story's creative director] is really passionate about the music," says Beeler. "He wanted to create that melodramatic drone." The studio worked with composer Brad Purkey, who created about 20 riffs on a slide guitar, which Seb Chevrel, Second Story's lead programmer, layered into Flash in 8-second bits (see "Streaming Sound," page 128). "The way we did it made it seem like a longer composition than it is," says Beeler.

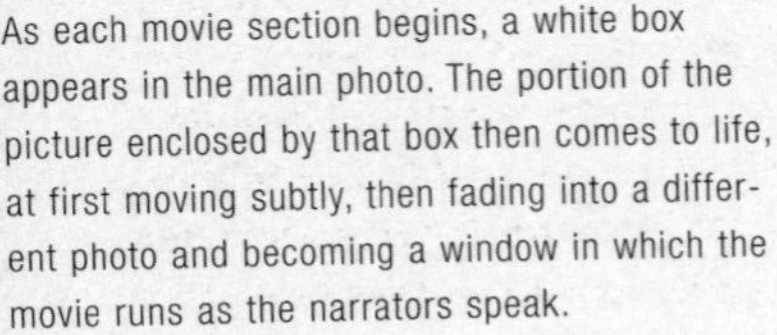
As each movie section begins, a white box appears in the main photo. The portion of the picture enclosed by that box then comes to life, at first moving subtly, then fading into a different photo and becoming a window in which the movie runs as the narrators speak.

> Rough and Shiny

"Usually, we let the content tell the story, and develop the visual part of the site out of the content," says Gabe Kean, Second Story's lead designer. In this case, he says, the design played on the contrast between the shiny, technical planes and the rough desert surrounding them.

One concern was that the site not seem too gloomy. AMARC is "like a graveyard," says Beeler, "desolate and isolated. We wanted to interject some life into it." The typography and the graphics bordering the screens provide an enlivening looseness—a way to bring out the quirkiness of the workers' characters.

The graphic elements used in the screens were pulled from details of the stories, says Kean. He gives an example: "When the planes come in, they go through this spraylat process, which is this white stuff they spray on the planes to protect them." The white-spray effect is seen around the edges of the screen. Other elements, such as the numbering and the blocky typography, come from military graphics.

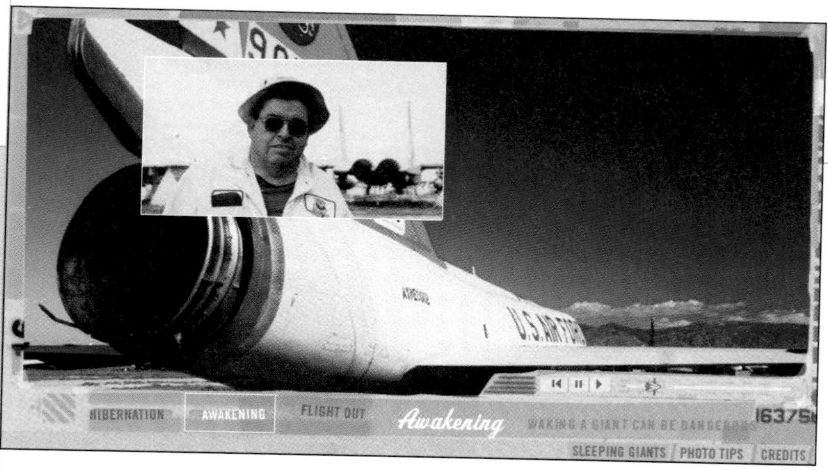

Clicking one of the three buttons at left takes viewers to a new section of the site. The movie controls move them back and forward through the narration and accompanying animations. Using the controls at the bottom right, viewers can jump to tips for taking photos of classic planes as well as site credits.

> Passive Activity

The site has an extremely simple structure. The stories are divided into three sections: Hibernation, Awakening, and Flight Out. The user's interaction is limited to choosing among those sections, and once within one, moving backward and forward through the story using a custom movie controller.

"We'd never done a project with interactivity that was so minimal," says Beeler. "We usually have lots of interactivity, so that you're not just sitting back listening." On this project, though, since the experience was more like watching a film, the team played with the idea of just leaving it at that, putting everything on autoplay. Sleeping Giants can, in fact, be experienced in that way. The only time the viewer really needs to do anything is to click the Continue arrow after each section introduction; otherwise, the stories play automatically, one section following another without user intervention. The simple interactivity that the site does offer, however, gives visitors some control over their experience, letting them jump ahead or repeat areas of interest. A movie producer might worry that a viewer stepping forward and back through reels may miss the arc of the film, but Kean says that wasn't an issue here. "It's a collage," he says. "It's not important to listen to it from start to finish."

The fact that interaction is optional may be one reason the navigation graphics are so unobtrusive. The buttons aren't well defined, and the colors fade into each other. The navigation generally melts into the general play of graphics around the screen's border. The most eye-catching detail is the movie controller—a little plane that moves along a mini-runway as the movie plays. According to Kean, the controller references the way planes are moved around AMARC; it also adds to the site's playfulness.

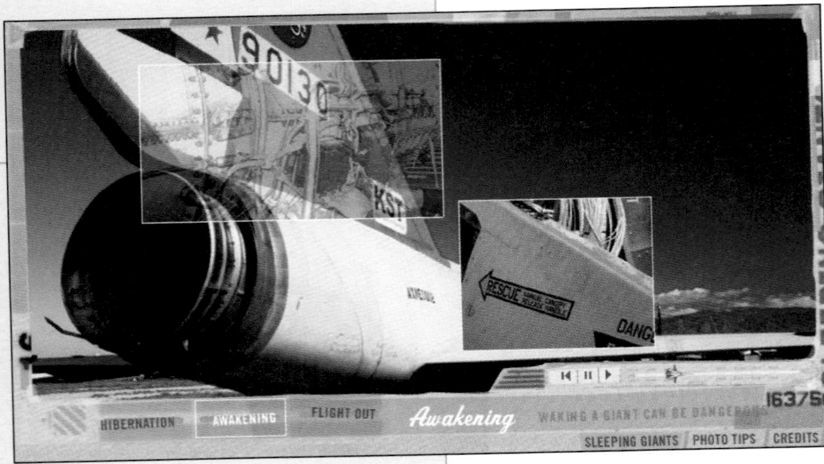

New animation windows pop up from time to time, adding more motion to the screen.

> Animated Stills

For a site showcasing still photography, Sleeping Giant has surprising life. The secret is the screen's constant, though often subtle, motion.

To prepare the photography, Aleen Adams, the site's producer, and Sam Ward, the interactive designer, created sequences from Kassnoff's photos. In addition, some photos were added from the libraries of Second Story staff, who had made their own trips to the desert. Tests uncovered a style of animation the team liked—a sort of panning across the stills and fading them into one another.

"It's a very traditional style in terms of documentary filmmakers," says Beeler. "We didn't ever want it to be absolutely still. We wanted to keep this subtle movement going." The studio also added its own touches to the traditional pan and zoom. The initial frame of each animation sequence surprises the viewer by bringing the background image to life. After the window that will hold the animation is drawn on the photo, the enclosed portion of the photo begins to move subtly, signaling the transition from still photo to animation.

To enliven the screen even more, a change in narrator often brings a change in window position as well. A second window is drawn onscreen and comes to life as the first one fades away.

The multilayered imagery makes for fast downloads as well as an interesting interface. Trying to animate a larger area of the screen would make for cumbersome downloads and sluggish playback. "If we had larger images, they'd really chug on some machines," says Beeler. Smaller image dimensions also allowed the designers to save the images at higher resolutions while keeping file sizes small.

> Down to a Minimum

Production, which took place over four weeks, was all about getting everything down to the smallest possible size. "It was mandatory that it stream over 56 K modems," says Beeler.

The team took different steps to minimize download times for different media. For the images, it was a matter of optimizing the JPEGs with careful cropping and compression. Then, they carefully timed the animation of the images to create enough movement to make things interesting while still keeping the pace slow enough to allow the next image to download without a pause in playback.

For the audio, it meant editing the original hour and a half of DAT tape down to about 10 minutes of narration. The next step was "making sure every pause was out of there," according to Beeler. Kean says that the fact that the original audio was of fairly poor quality actually worked to their advantage. "You could hear engines and background sounds," he explains. The team found that saving at a lower compression actually minimized the noise. They used a setting of 16 kHz, compared with their usual standard of 44 kHz.

The audio was set to "streaming" to mix the music and narration in a single stream.

With the assets optimized, the final step was testing and fine-tuning playback. An important element of that was the text-based introduction screens, which serve the dual purpose of setting the scene for the upcoming movie and keeping the viewer occupied while the movie begins loading. "We couldn't make the load time go away, so we were just trying to hide it," Beeler says.

The intro screens originally had a lot more text—three paragraphs each—but the team knew that was more than they could expect viewers to read. They edited the screens down to a single line but found that didn't hold the viewer's attention long enough. Once the movie was in place, the team was able to see the intro screen in the final layout and in the context of the movie download. In the end, the screens were edited word by word to create the right balance of page layout and reading time.

UNDER THE HOOD
STREAMING SOUND

For Sleeping Giants' leisurely soundtrack, Second Story found that the simplest approach was also the best.

Musician Brad Purkey created a dozen guitar riffs of about 8 seconds each, which Seb Chevrel, Second Story's technician, then digitized and optimized using Macromedia's Sound Edit. Chevrel then became a composer as well as a Flash programmer: He was responsible for determining how the individual riffs would be combined on the timeline, creating the score of the movie.

The music files were the last element to be placed on the timeline—after the interview files were in place and the animations were complete (**Figure 1**). "That allowed us to precisely compose synchronized music using hardly any additional bandwidth," says Chevrel. By setting the audio to "streaming" to mix the music and narration into a single streaming file, Chevrel was able to get the bandwidth down to 24 Kbps, which he calls "the minimum acceptable quality for a narration and music mix."

Using short clips and placing them last also allowed Chevrel to arrange the music in ways that wouldn't interfere with the narration. "It ended up working extremely well, giving the feeling of a random, slow composition, even though it was a low-tech approach," says Chevrel.

Figure 1

The timeline includes three layers for the guitar track. Chevrel placed those files last, making sure that the guitar riffs didn't interfere with the narration.

At the end of the movie, the site comes to a stop on a still title frame. No action is suggested, though visitors can use any part of the navigation to repeat parts of the movie or go to the ancillary materials at the bottom right.

> A Leisurely Pace

In timing the intro text, it was probably safe to assume that the visitor would be reading the text at a pretty relaxed pace. The music, the narration, and the pace of the animations all combine to create a loping, leisurely tone without ever dragging. It's a tone that's appropriate to the topic, which is all about waiting: The planes sit in the desert for a decade or more, waiting to be put back into service. The workers have been there for decades themselves. Their stories, and the way they speak, all signal patience, slowness, carefulness—and the interface falls right in step. Sleeping Giants is a study in how well a simple structure and complex effects can go hand in hand. ■

SPOTLIGHT
MUSIC AND SOUND

Only five of the dozen sites profiled in this book use sound at all, and of those, three use it very little.

iHotelier's OneScreen provides audible feedback for clicks, but no other sounds.

The MINI USA site uses sound sparingly. Clicks supply feedback to menu choices, bits of music signal the download of a new section, and appropriate sound effects accompany surprises such as a lightning flash or a helicopter's approach. The clicks, whirs, and thunderclaps add a snappy punctuation that is in keeping with the jauntiness of the site as a whole.

On Bud Greenspan's Ten Greatest Winter Olympians, sound is used just once. In the site's introduction, a voice-over by Greenspan introduces the site's theme. It's a powerful way to interject Greenspan's personality into a site meant to introduce him to the audience.

In contrast, sound is the preeminent medium in Sleeping Giants. The guitar soundtrack creates the lonely, Old West tone, while voice-overs by the AMARC workers tell the story of the place. Together, they heighten the cinematic feel that is the hallmark of the site.

Testimony: A Story Machine, like Sleeping Giants, is a storytelling site with a soundtrack. Quiet background sounds, though hard to identify, suggest a mood for each scenario. Like the illustrations, they're chosen to evoke specific emotions and images that relate to the murder-mystery theme.

On Bud Greenspan's Ten Greatest Winter Olympians, the sound of Greenspan's voice creates a feeling of intimacy.

A munching sound introduces Testimony: A Story Machine. It begins during the initial loading sequence, before any images appear. The first image, shown here, solves the sonic mystery.

In each case, sounds are used for particular, consciously crafted effects that enhance the site's content and further its goals. Sound can never be used lightly, but in some cases, it's well worth its considerable bandwidth (and load-time) requirements. Most of the sites highlighted in these pages rightly determined that sound wouldn't add enough value to justify its bandwidth.

Interestingly, none of the sites that do use sound offer what I normally consider a necessity—a "sound off" option that lets users silence the sound if it's likely to annoy others (or embarrass the user).

You should almost always offer the option of silence. I can see why Sleeping Giants doesn't; the site would be meaningless without sound. But on sites like Testimony: A Story Machine, a "sound off" option would be useful. I asked the creator of Story Machine about it, and he agreed it was an oversight. He also apologized nicely to my husband, who—working in the same room where I was playing the site again and again—was being driven insane.

You hear the helicopter before you see it. Because sound is used sparingly on MINI USA, its rare appearances add an element of surprise.

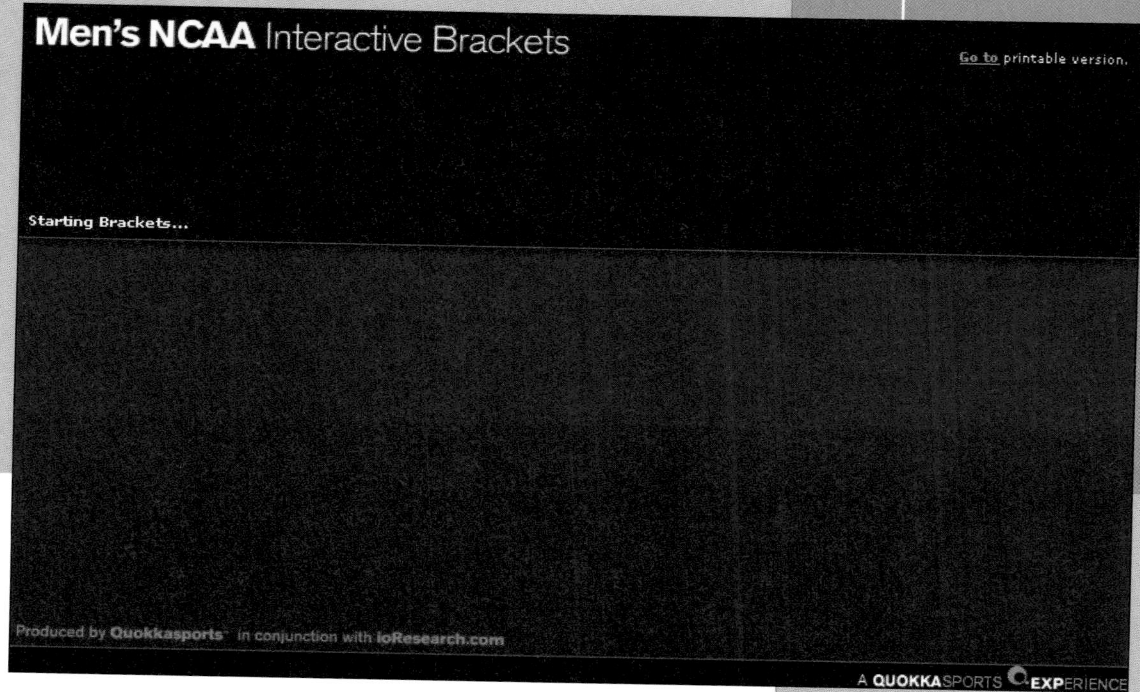

CHAPTER

NCAA Final Four Brackets

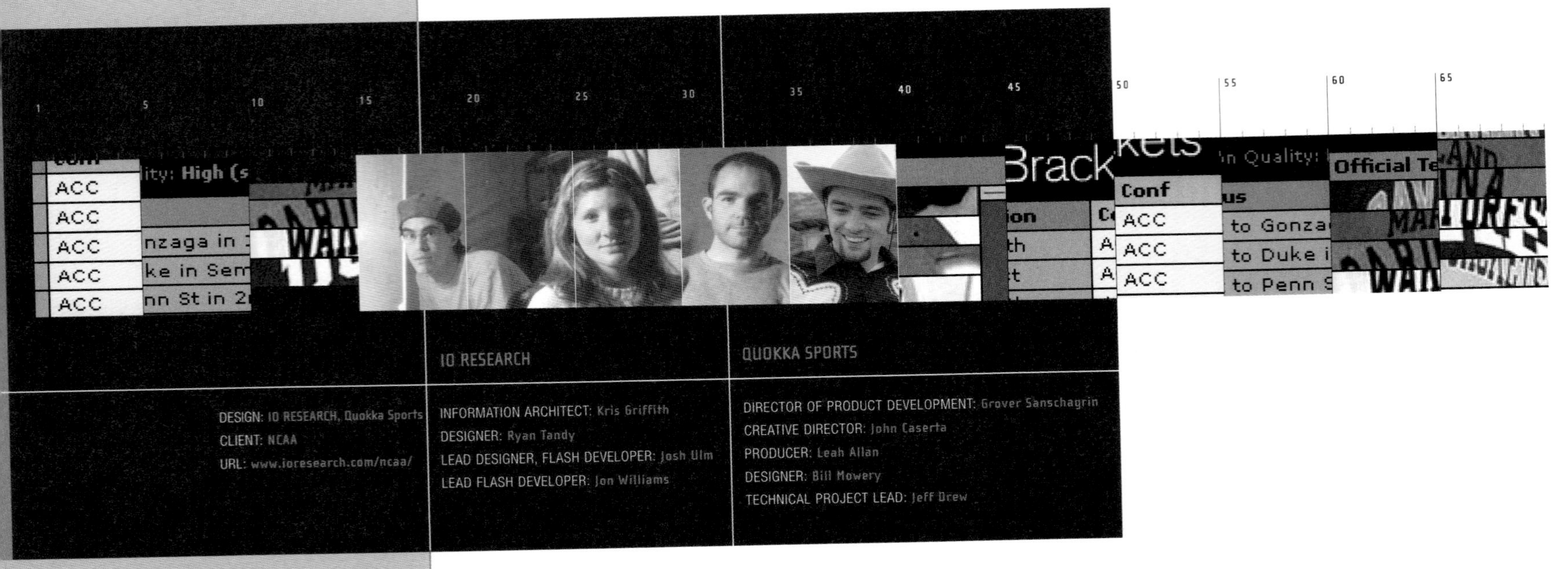

IO RESEARCH
QUOKKA SPORTS
DESIGN: IO RESEARCH, Quokka Sports
CLIENT: NCAA
URL: www.ioresearch.com/ncaa/
INFORMATION ARCHITECT: Kris Griffith
DESIGNER: Ryan Tandy
LEAD DESIGNER, FLASH DEVELOPER: Josh Ulm
LEAD FLASH DEVELOPER: Jon Williams
DIRECTOR OF PRODUCT DEVELOPMENT: Grover Sanschagrin
CREATIVE DIRECTOR: John Caserta
PRODUCER: Leah Allan
DESIGNER: Bill Mowery
TECHNICAL PROJECT LEAD: Jeff Drew

CHAPTER

NCAA Final Four Brackets

INTRO

Most sports fans are familiar with the "brackets" layout commonly used to map a sports tournament's matchups. For the NCAA basketball finals, Quokka Sports exploited and expanded the well-known structure by making it interactive: a window into the games, the teams, and their merchandise.

Pictured: (from left) Jon Williams, Kris Griffith, Josh Ulm, John Caserta

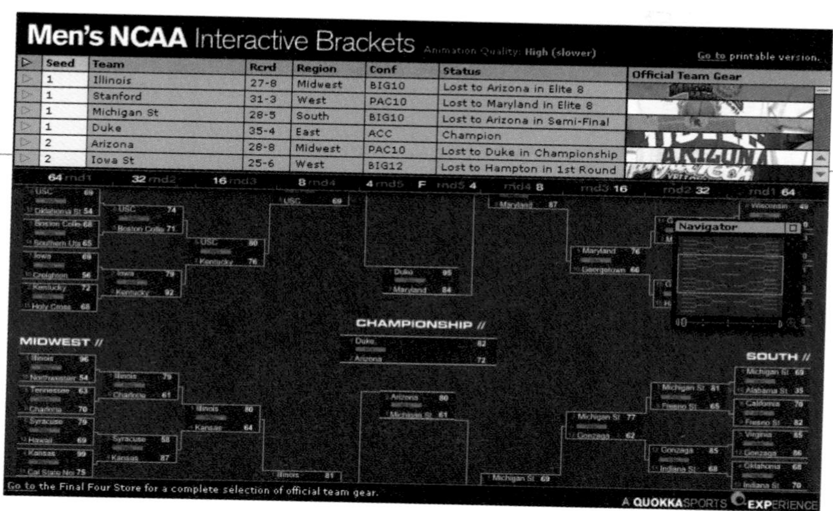

The brackets layout provided an interactive interface to information about each game and each team.

For basketball fans, the most exciting time of year is March, when the National College Athletics Association (NCAA) organizes the final matchups of the country's top teams. Over a period of four weeks, 65 teams play 64 games in a fight to the finish.

The traditional method of illustrating this inexorable march toward victory is with *brackets*—a layout that shows the broad field in each region being narrowed to four regional champions, then to the final two winners, who meet, appropriately enough, in the middle of the map, with the names of their fallen brethren ranked behind them. It's a layout familiar to sports fans—from grade-school kids to adults participating in office pools.

It is appropriate, then, to use this time-honored, immediately recognizable layout to show the tournament's progress on the Web. But while the bracket layout provides an efficient means of displaying information, it is unwieldy in scale. Quokka Sports, working with IO Research, found a way not only to display the brackets on the Web, but to exploit them as an interface for navigating through all sorts of other information about the 2001 NCAA finals, hosted on FinalFour.net, the official site of the NCAA Basketball Championship.

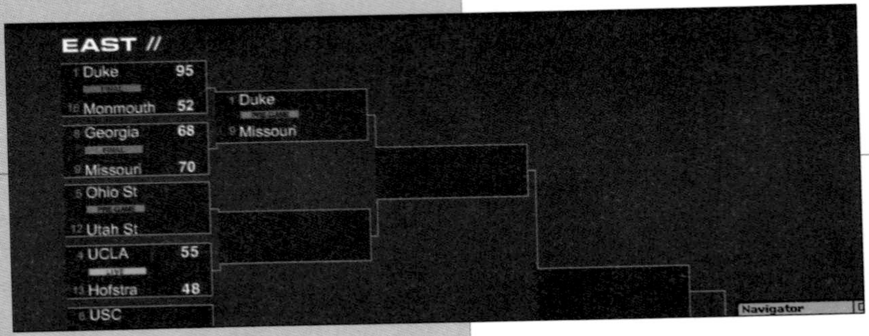

EAST //

1 Duke	95	
16 Monmouth	52	
8 Georgia	68	
9 Missouri	70	
5 Ohio St		
12 Utah St		
4 UCLA	55	
13 Hofstra	48	
6 USC		

1 Duke
9 Missouri
Navigator

As a game began, the status bar in its game box turned green, and the score would be updated every few minutes. A final score was indicated by a red status box.

> Doing Brackets Right

"As a basketball fan, I had been thinking about how to do the brackets online for years," says John Caserta, creative director of sponsor-related projects for Quokka Sports, an online sports-coverage company based in San Francisco. "I didn't want to go on the Web and see the same thing I'd seen in print. I wanted it to be computerized." He and Grover Sanschagrin, Quokka's director of product development for project accounts, cooked up the basic concept for the interactive brackets and proposed the project to the NCAA, which hired them for the job.

The interactive brackets Quokka proposed offered decided advantages over traditional brackets, which are frozen as a still schematic. Quokka's brackets, in contrast, came to life as the tournament progressed.

As the NCAA determined standings and schedules, bracket information was filled into the appropriate game boxes. A colored bar in the center of each box indicated the game's status. Before a game began, its square was gray and read "Pre-Game." Once a game began, that square turned green and read "Live," and the game score, updated every few minutes, was displayed to the right of the teams' names. At the game's end, the box turned red and read "Final," with the final score displayed to the right.

Basketball fans could keep the brackets up on their screens during game days and watch the tournament's progress in something approaching real time. The brackets display was able to simultaneously convey the excitement of a live game as well as a sense of where the tournament as a whole was heading: Who was advancing, and who had been defeated? Who would emerge from each region to win a place in the Final Four? When was the next game? What was going on right now? Action was taking place in the four corners of the country—and of the brackets.

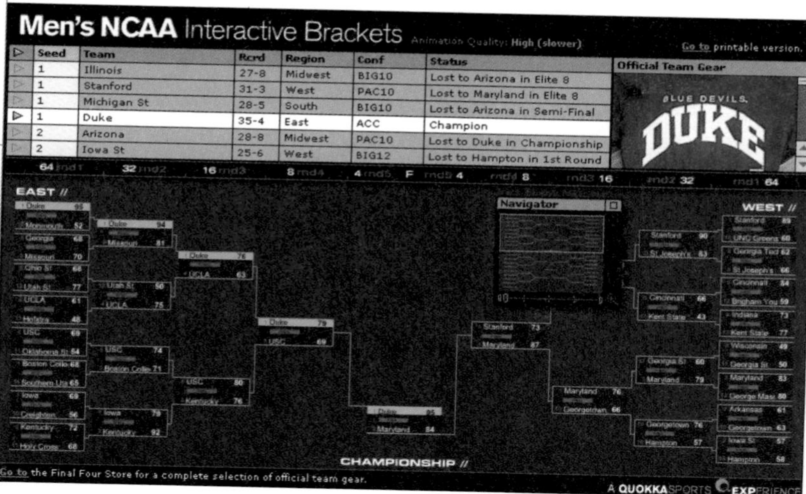

The table at the top of the screen let users follow their favorite teams. Clicking a team's name in the table highlighted that team's positions in the brackets and called up an image of the team's gear (to the right of the table), which was offered for sale through the site.

> The Story Behind the Interface

The brackets display was only the first of the schematic's uses. "It was important to Quokka that viewers not be limited to viewing the current games, or to any other narrow focus," says Kris Griffith, the project manager at IO Research, Quokka's development partner for the project. "They wanted users to be immersed in the whole, able to be drawn in and out of a holistic view based on the tournament's events."

Taking the users' point of view, IO Research posited that they would want to follow the tournament as they would a story. "Users are interested in tracking their team or their conference to see how their characters play into the story," says Griffith.

To meet both these requirements, Quokka and IO Research supplemented the bracket display (the holistic, macro view) with additional controls and information. Different interactions let users zoom in on the action—following their characters' trajectories through the drama.

By clicking the team's name in the team table above the brackets, for example, users could see at a glance the team's position in the brackets. Clicking the brackets themselves opened new windows with detailed information about a specific game or team.

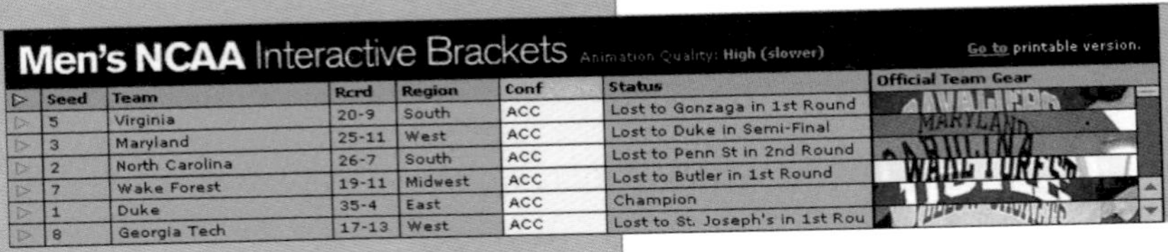

Men's NCAA Interactive Brackets Animation Quality: **High (slower)** Go to printable version.

Seed	Team	Rcrd	Region	Conf	Status
5	Virginia	20-9	South	ACC	Lost to Gonzaga in 1st Round
3	Maryland	25-11	West	ACC	Lost to Duke in Semi-Final
2	North Carolina	26-7	South	ACC	Lost to Penn St in 2nd Round
7	Wake Forest	19-11	Midwest	ACC	Lost to Butler in 1st Round
1	Duke	35-4	East	ACC	Champion
8	Georgia Tech	17-13	West	ACC	Lost to St. Joseph's in 1st Rou

Official Team Gear

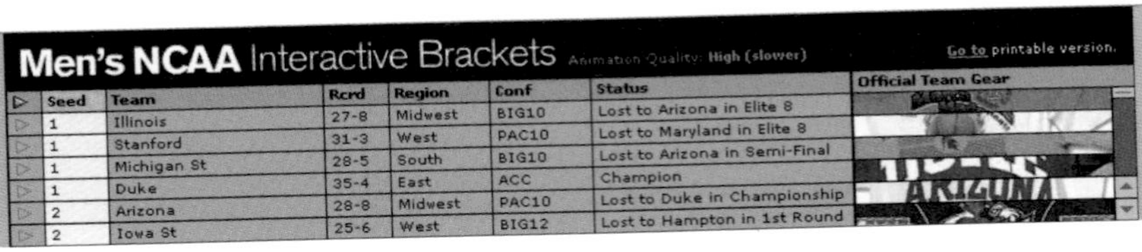

Men's NCAA Interactive Brackets Animation Quality: **High (slower)** Go to printable version.

Seed	Team	Rcrd	Region	Conf	Status
1	Illinois	27-8	Midwest	BIG10	Lost to Arizona in Elite 8
1	Stanford	31-3	West	PAC10	Lost to Maryland in Elite 8
1	Michigan St	28-5	South	BIG10	Lost to Arizona in Semi-Final
1	Duke	35-4	East	ACC	Champion
2	Arizona	28-8	Midwest	PAC10	Lost to Duke in Championship
2	Iowa St	25-6	West	BIG12	Lost to Hampton in 1st Round

Official Team Gear

Clicking a column heading in the team table sorted the teams by that item—which let viewers quickly see how their conference was doing (left) and who the top teams were (right). It even let them check the status on a custom list of teams (facing page).

> Mediated Live

For a detailed look at a particular game, a fan could click the game's status bar. This would launch a new window holding different information, depending on the game's status. Before a game began, the page held links to a team's page on FinalFour.net as well as information about the upcoming game (time, location, and so on). During a game, the page added live text coverage of the game, updated every few minutes. After the game, the page included a game summary and the final score.

The live game coverage was provided courtesy of technology from Total Sports, a company Quokka had recently acquired. Total Sports, which specialized in live basketball coverage for the Web, had been working with the NCAA to provide live reports of its games on the NCAA's FinalFour.net Web site.

The up-to-the-minute game data—who scored, from where, and how; who fouled, against whom; and so on—was input into a special program by reporters sitting ringside at the stadium. Total Sports' proprietary software then saved that information in real time into an XML file, which was uploaded to the brackets site every couple of minutes.

Josh Ulm, director of IO Research, says the project team tested different upload intervals to find the optimal rate for uploading and the most efficient method of updating the site. In the end, the team

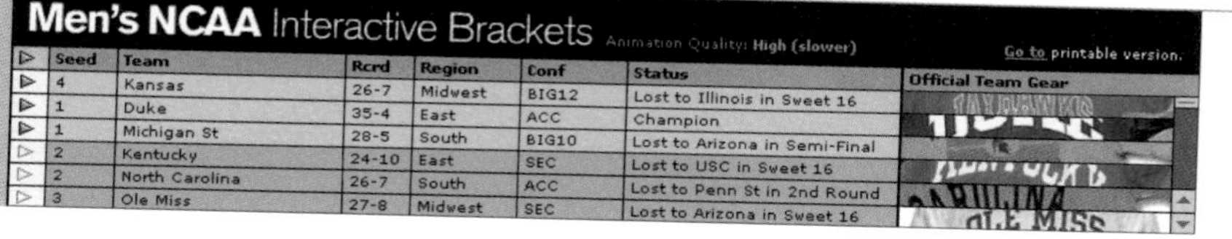

Men's NCAA Interactive Brackets Animation Quality: **High (slower)** Go to printable version.

▷	Seed	Team	Rcrd	Region	Conf	Status
▶	4	Kansas	26-7	Midwest	BIG12	Lost to Illinois in Sweet 16
▶	1	Duke	35-4	East	ACC	Champion
▶	1	Michigan St	28-5	South	BIG10	Lost to Arizona in Semi-Final
▷	2	Kentucky	24-10	East	SEC	Lost to USC in Sweet 16
▷	2	North Carolina	26-7	South	ACC	Lost to Penn St in 2nd Round
▷	3	Ole Miss	27-8	Midwest	SEC	Lost to Arizona in Sweet 16

Official Team Gear

decided that the (100 KB–plus) data file was too much for Flash to render on the fly through its own XML filter. Instead, they used Macromedia Generator to turn the XML file into a SWF file, and then read that into Flash.

> Sorting Out the Data

In addition to updating the scores and the live game report, Quokka's live feeds updated the Status column in the team table. More than a way to find a team in the brackets, the table served as an at-a-glance index of the teams' (the characters') current status in the tournament.

"Users would want to get quick access to lists of the teams that have been eliminated or that remain, of remaining teams in their conference, or of teams by rank, in hope of maintaining their office-pool brackets or to search for Cinderella stories," says Griffith. For that kind of at-a-glance information, the designers determined that a table format would be more efficient than the brackets.

Not only did the table provide team information in a nutshell, it also let users sort teams by any number of criteria. Clicking a column heading sorted the teams by that item—a behavior familiar to anyone who's used Microsoft Excel, the Macintosh Finder, or Qualcomm's Eudora email program (among other popular applications). Users could also sort the list to bring a set of teams they had chosen to the top of the list. A "selected" icon would be highlighted in the first column of the table, and clicking that column heading would bring user-selected teams to the top.

Griffith says that Seed, Team, Record, Region, and Conference columns were obvious choices for a table of this kind. The Status column was added to accommodate the current information available in the live feed. Users could also sort by Status to find out which games were currently live.

The need for the "selected" column became clear when the companies were designing the site's interface. It became a way for users to home in on the specific teams they wanted to follow, since sorting by that column brought the selected teams to the top of the list. Testing showed that turning the selection into a toggle—one click to turn it on, and another to turn it off—would be the easiest way to manage changing selections.

UNDER THE HOOD
PARSING XML

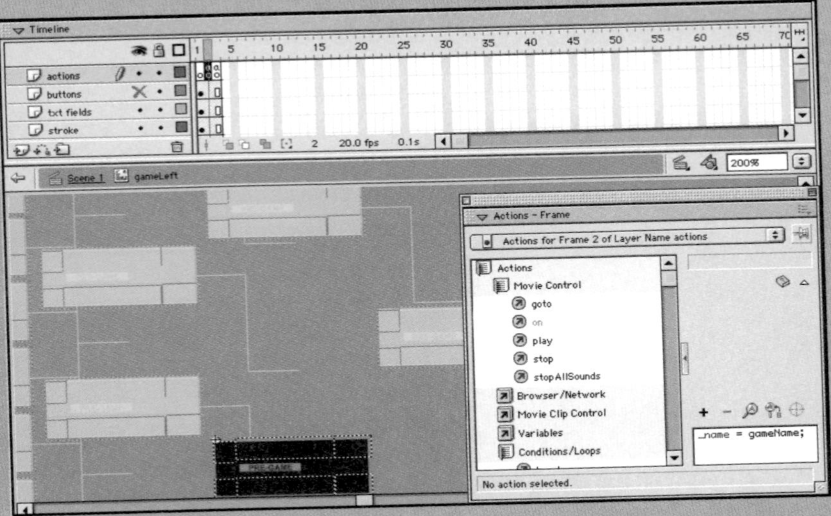

Figure 1
The game movie clip has an onClipEvent (load) action that provides the name for that instance.

During the tournament, game information was uploaded to the brackets every few minutes, letting Web users follow the action of games in progress as well as the march of advancing teams at the conclusion of each contest. That meant asking Flash to parse upwards of 100 K of XML in almost real time.

In the 2001 tournament, using Flash 5, IO Research found that Flash's XML-parsing skills weren't up to performing the task at the speed needed. Their answer at the time was to feed the XML file through Generator, which parsed the file and generated the SWF. With the improved XML-handling skills of Flash MX, however, Generator is no longer required, and Jon Williams (now at shovemedia.com) has created a simple XML parser that can handle the XML feed with the requisite speed.

The second part of the solution is a set of movie clips that uses the data feed to automatically update the brackets display—not only filling in new game scores and other data but also figuring out which game boxes need to be redrawn.

In the brackets layout, each box is an instance of a game movie clip, which is completed with the proper game information, placed in the correct position, and connected to the surrounding boxes with the appropriate connecting lines when the data is uploaded. As each game clip is loaded, it runs an onClipEvent (load) action that tells the clip its own gameName (**Figure 1**), plus the name of the

```
gameInit (this)
gameInit = function (mc) {
    connectToWinnerGame (mc, mc.winnerGameName)
    //[snip]
}

connectToWinnerGame = function (mc, winnerGameName) {
    var winnerGame = mc._parent[winnerGameName]
    var targetAnchor=""
    if (mc._y < winnerGame._y) {
        targetAnchor="teamaAnchor"
    } else {
        targetAnchor="teambAnchor"
    }

    var startX = mc.winnerPath._x + mc._x
    var startY = mc.winnerPath._y + mc._y
    var endX = winnerGame[targetAnchor]._x + winnerGame._x
    var endY = winnerGame[targetAnchor]._y + winnerGame._y
    mc.winnerPath._xscale = endX - startX
    mc.winnerPath._yscale = endY - startY
}
```

Figure 2

Frame 3 of the *game* movie clip includes the `gameInit` function, which uses the `connectToWinnerGame` function to control how the lines are drawn from one game box to the next game in the contest.

game the winner will play in. A `connectToWinnerGame` function (**Figure 2**) tells the *game* clip how to connect to the next game. Each *game* clip has two empty movie clips, `teamaAnchor` and `teambAnchor`. The `connectToWinnerGame` function figures out which anchor to use, based on whether the next game is positioned above or below the current game in the brackets. It then draws the line—a movie clip called `winnerPath`—which stretches out, then up or down, and out again to meet the next box, based on that box's coordinates.

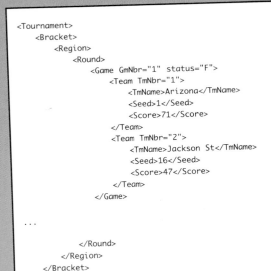

```
<Tournament>
    <Bracket>
        <Region>
            <Round>
                <Game GmNbr="1" status="F">
                    <Team TmNbr="1">
                        <TmName>Arizona</TmName>
                        <Seed>1</Seed>
                        <Score>71</Score>
                    </Team>
                    <Team TmNbr="2">
                        <TmName>Jackson St</TmName>
                        <Seed>16</Seed>
                        <Score>47</Score>
                    </Team>
                </Game>

 ...

            </Round>
        </Region>
    </Bracket>
</Tournament>
```

Figure 3

The XML file has a node structure like this, with game data included for as many teams as are playing the current round.

The information needed to initiate all of this drawing comes from the XML file, whose structure is shown in **Figure 3**. The parent node, Tournament, has descendent nodes that include Bracket, Region, Round, and Game (which contains each team's name, seed, and score).

The parser (**Figure 4**) loops through each node, storing the name of each and its assigned name in variables. As variables are assigned values, a series of "if" statements checks those values against the expected structure to ensure that it's reading in the appropriate data and that it only stores the data that's needed. If these conditions are met, the program continues, until it reaches the Game node. It then stores the game data (game number, status, the name and seed for each team, and the score), and pushes the variable into the text-field slots in the appropriate game clip.

```
gameData = new XML()
gameData.ignoreWhite = true
gameData.onLoad = populateData
gameData.load ("bracket2.xml")

populateData = function () {
   var nodes = this.childNodes[0].childNodes //Get <Tournament> children
   for (var i = 0; i<nodes.length; i++) {
      var tournElm = nodes[i]
      var tournElmName = tournElm.nodeName

      if (tournElmName == "Bracket") {
         var bracketNodes = tournElm.childNodes //Get <Bracket> Children
         for (var j=0; j<bracketNodes.length; j++) {
            var bracketElm = bracketNodes[j]
            var bracketElmName = bracketElm.nodeName
```

Figure 4

The parser loads the contents of the XML file (bracket2.xml) into a new gameData file and loads the populateData function. That function loops through the XML file, storing the contents of each node in variables and then assigning the data to the text fields of the proper game movie clips.

```
            if (bracketElmName == "Region")
               var regionNodes = bracketElm.childNodes //Get <Region> children
               for (var k=0; k<regionNodes.length; k++) {
                     var regionElm = regionNodes[k]
                  var regionElmName = regionElm.nodeName

                  if (regionElmName == "Round") {
                     var roundNodes = regionElm.childNodes     //Get <Round> children
                     for (var l=0; l<roundNodes.length; l++) {
                           var roundElm = roundNodes[l]
                     var roundElmName = roundElm.nodeName
                     if (roundElmName == "Game") {
                        var gameNumber = roundElm.attributes.GmNbr      // STORE GAME DATA
                        var status = roundElm.attributes.status
                        var gameNodes = roundElm.childNodes  //Get <Game> data
                        for (var m=0; m<gameNodes.length; m++) {
                           var gameElm = gameNodes[m]
                           var gameElmName = gameElm.nodeName

                           if (gameElmName == "Team") {
                              var teamNodes = gameElm.childNodes       //Get <Team> data
                              var teamNumber = gameElm.attributes.TmNbr          // STORE TEAM DATA
                              for (var n=0; n<teamNodes.length; n++) {
                                 var teamElm = teamNodes[n]
                                 var teamElmName = teamElm.nodeName

                                 // STORE TEAM NAME
                                 if (teamElmName == "TmName") var TmName = teamElm.childNodes[0]
                                 // STORE SEED
                                 if (teamElmName == "Seed") var Seed = teamElm.childNodes[0]
                                 // STORE SCORE
                                 if (teamElmName == "Score") var Score = teamElm.childNodes[0]

// POPULATE TEXTFIELDS
                           if (teamNumber == "1") fieldSet = "a"
                           if (teamNumber == "2") fieldSet = "b"
         _root["game"+gameNumber]["team"+fieldSet+"Seed"].value = Seed
         _root["game"+gameNumber]["team"+fieldSet+"Name"].value = TmName
         _root["game"+gameNumber]["team"+fieldSet+"Score"].value = Score
         _root["game"+gameNumber].gameStatus.gotoAndStop (status)
         trace ([gameNumber, TmName,"p"])

   }}}}}}}}}

}
```

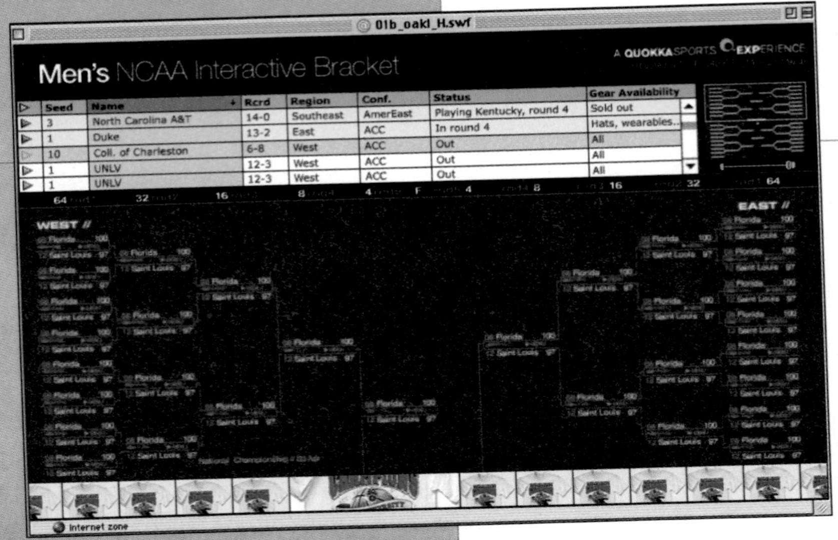

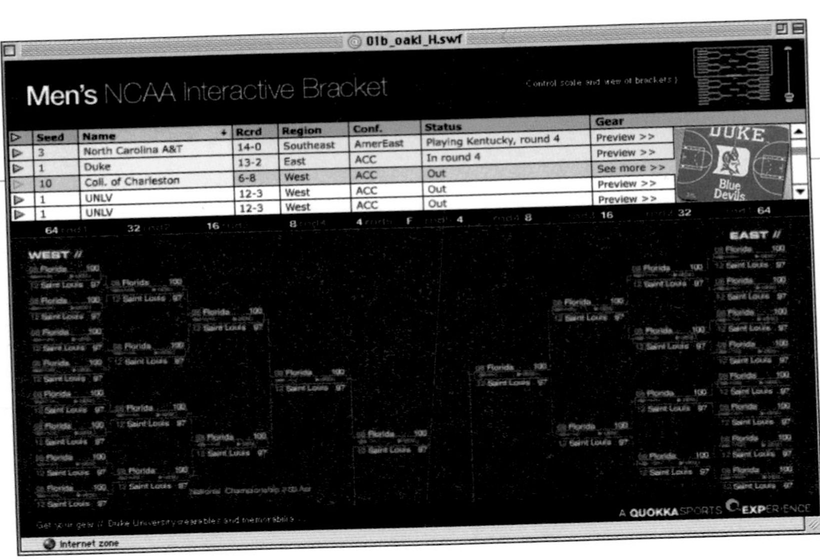

Caserta sketched out a variety of approaches for adding merchandise to the main brackets page. In one (left), a Gear Availability column was added to the table, with pictures of the gear arrayed across the bottom of the page. Another (right) was similar to the final approach but offered a different interaction with the gear window.

> A Word from the Sponsors

The site designers needed to include one other type of information on the screen: a place for sales. In a way, this was the most important part of the site, since Quokka had proposed the project to the NCAA as a money-making proposition, paid for by sales of team equipment during the tournament. In fact, the Quokka team that developed the site was formed especially for such ventures. During Quokka's coverage of the Sydney Olympics for CNBC, the company pioneered methods for garnering commercial support of sports coverage on the Web, and it was now developing its ideas into a business model for one of its business units.

For this site, selling sports gear seemed the most promising means of support. "There's a large demand by fans for gear, and there's a lot of traffic coming to the site after wins," says Caserta.

In brainstorming ways to get visitors to buy, IO Research first proposed using storytelling: video montages of the teams' play would be presented to work up fans' excitement for their teams. Quokka was worried, though, that this approach would remove the store

Men's NCAA Interactive Brackets Animation Quality: High (slower) — Go to printable version.

Seed	Team	Rcrd	Region	Conf	Status
1	Illinois	27-8	Midwest	BIG10	Lost to Arizona in Elite 8
1	Stanford	31-3	West	PAC10	Lost to Maryland in Elite 8
1	Michigan St	28-5	South	BIG10	Lost to Arizona in Semi-Final
1	Duke	35-4	East	ACC	Champion
2	Arizona	28-8	Midwest	PAC10	Lost to Duke in Championship
2	Iowa St	25-6	West	BIG12	Lost to Hampton in 1st Round

Official Team Gear

Men's NCAA Interactive Brackets Animation Quality: High (slower) — Go to printable version.

Seed	Team	Rcrd	Region	Conf	Status
1	Illinois	27-8	Midwest	BIG10	Lost to Arizona in Elite 8
1	Stanford	31-3	West	PAC10	Lost to Maryland in Elite 8
1	Michigan St	28-5	South	BIG10	Lost to Arizona in Semi-Final
1	Duke	35-4	East	ACC	Champion
2	Arizona	28-8	Midwest	PAC10	Lost to Duke in Championship
2	Iowa St	25-6	West	BIG12	Lost to Hampton in 1st Round

Official Team Gear

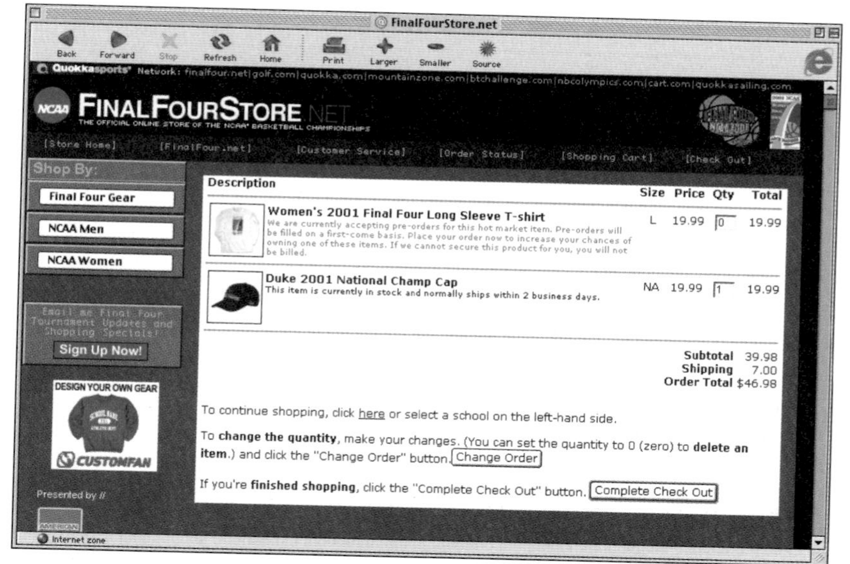

In the final design, an Official Team Gear window displayed a collage of team jerseys (top). Rolling the pointer over a team's row showed that team's merchandise in the window (center). Clicking in that window opened a store window (bottom).

too far from the main page—and from the information that users were there to get. Instead, the company brought out a simpler idea that everyone was happier with: featuring the team gear on the main brackets page.

The final design for this approach merged commerce and the users' interaction with the brackets. A merchandise window was arrayed next to the table, in a new Official Team Gear window. Rolling the pointer over a team row in the table would bring up that team's merchandise in the window. "Since the interaction model prescribes that the table runs the brackets, it follows that the table should run the merchandise viewer as well," Griffith notes.

This interaction offered a couple of other advantages as well: The fact that the merchandise display changed as the user's pointer rolled over the table not only made the connection between the two areas clear, it produced an eye-catching visual effect that drew attention to the sales. It also ensured that users saw the merchandise they were most interested in—the products linked to the teams they were interacting with in the table.

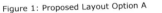

BRACKET (ROLL OVER AREA TO ENLARGE) Printable version

CATEGORY (CLICK ON CATEGORY TO SORT)

Seed	Name (Record)	Region	Conf.	Status
1	Duke (31-4)	East	ACC	In rnd 3
1	Purdue (xx-xx)	West	XXX	Out
1	Team Name (xx-xx)	Southeast	XXX	In rnd 3
1	Team Name (xx-xx)	Midwest	XXX	Playing
2	Team Name (xx-xx)	East	ACC	In rnd 3
2	Team Name (xx-xx)	Midwest	XXX	In rnd 3
2	Team Name (xx-xx)	Southeast	XXX	In rnd 3
2	Team Name (xx-xx)	West	XXX	Out
3	Duke (31-4)	East	ACC	Playing
3	Purdue (xx-xx)	West	XXX	In rnd 3
3	Team Name (xx-xx)	Southeast	XXX	In rnd 2
3	Team Name (xx-xx)	Midwest	XXX	Out
4	Team Name (xx-xx)	East	ACC	Out
4	Team Name (xx-xx)	Midwest	XXX	Playing
4	Team Name (xx-xx)	Southeast	XXX	In rnd 3
4	Team Name (xx-xx)	West	XXX	In rnd 3

SPONSOR MESSAGE

Quokka's original proposal already encompassed the interplay of the table and brackets, but envisioned a more equal use of space for each element.

> Juggling Space

Quokka's original proposal to the NCAA included a schematic showing how all of these elements might fit on a computer screen. As the project developed, though, so did the screen design.

After discussions with Quokka and an analysis of expected user goals and interactions, IO Research drew up a new schematic. "In general, well-designed images are the quickest and clearest way for users to gain an at-a-glance understanding of a concept," explained Griffith in the design proposal to Quokka. "An information image—the brackets—will also have a better shot at intriguing users and encouraging them to delve deeper into the sports coverage than table-formatted information." The brackets became the focus of the screen as well as the way to access team and game information. The table would act as a tool to manipulate the information on the screen.

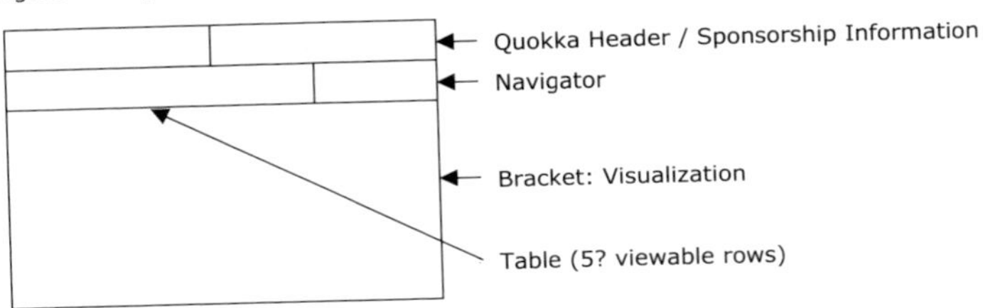

After analyzing expected user goals and interactions, IO Research proposed a design with a greater focus on the bracket information.

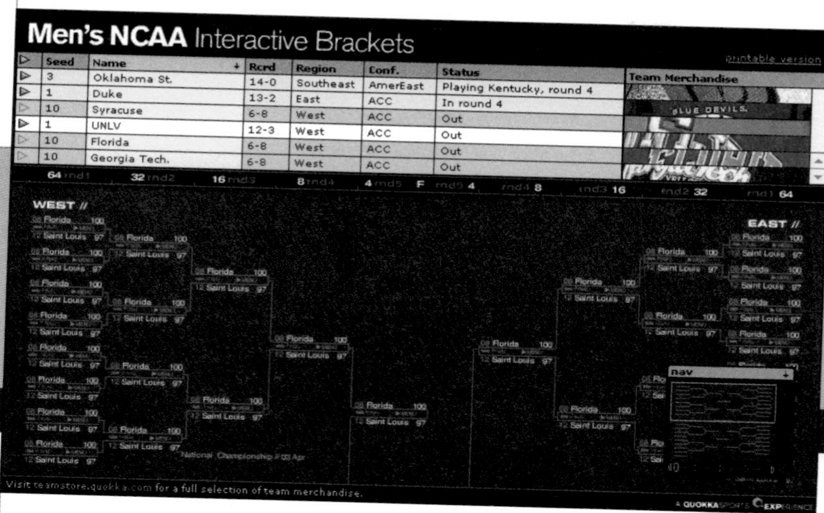

After the sponsorship integration was sorted out, this schematic showed the final plan.

In their studies the designers experimented with different layouts for the various screen elements, focusing on how to make the all-important brackets readable within a 600-by-800-pixel window. Clearly, it would be impossible to display the entire tournament schedule in any readable size. Yet the brackets could not be completely unreadable in the default view. “People like to see things,” says Caserta. “They get impatient if they have to roll over something to see it.” The designers decided on certain guidelines: Users should be able to at least distinguish completed, live, and uncompleted games, and to make out the bracket regions in the default display. There would also need to be some kind of zooming capability so that users could get a clearer view of particular details.

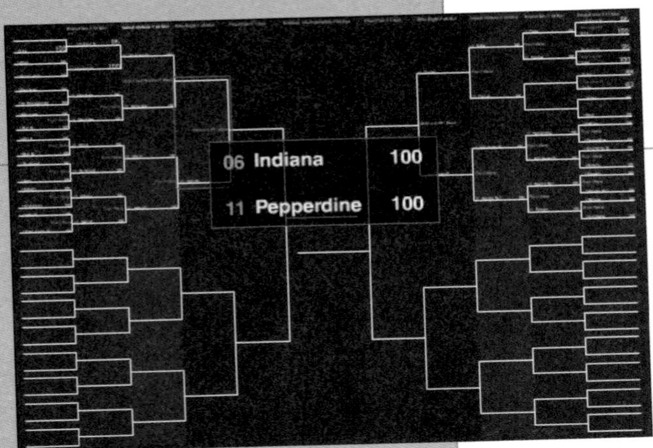

Quokka and IO Research explored several methods for magnifying areas of interest in the brackets. Above, a window pops up to show the area pointed to, while a rectangle on the zoomed-out version shows the area being displayed. Facing page, left, a slider controls the zoom level while the user clicks and drags to move the brackets within the window. Facing page, right, the area beneath the pointer is magnified in a pop-up window.

> Ways to Zoom

For the zoom capability, Caserta initially envisioned a sort of magnifying effect attached to pointer movement. "I wanted to get away from geeky controls," says Caserta. Instead, he preferred direct manipulation of data, with the user pointing directly to the chosen item to zoom in on rather than making abstract connections to a tool.

In this case, though, the sort of "fish-eye" effect Caserta imagined proved impractical. Magnifying the smallest logical unit of information—a game—resulted in so much of the screen's being covered that users had trouble making the connection between the magnified area and its context in the brackets. The team considered making the magnified area slightly transparent, so that users could see the area underneath and make that connection, but this option wasn't feasible at the time, before the introduction of Flash MX. Says Griffith, "With the already slow performance of the system, adding transparency would have really killed it."

The team solved the problem by using a control they called the Navigator, which offered a thumbnail view of the brackets, overlaid by a rectangle showing the current window boundaries. A slider along the bottom let users manipulate the zoom level. By dragging the window, users could change the bracket area displayed.

Ulm says the team looked at numerous examples in a variety of media, including print, to arrive at its magnification solution. He cites MIT's Media Lab as a source for many influential ideas. The Navigator design, in fact, was based on a customization of a control that had been in use for a while. "Photoshop uses a Navigator," Caserta notes. "It's also a carryover from CD-ROM design; scroll bars weren't used that much in CD-ROMs."

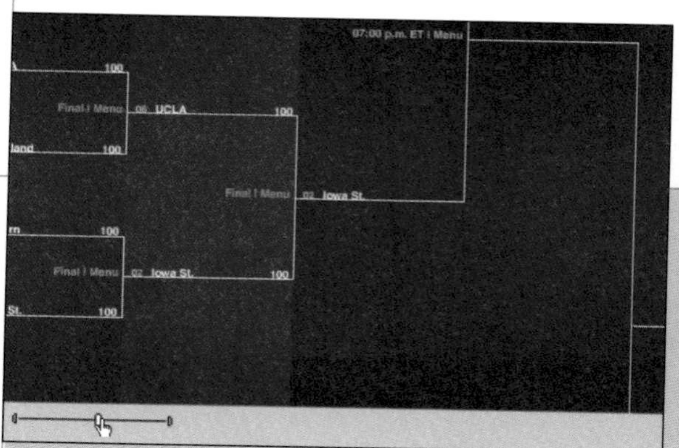

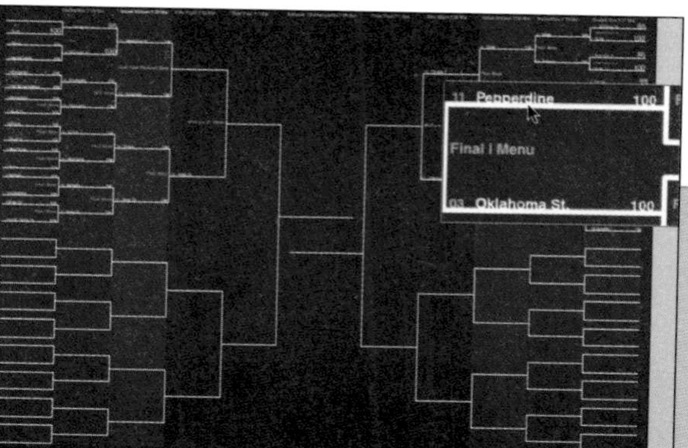

Originally anchored above the brackets next to the table, the Navigator became a floating element when the sponsorship area was connected to the table. "Once we realized how precious the aspect ratio and screen real estate were, it seemed impossible to anchor the Navigator," says Griffith. As a floating palette, the Navigator was now controlled by the user. "They could choose what information was important to their focus, and what was unimportant and could be covered by the Navigator," she explains.

As the tournament progressed and teams fell away, the designers assumed that the users' focus would likely change—and so they made the default view of the brackets change as well. As each round was completed and the games listed at the outer boundaries of the brackets receded into the past, the default zoom level increased to focus on the central part of the chart, showing the games still to be played. The marks on the zoom bar were also keyed to tournament stages. Moving the bar to a different mark changed the zoom to show the next round in the championship.

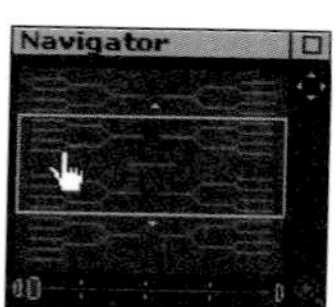

The Navigator let users change their view of the brackets, moving the window to focus on different sections of the schedule or moving the slider underneath to change magnification.

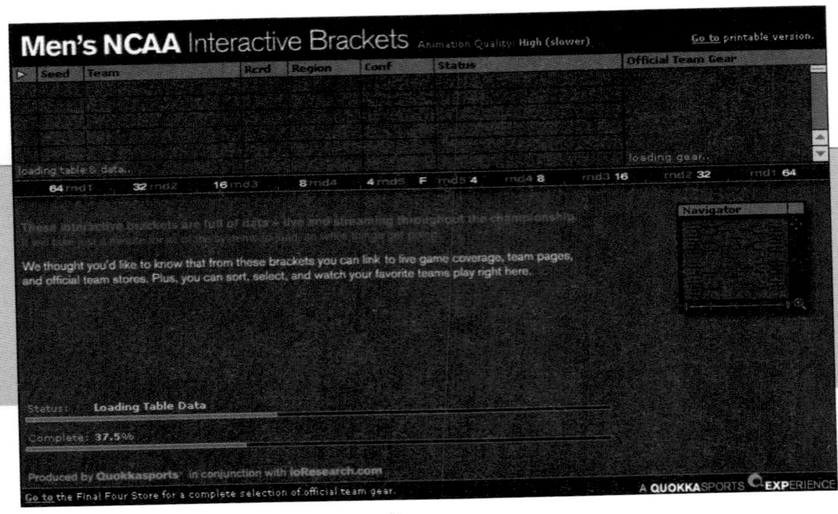

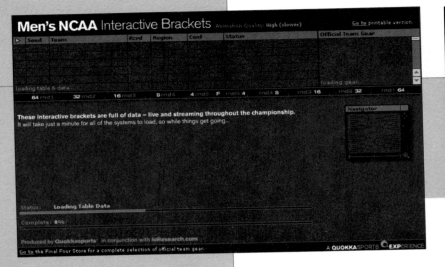

> A Short Primer

While not unprecedented on the Web, the Navigator was far from a familiar interface element to most users. To make sure that visitors knew how to manage the tool and the other features of the brackets, the designers made use of the site's loading time to provide a primer on their use.

As the program and all its data loaded, gauges at the bottom of the screen alerted users to its progress. (They also served notice of the program's complexity: The display changed several times during the process to note the different types of data being loaded—table data, brackets module, game data, and so on.) In the area that would be filled by the brackets, three short paragraphs of introduction were displayed—one by one, so that the user would focus on and absorb each point separately. Alongside the third paragraph, describing the Navigator, an animated version of the Navigator demonstrated the use of its various controls. When the animation was complete, the user was given the option of replaying it for a refresher.

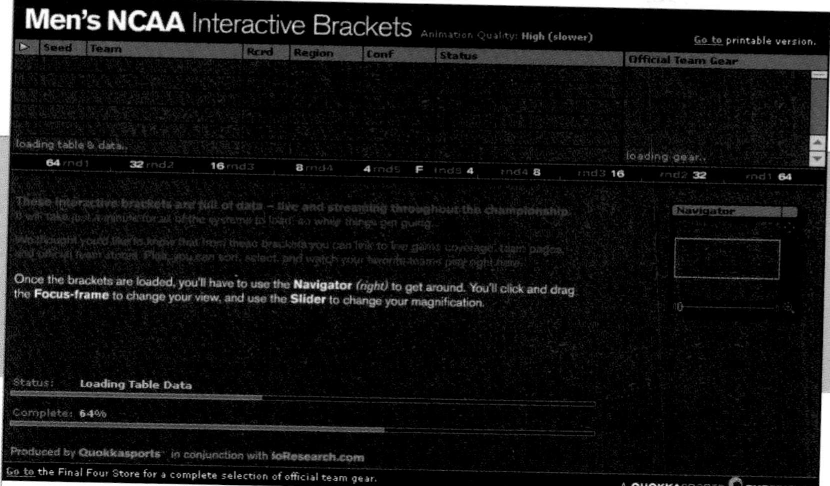

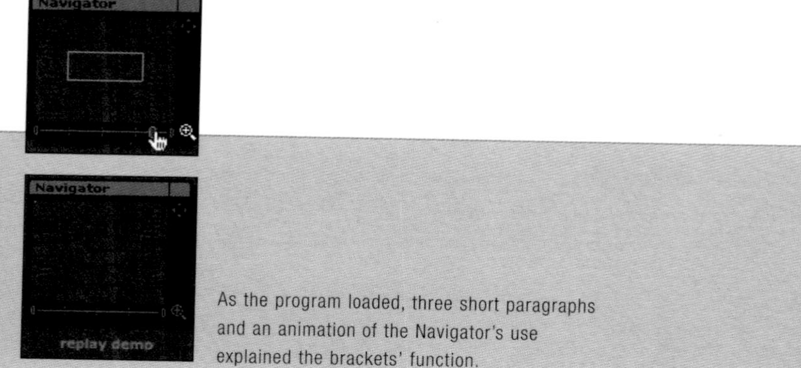

As the program loaded, three short paragraphs and an animation of the Navigator's use explained the brackets' function.

When the program and data finished loading, the brackets appeared in the space where the instructions had been displayed. The Navigator remained in place, now ready to control the bracket display. Because the Navigator didn't move, the user didn't need to make any abstract connections or search for the Navigator in its new context. This process demonstrates a clever use of loading time and a skillful example of online training. Caserta felt the primer addressed most of his worries about the users' needing to learn a special interface for the Navigator. "The how-to animation really helped," he says.

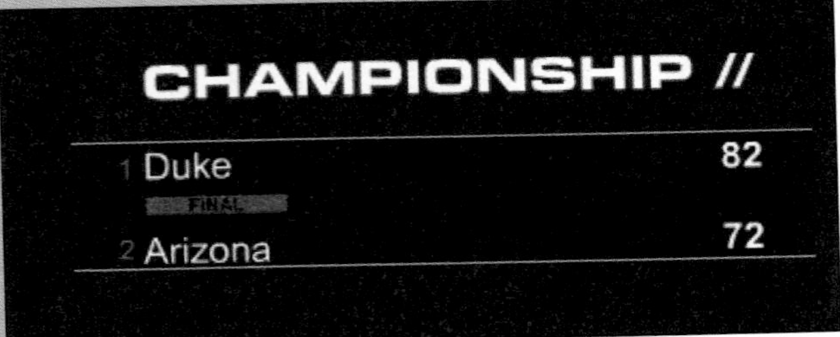

Tandy chose Helvetica Neue for the brackets display because of the way it worked at small sizes, large sizes, and in reverse, as well as for its style, which he says "fit in nicely with the overall minimal design."

> Math and Typography

At the default zoom level and focus, exactly half of the brackets (a slice from the center, focused on the championship game) were visible in the window. Amazingly, the type in each game box was, just barely, readable without zooming. Ryan Tandy, the designer at IO Research responsible for the layout, says that a combination of high-tech work with the programmers and old-fashioned typography did the trick.

The problem was complicated by the fact that the layout had to work at both the default size and at various magnifications. Programmer Jon Williams worked out the proportions; it was then Tandy's job to fit the brackets within them. The final layout modified the traditional brackets layout, switching the regions' accustomed positions to create an aspect ratio that would work in 400 by 800 pixels (the 600-by-800-pixel screen minus 200 pixels for the heading and table) and a layout that would break into logical parts at the default zoom level.

The next step was picking a typeface that would also work at different zoom levels. "Since the primary goal was 'small, small, small,' our first tendency was to look at pixel-based typefaces, using no anti-aliasing," says Tandy. But realizing that this would compromise readability at larger magnifications, he decided to use a traditional typeface.

Working in Flash with a prototype of the Navigator, Tandy tried different sans-serif fonts at varying magnifications. "The Flash authoring environment is almost identical to the view in the Player," he notes, which means he was able to see a true representation of how the type would look with Flash's scaling and anti-aliasing. Finally, Tandy settled on the typeface Helvetica Neue.

Animation Quality: High (slower)

Animation Quality: High (slower)

Animation Quality: Low (faster)

A toggle between high- and low-quality settings was dimmed until the user pointed to it.

CHAMPIONSHIP //
1 Duke
82
FINAL
2 Arizona
72

The high-quality display (top) anti-aliased the type. The low-quality setting (bottom) gave users the option of speeding up their screen display by trading off type quality.

Tandy chose a sans-serif typeface for two reasons. "I wanted a sans-serif type to work with the modern look we had in the whole interface," he says. "Also, serifs get noisy at small sizes." Among sans serifs, he says, the best types for small sizes are those with large counters (the spaces inside the letter forms), a medium-size x-height, and good contrast. In his tests, Helvetica Neue stood out for these features as well as for the way its letterspacing and kerning worked at the sizes he needed. "The crossbars and arms in other sans-serif fonts seemed to collapse when zoomed out," says Tandy. Helvetica Neue worked similarly well in the reverse states used when the team names were highlighted.

To design the layout, Tandy also fine-tuned the amount of information in the brackets. "We got a list of all the data available in the stream, which included lots of options," he says. "But with 65 matchups, you really had to pull back. The final display showed just the team, score, and status (Pre-Game, Live, or Final) for each game.

> User-Chosen Trade-Offs

At the top of the brackets display was a subtle option, offering the viewer the option of high-quality (slow) or low-quality (fast) animation. The control simply toggled the high-/low-quality setting, a standard feature of Flash movies that turns anti-aliasing on (for high quality) or off (for low).

On fast systems, there's barely any difference between the two settings: The system will anti-alias the text if it can do so without slowing the movie below its specified frame rate. If it can't, the type will look jaggy, but the screen redraw will be much speedier after a change in framing or zoom level.

"One of the brackets' biggest downfalls is its performance," says Griffith. "With all the live data being displayed dynamically, and with Flash needing to render all of this information every time you organize the table or view the brackets differently, it bogged down user systems." The quality control was the one feasible way to speed performance, she says.

The Internet after the boom? In 2002, the NCAA returned to static GIF and PDF versions of the brackets.

> A Flash in Internet History

The 2001 tournament was a brief, shining moment for the concept of interactive brackets. In 2002, FinalFour.net presented the brackets in static GIF and PDF formats, accompanying live Webcasts and live audio of the games. Like most other Internet businesses that looked to future, rather than immediate, payoffs, Quokka went out of business in 2001, soon after the brackets were launched, dispersing much of its intellectual property in the process. The downturn in the Internet economy affected FinalFour.net as well, and cost-cutting there made it impractical to try to rebuild the interactive brackets.

Like a lot of the ideas cooked up during the Internet boom, though, the effect of projects like these interactive brackets may linger longer than the venture capital money that made their first appearance possible. As Ulm puts it, "I think what's most powerful here hints at something larger than this application. In the interactive brackets, users are encouraged to interact with information and observe it from their own distinct perspective. We were creating a way for users to create their experiences." Quokka, IO Research, and other designers experimenting with new types of interaction during the boom may have planted—and may still be planting—seeds that will come to fruition and be commonplace in years and on Web sites to come. ■

SPOTLIGHT
USER TESTING

Every interactive interface should go through user testing—and that goes double for interfaces that, like most in this book, have interactive elements that are unique to the site.

It's notable that almost none of the designers here carried out formal user testing of their interface designs. Most of them took a more informal route—showing their sites to friends, colleagues not involved in the development, and others who came to the design fresh.

This approach wouldn't work for a site designed for a particular audience—say, one that was automating a specialized work procedure, or a site specifically geared to young mothers. For sites like these, you need to test with people who belong to the intended group of users. But even informal testing is immeasurably better than no user testing at all.

The bottom line is this: Whether you do it on your laptop with your roommate after work, or you recruit a demographically correct audience to view your site as you take notes behind a two-way mirror, you need to test. You must show your interface to at least three or four people who have never seen it before, and you must watch how they interact with it. And then you must believe what they say and what you see. Humility is the high road to good interface design.

CHAPTER

HANDSPRING AD

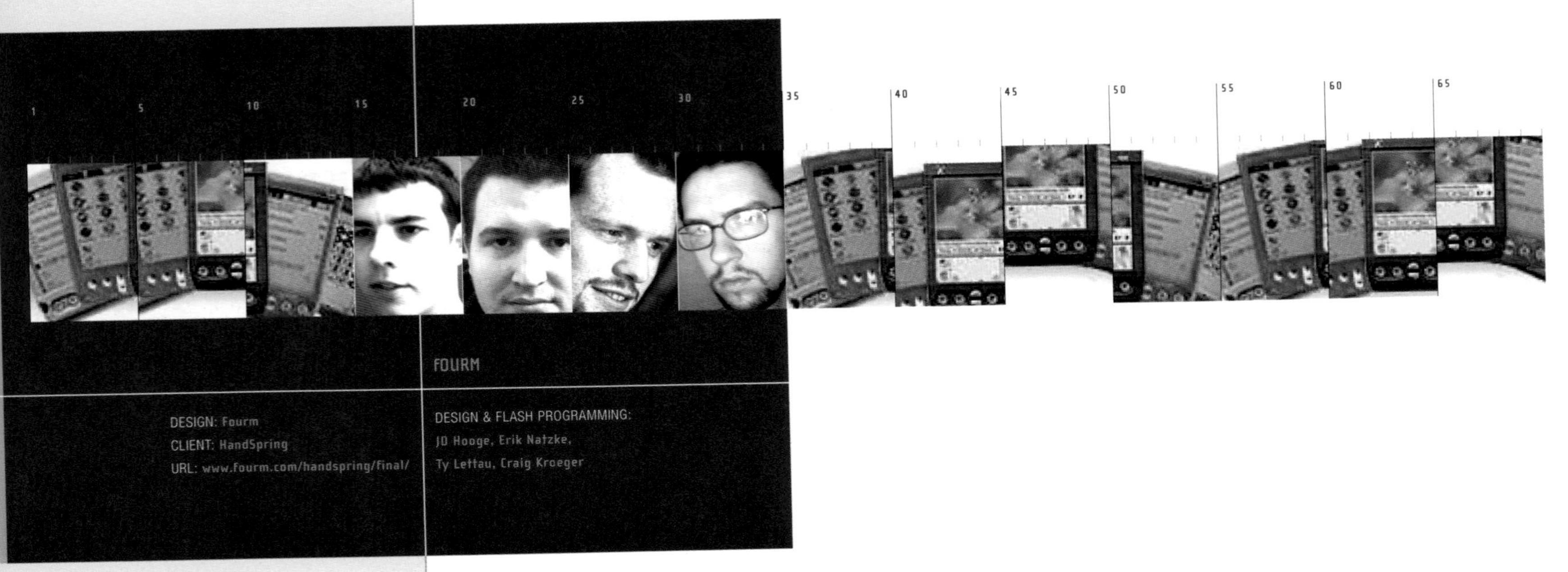

DESIGN: Fourm
CLIENT: HandSpring
URL: www.fourm.com/handspring/final/

DESIGN & FLASH PROGRAMMING:
JD Hooge, Erik Natzke,
Ty Lettau, Craig Kroeger

CHAPTER

HANDSPRING AD

INTRO

Flash ads can hold a whole site's worth of information in a banner. Studies have shown that Flash ads get 340 percent more user response than static banners. Here's the catch: You have to do it all in 25 K.

Pictured: (from left) JD Hooge, Erik Natzke, Ty Lettau, Craig Kroeger

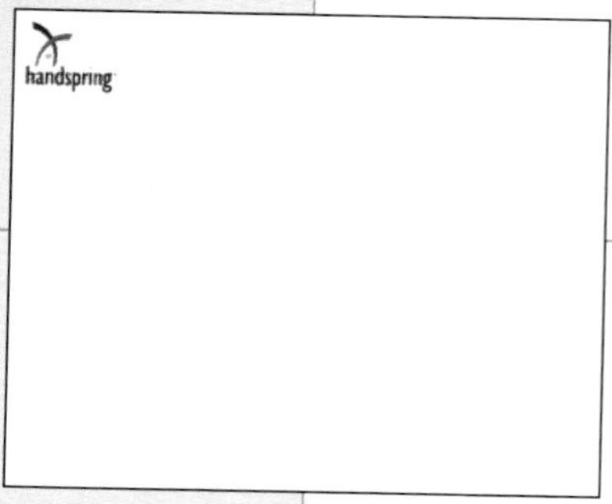

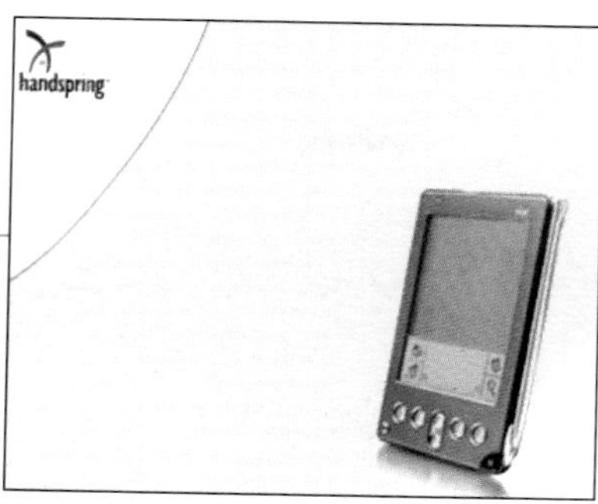

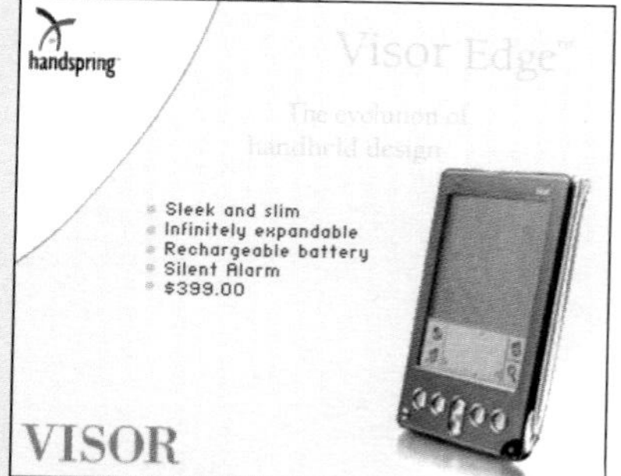

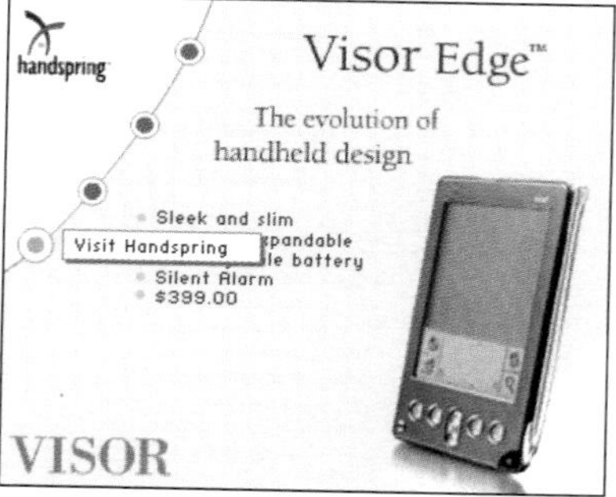

After the opening animation (shown on page 157) is complete, the ad's "home page" builds, with each element sliding into place from offscreen. When the content is in place, a label flashes on each button to indicate its function.

Banner ads on the Web are a problem no one has found a way to solve. They're necessary, but they're annoying. And at this point, people tend to recognize ads without even looking at them directly. In fact, tests show that Web users are so used to ignoring anything resembling an ad on a Web page that they don't even notice ad banners anymore. To get viewers' attention, advertisers often sink to the most annoying devices: loud colors, flashing animations, and pop-up windows. And if users actually click an ad (which relatively few do), they are taken off the host site's page—to the annoyance of the host site and, often, to the confusion of the user.

To battle these trends, sites that accept advertising often put strict limits on the types of files and effects that advertisers can use. At minimum, the host site will specify maximum dimensions and file size. Some also limit the types or amounts of animation you can include.

In mid-2001, CNET, the online computer information network, invited HandSpring, maker of palmtop computers, and a few other advertising clients to see what they could do with Flash in a new rich-media ad program CNET was launching. HandSpring came to Flash experts Fourm to see what they could cook up.

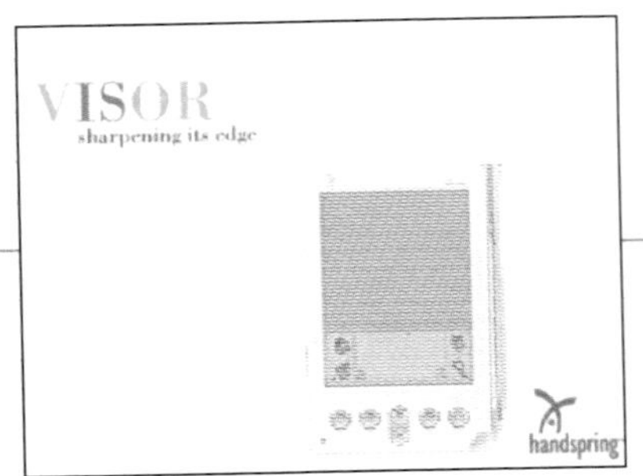

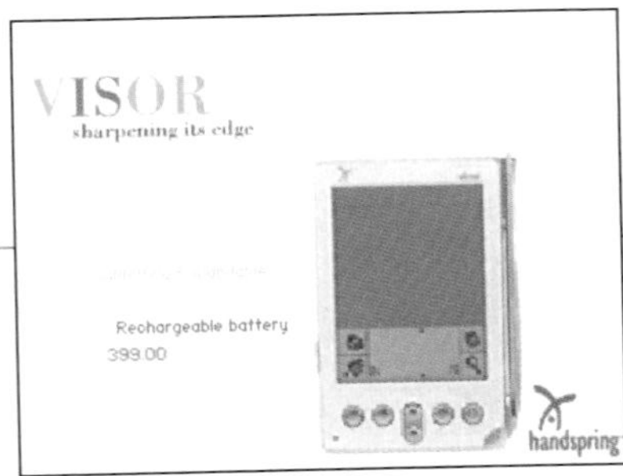

> Making Ads Work

According to Brendan Kyle, advertising and promotions manager at HandSpring, CNET's initiative to offer Flash ads was an attempt to revive the perceived value of banner ads. "Basically, the whole banner-ad industry has gone into a tailspin, in terms of how valuable people think online ads are and how much sites can charge for banner ads," says Kyle. "CNET was looking for new ways to make advertisers happy."

According to Kyle, HandSpring almost said no. Given the consumer backlash against annoying ads, the company worried that launching an animated ad might do its brand more harm than good. In the end, though, HandSpring decided this would be a good opportunity to test the waters.

> Re: Fourm

Armed with a sample Flash ad that another online network had created, HandSpring approached Fourm Design, a Wisconsin-based company that specializes in Flash development and had worked with HandSpring's ad agency, Leo Burnett.

"We liked the way the sample ad worked, with a tab interface, but we wanted something that would fit our brand better," says Kyle.

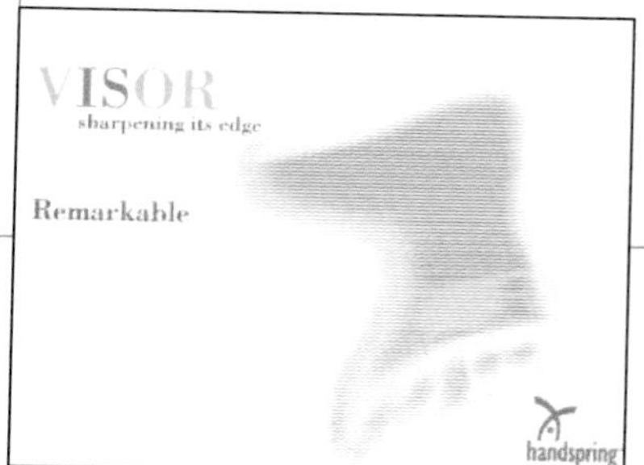

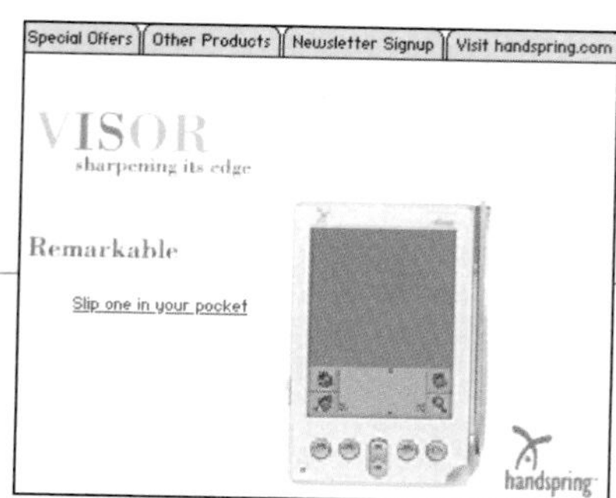

Some of Fourm's first comps were based on a longer introductory animation, resolving to a tab interface.

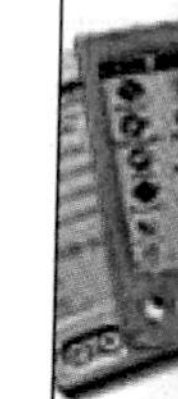

To Fourm's eyes, the sample ad wasn't interactive enough. "It was basically a static layout implemented in Flash," says Fourm's creative director for the project, JD Hooge. "When we do Flash work, we think of the interactivity as the first priority."

Playing it conservatively, the Fourm team came up with several designs that worked with the tab format HandSpring had liked. Their designs hewed closer to HandSpring's corporate style (which Kyle characterizes as "clean, with lots of white space and simple product shots") and made use of opening animations to introduce the company's branding messages.

"At the beginning we were going, 'This is HandSpring. We can't get too crazy,'" says Hooge. "We didn't want to give them something too off-the-wall." To Fourm's surprise, though, HandSpring asked it to push the boundaries more. "We didn't want anything too flashy or fast-moving," says Kyle. "We didn't want something that would totally distract people. But we wanted something that when people see it, they know they can interact with it. And when you clicked on it, we wanted it to do something."

The end design was clean, with subtle animation and a non-traditional navigation method that everyone felt hit the right balance between liveliness and subtlety.

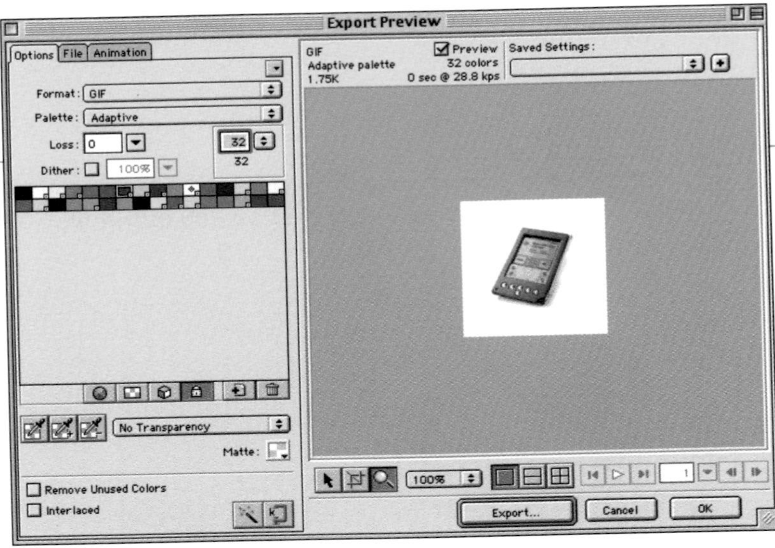

Graphics optimization was key to getting the movie down to the file sizes allowed by CNET. Fourm shrank graphics files by using Macromedia Fireworks to view and optimize the number of colors used in each illustration. In this case, they were able to reduce the number of colors in a product shot from 256 (left) to 32 (right) and from 4 K to under 2 K.

> Design Within Constraints

When creating Internet ads, designers are used to working within the host site's guidelines for ad dimensions, file size, and other attributes. Such limits, though, are particularly challenging for multimedia files. Among the restrictions CNET set were a maximum file size (for all assets) of 25 K, and no more than 5 seconds of animation.

"File preparation was a grueling process," says Hooge. "You say, 'OK, this movie is 12 K. I've got to lose 4 K. How am I going to do that?'"

Hooge says he found the most space savings by optimizing the images using Macromedia's Fireworks. "You can go right into the images and say, 'OK, there are 26 blues in this product image, and I can probably get away with 6 blues.'" And on the Internet, don't forget, color choice is complicated by the vagaries of the systems people use to view your work. As Hooge puts it, "Of course, then you have to test that on 200 different monitors and 20 different systems and everything."

Other savings were achieved by performing small tricks in the Flash SWF files. Hooge found, for instance, that he could reduce file sizes by cutting off a frame as soon as the graphic in it became transparent. The optimization was more challenging than it might have been because the ad used a lot of tweening, rather than employing movie clips, for animation.

Hooge says he uses tweening relatively rarely. "If I can do it with ActionScript, I will," he says. However, in this case, the design used lots of blurring to accentuate motion, so tweening it was. Hooge says he probably could have animated the movement of the navigation, which slides into the frame along a curved line, with ActionScript, "but I would have had to jump through a lot of hoops to do it." (He created the ad in Flash 5 but exported it to Flash 4 in order to reach the maximum audience, as specified by HandSpring.)

The file-size restrictions also called for some changes to the design itself. In the final design, the navigation buttons move in and settle along the left side of the ad. On lower-level pages, the navigation is on the right side. Originally, Hooge says, he envisioned the navigation moving to a new side on each click, but that effect wasn't possible within the file-size guidelines. Sound was another sacrifice. Hooge says that while they had no plans for an elaborate soundtrack, even simple audio click feedback was ruled out by the size restrictions.

In the end, says Hooge, the ad design guidelines were just a design problem to solve, like any other. By the time the project was complete, Hooge says, he had learned a lot about file optimization. He was even sort of proud of himself: "When you're done, you say, 'I can't believe we did this in 25 K.'"

> Timing Is Everything

The team paid sharp attention to the fine line between attention-getting and annoying when it comes to online ads.

After the initial, short animation of the HandSpring name, the ad resolves to a sort of home page. (Fourm designed the animation, in which the HandSpring logo does its own handspring, kicked into the air by the last part of the name.) After all the home page elements slide into place, labels for the page's four navigation buttons take turns presenting themselves and then fading away. After that, the page is static until the user interacts with it.

"The user has to activate the ad," says Hooge. This is in contrast to the usual action of banner ads, which continually loop their animation. The main purpose of the opening animation was to make the ad look interactive. The point here was for it not to act like the typical banner ad.

Says Hooge, "We were very careful about making sure people knew how to interact with the ad," particularly at the end of the animation. At first, the button labels were to appear only on rollover, but the team decided that flashing the labels as part of the intro would make the interaction more clear.

Special Offers

Second-level pages (accessed from the button navigation) add another, user-selected level of information, without leaving the host page. The illustrations in this row show the secondary pages available from each of the main navigation buttons.

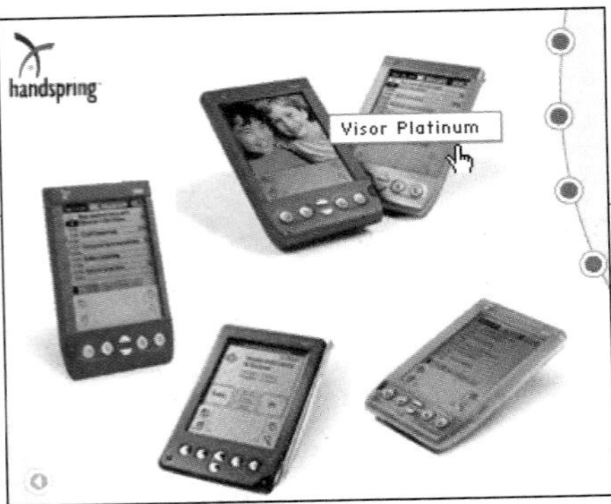

Visor Handhelds

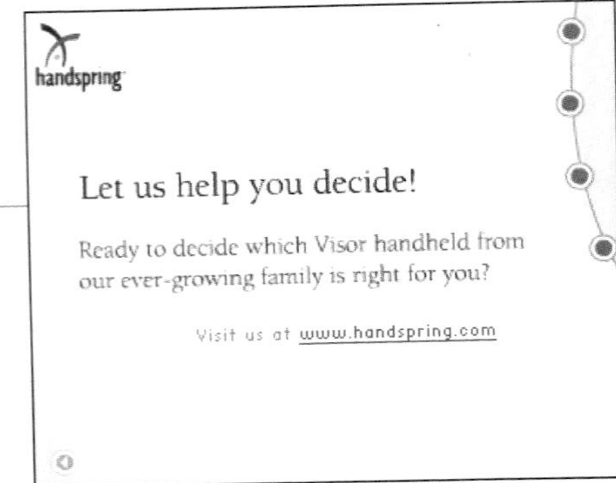

Visit HandSpring

The team had to think carefully about when, as well as what, to animate. "We had to consider what happens if the ad is at the bottom of the page, and you have to scroll down to see it," says Hooge. The designers didn't want the animation to end before the viewer had even seen it. They considered ways to stretch the animation to accommodate latecomers, but in the end, the decision was again directed by the guidelines: CNET had capped the animation time on the home page at 5 seconds. Viewers who get there late just see the still home page.

> Site in a Box

Probably the most valuable feature of Flash advertisements is the complex interactivity they offer. "It's not just click and chase the monkey," as Hooge puts it. Users following one path in their browsing are sometimes reluctant to click a banner ad, whose action will take them to an entirely different site. Traditional, GIF-based ads can only offer a single level of information before taking you off to another Web page. If they take advantage of GIF animation, the ads can rotate through a couple of different pages, but without regard to the viewer's interests or reading speed. The HandSpring ad shows how a Flash ad can comprise a whole minisite in a few hundred pixels of space, offering an engaging interactive experience—and a lot of information—without taking the viewer away from the host page.

Win a Free Visor Edge

On third-level pages, like this one, a Return button lets users move up a level without using the main navigation (or the browser Back button).

The HandSpring ad is a mini Web site with three levels, including Home. Each of the four navigation buttons takes the user to a secondary page. From there, blue underlined links take the user to more information on the HandSpring site (launched in a new window). The Visor Handhelds page (shown on the facing page, center) links deeper, to individual pages outlining the features of each model (bottom left).

On secondary pages, the navigation moves to the right side of the ad box, while a button appears at the lower left, to take the user back home. On the third-level pages, a second button appears at the center of the left edge, which takes the user back to the main products page. Hooge points out that those "back" buttons aren't strictly necessary, since all the information on the site can be accessed via the main navigation buttons. "We really only put the Home buttons there so people could see the cool animation again," he says. Adding them, of course, also gives users a sense of the site's structure and a logical, flexible way to navigate it.

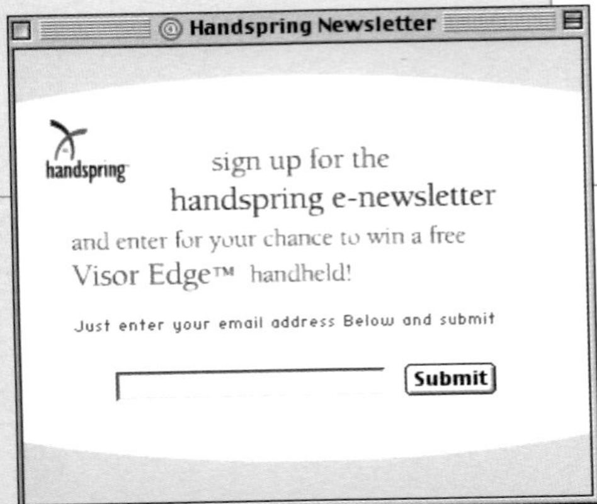

An HTML window pops up when the user clicks to sign up for the newsletter. This was Fourm's way of getting the code for delivery to the database out of the SWF file, so that clients could manage it themselves.

> Click-Through Tracking, the Flash Way

Part of producing Web ads is building in a way to track user response to them. Advertisers want to measure *click-through*—the rate at which users click an ad to find out more—in order to gauge an ad's value on that Web site.

For a regular banner ad, this measure is simple. The Web site only needs to track a single click. The first click takes the user to the advertiser's Web site, where the advertiser can do its own tracking.

For Flash ads, the site hosting the ad has more to track. Advertisers want to know what parts of the Flash ad visitors have viewed before clicking a link that takes them to the advertiser's site.

Now that Flash ads have become more common, major Web ad-serving networks, such as DoubleClick and 24/7 Media, have agreed on a system of doing just that. The HandSpring ad, though, was launched before the joint system was agreed on; CNET created its own, similar system (see "Tracking Clicks in a Flash Ad," page 168).

> A Little HTML

One structural anomaly had me puzzled. If the user decides to sign up for the HandSpring newsletter, a separate window with an HTML form pops up, into which the user types and clicks to submit his or her information. Why not just have the form in the Flash box?

Hooge cleared up the mystery: It turns out that as Fourm was finishing the project, HandSpring still wasn't sure how it was going to capture visitors' contact information. Delivering an HTML form saved the client from having to go into the Flash files to change them once the capture method was hammered out—and saved Fourm from having that task hanging over its head after the rest of the project was complete. Perhaps not the optimal solution, but a practical one.

> Use Judiciously

HandSpring's Kyle says he's happy with the results of the Flash ad for his company, although he thinks HandSpring will continue to use rich-media ads like this one sparingly, mostly due to the development costs associated with them.

Kyle notes that developing a fully interactive message is a lot more time-consuming than doing a billboard-type banner ad. "I have an in-house guy who can crank out GIF banners in about a minute," he says ruefully. On product launches or other occasions when the goal is to get attention or provide detailed information, a Flash ad is a route to consider. "It's a branding tool," Kyle says. Interactive ads get and keep attention, and when they're well done, they associate the company that publishes them with the cutting edge.

Apparently, more and more advertisers are finding the right use for these attention-getting banners. According to a study by the technology-analysis firm Jupiter, 30 percent of advertisers are planning to dedicate more than 10 percent of their ad budgets to rich-media advertising in 2002, and more than 54 percent of Web advertisers have already used Flash ads. ■

For Flash advertising statistics and more on Flash advertising, see the Rich Media Advertising Resource Center on Macromedia.com.

UNDER THE HOOD
TRACKING CLICKS IN A FLASH AD

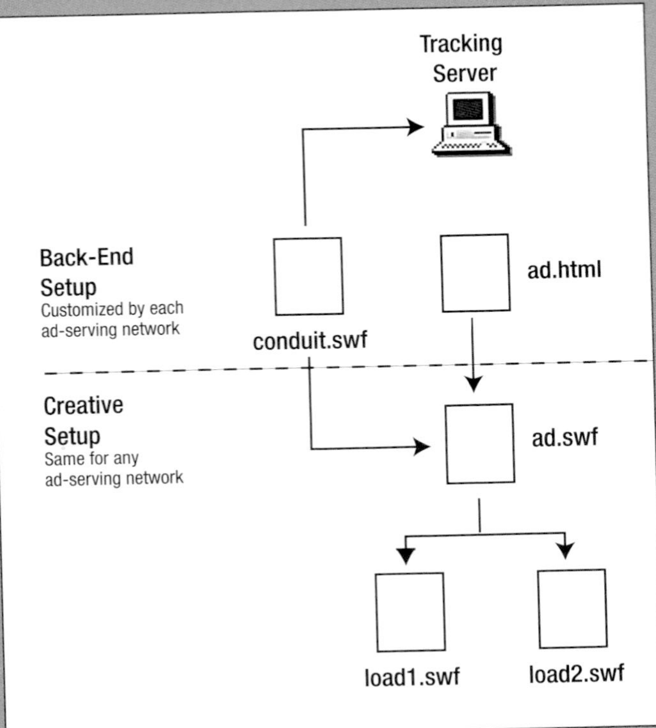

Figure 1
The ad created by the designer works with a conduit.swf file on the ad server's network. The conduit.swf file relies on predefined variables to do its job: gather information about the tracked events and then fulfill the file requests.

For traditional banner ads, it's easy to measure click-through, the number of times an ad interests viewers enough that they click it to find out more. When a viewer clicks a GIF banner, a call is made to the advertiser's server, and those calls can be easily tallied. For Flash ads, though, the user can click many times, and get a lot of information about the advertised product, without ever involving the host server—instead, all of the interactivity is managed within the Flash movie. To get an accurate click-through count, Web sites that accept Flash ads ask the Flash programmers to embed special codes in the movies to make the necessary calls to the server so that each click can be counted.

When CNET began accepting Flash ads, it devised its own method of logging click-throughs on the ad's pages and options; Fourm developer JD Hooge used this method to create the HandSpring ad. Recently, however, CNET began offering a new method, which takes advantage of the extension capabilities of Flash 5 and Flash MX to streamline the system for ad creators. The new system can track almost any user action—including clicks for more information within the Flash movie, and even internal events such as rollovers.

Like the standard method of tracking GIF-based ads, the CNET system sends calls for actions through a tracking system that can log the request before forwarding it to the server. Since there aren't necessarily any calls for new files to trigger the tracking, though, the CNET method uses Flash to generate the redirect code. Then, a conduit.swf file on the ad host's server gathers information about the user's requests and executes the requested events (**Figure 1**). Most of the code is hidden from the ad creators, who must simply be sure to use the variables in the ad that the conduit.swf file is waiting to receive.

For the ad creator, the first step is to download and install the MTK (Multi-Tracking Kit) extension from CNET. Installing this extension, like any other, requires the use of Macromedia's Extension Manager, available from the Macromedia Exchange for Flash (www.macromedia.com/exchange/flash).

Once the extension is installed, you can access it from Flash MX's File menu. Choosing File/Open From Template and clicking Ads in the Category list should display a Category item called MTK Template (**Figure 2**), which is CNET's ad template.

Designers then create their ads in the template file, using no special procedures except one. For links they want to track, they don't write the `getURL` or `loadMovie` ActionScript commands that activate the link—those actions are taken care of by code already in the template, in tandem with the conduit.swf file. When the ad is complete, the designer attaches that special code to the controls in the ad. To do that, you expand the Multi-Tracking Code layer folder in the timeline, select Frame 1 of the Links and Descriptions layer, and open the Actions panel (if it's not already open).

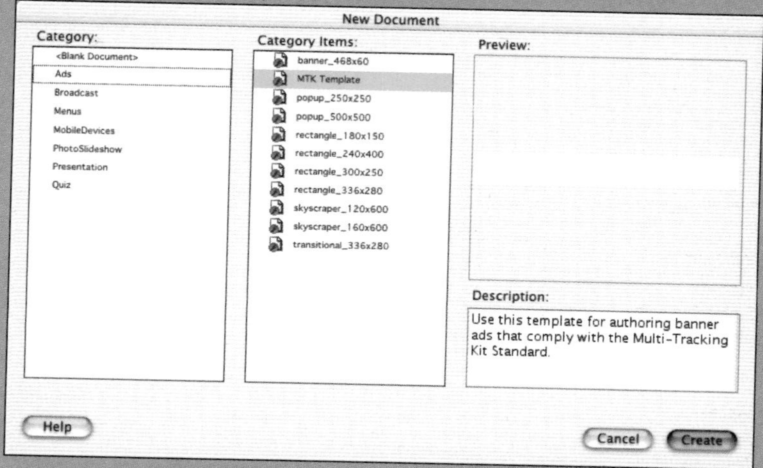

Figure 2

After the Multi-Tracking Kit extension is installed, the MTK template should appear in the Ads category of Flash's New From Template menu.

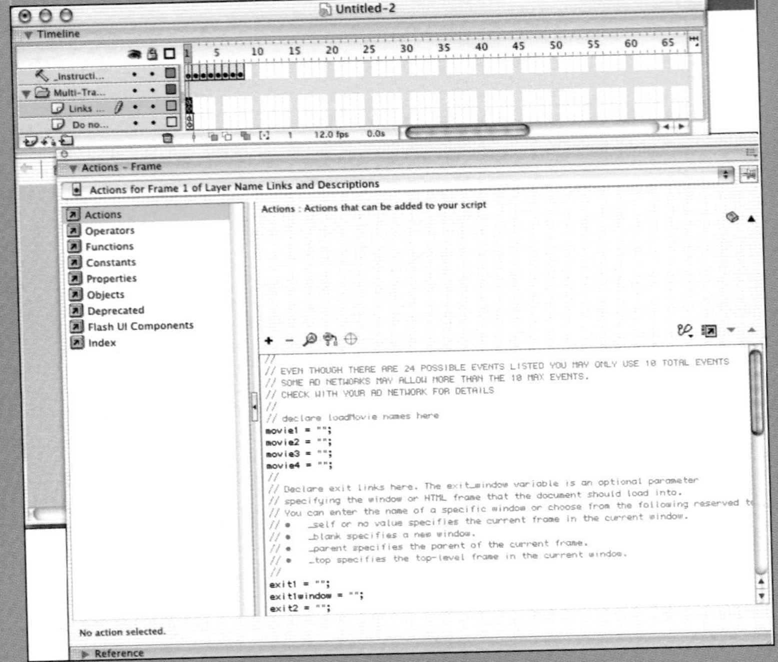

Figure 3

The Links and Descriptions script, provided as part of the template, assigns variables for each action that will be tracked. The designer types in identifying information for each movie load, exit link, and user event.

In the script that appears there (**Figure 3**), the designer adds information about the movie loads, exit links, and chosen user events to track. The script can track as many as four movie loads, ten exit links, and ten user events.

For the movie loads, type the name of each movie whose selection is to be tracked between the quotation marks in the definitions of the `movie1` through `movie4` variables. (For the HandSpring ad, Hooge would type *special_offers.swf* for `movie1`, *visor_handhelds.swf* for `movie2`, and so on.)

For the exit links, type the target addresses for each of the links to outside sites. A second line for each exit variable lets the designer specify the window in which to open the link. So, for example, for the link from the Visor Platinum page (see page 165), Hooge might type

```
exit1 = "http://www.handspring.com/products/visorplatinum/index.jhtml"
exit1window = "handspring"
```

If there are events to track, the designer would describe those events in the definitions of the `eventxdesc` variables. (Since there are no significant user events to track in the HandSpring ad, Hooge would leave those lines blank.)

With those variables defined, the designer's next task is to link each variable to the objects they're meant to track. In the HandSpring ad, Hooge would select the Check It Out link on the Visor Platinum page, open the Actions panel, and double-click Exit under Multi-Tracking Actions (**Figure 4**). In the template script,

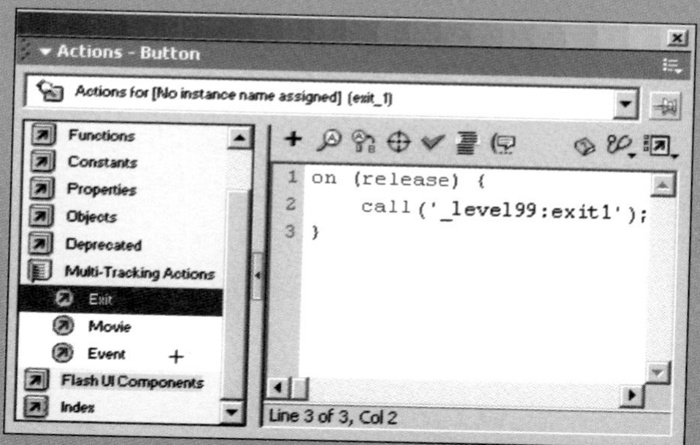

Figure 4

With the variables defined, the designer ties the object for which `loadMovie` or `getURL` events will be tracked with the variable names defined for them. To do that, you simply type the assigned variable number in the predefined event script template.

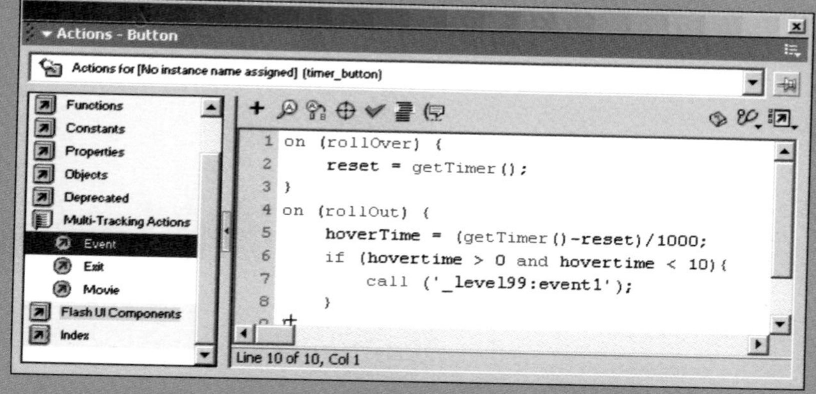

Figure 5

For user events, the developer provides the script for the action that will be tracked in the predefined event script template.

the only thing to do is type in the number of the exit variable assigned to this link. The `onRelease` command in the script now references that variable. Do the same for the other exit links from the ad, selecting the button, double-clicking the Exit line, and specifying the correct variable.

A similar process is used for movie loads: Select the button that triggers the first movie load you'd like to track, open the Actions layer, and this time, double-click Movie under Multi-Tracking Actions. As with the exit links, specify the right `moviex` variable. So for HandSpring, Hooge would click the Special Offers button, double-click the Movie layer, and type the assigned number. He'd then do the same for the other three buttons.

User events are a bit, but not much, more complex. As with the other actions, select the object that triggers the event, open the Actions panel, and double-click Event. Then, after selecting Expert mode from the pop-up menu in the upper-right corner of the panel, add the script that triggers the tracking (**Figure 5**). With the proper code attached to the exit links, movie loads, and events, the ad creator's work is finished.

At press time, CNET was working with Macromedia and the Interactive Advertising Bureau (a consortium that sets standards for Internet advertising) to make this method a standard system for the leading advertising networks. If that push works as planned, Flash ad designers could create just one ad, employing this method, for use with almost any ad network.

SPOTLIGHT

ACCESSIBILITY FOR FLASH

According to the U.S. Census Bureau, almost 20 percent of the United States population has some type of disability—auditory, motor, visual, or cognitive; temporary or permanent—a significant slice of any potential audience.

Until recently, those people were left out in the cold when it came to Flash sites. Assistive technology, such as the screen readers designed to help the visually impaired, couldn't penetrate the Flash format. Now, Flash Player 6 and Flash MX go a long way toward alleviating this problem, but creating Flash content that's truly accessible to people with disabilities still takes some effort.

Flash Player 6, used with Microsoft Internet Explorer, can now communicate with any screen reader that uses Microsoft's Active Accessibility (MSAA) protocol. This means that conforming screen readers can read text elements, buttons, and input text in any Macromedia Flash content created with Flash 4 or later.

Although this new capability makes the Flash format penetrable by screen readers, it doesn't mean that Flash movies will be understandable or even necessarily usable by a disabled person. To achieve these goals, designers must understand how Web users with disabilities interact with Web pages, and how the assistive technologies they use interact with Flash. Then, designers must make sure their movies work in ways that don't create blockages or annoyances to those users.

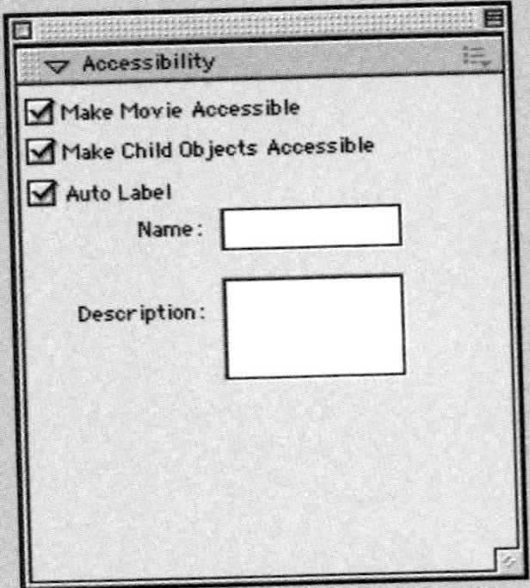

Flash MX's Accessibility Panel lets developers add text labels and descriptions to nontext elements of movies, making that content available to screen readers. It also lets you make elements of the movie that do not include content inaccessible.

In general, a few simple changes, which shouldn't effect the punch of your designs, should do the trick. For instance:

Make your page's content accessible to screen readers. By default, a screen reader working with Flash Player 6 will read all text content plus buttons and text field labels. However, it won't read any descriptions of graphic elements, movie clips, or other nontext elements unless you add those descriptions yourself. Flash MX's new Accessibility panel lets Flash developers add text equivalents for nontext elements. It also lets developers make objects that have no important content "inaccessible" (so that they're ignored by screen readers). The panel lets you group objects under a single description, if they make the most sense that way.

Avoid looping animations. Screen readers accommodate the dynamic nature of Flash pages by recognizing when the page content has changed and returning to the top of the page to read it again when a change occurs. This can quickly become annoying if the change is simply repetitive—especially if it's a meaningless effect, such as the animation of a button.

Recognize which elements won't be readable at all, and choose other types of controls if necessary. Controls like scroll bars, list boxes, invisible buttons, and actions associated with the down state of buttons don't work well with assistive technologies.

Remember users who can't use the mouse. Users with motor problems may not be able to use the mouse, relying instead on the Tab key to navigate pages and on keyboard shortcuts to execute commands. Users may also use touchscreens, head pointers, and other assistive devices. You can accommodate these users by offering keyboard equivalents, placing elements on the stage with an eye to their Tab order, and avoiding effects, such a rollovers, that rely on the mouse.

Just as you consider how an HTML page will play in different browsers, or how your color palette will appear on different monitors, you need to think about how your movie will play with different assistive technologies. For more information, turn to Macromedia's Web site (www.macromedia.com/macromedia/accessibility/), where you'll find lots of information about (and guidance for) creating accessible content with Flash.

CHAPTER

BUD GREENSPAN'S 10 GREATEST WINTER OLYMPIANS

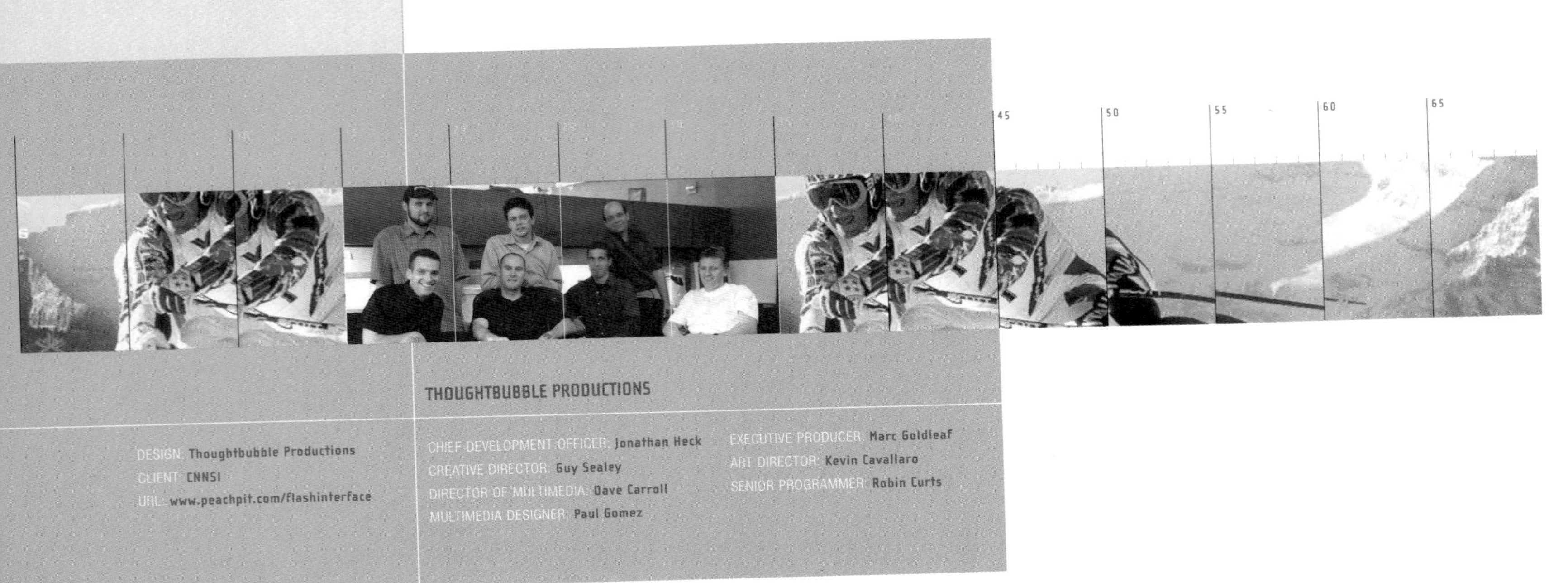

THOUGHTBUBBLE PRODUCTIONS

DESIGN: **Thoughtbubble Productions**
CLIENT: **CNNSI**
URL: **www.peachpit.com/flashinterface**

CHIEF DEVELOPMENT OFFICER: **Jonathan Heck**
CREATIVE DIRECTOR: **Guy Sealey**
DIRECTOR OF MULTIMEDIA: **Dave Carroll**
MULTIMEDIA DESIGNER: **Paul Gomez**

EXECUTIVE PRODUCER: **Marc Goldleaf**
ART DIRECTOR: **Kevin Cavallaro**
SENIOR PROGRAMMER: **Robin Curts**

CHAPTER

BUD GREENSPAN'S 10 GREATEST WINTER OLYMPIAN

INTRO

CNNSI had three goals for a minisite running in the weeks before the 2002 Winter Olympics: to gather names for a sweepstakes, to make sure the Olympics audience knew about Bud Greenspan, and to let users vote for their favorite all-time Winter Olympians. Thoughtbubble Productions used Flash to accomplish all those activities in a single page.

Pictured: (from left, back row) Robin Curts, Marc Goldleaf, Jonathan Heck; (front row) Dave Carroll, Kevin Cavallaro, Paul Gomez, Guy Sealey

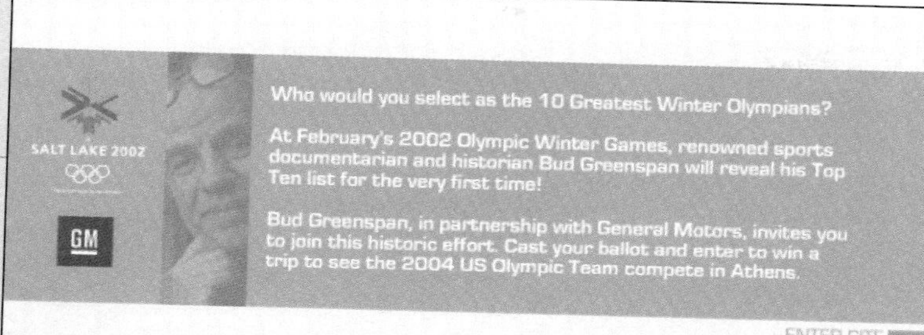

SALT LAKE 2002
GM
Who would you select as the 10 Greatest Winter Olympians?
At February's 2002 Olympic Winter Games, renowned sports documentarian and historian Bud Greenspan will reveal his Top Ten list for the very first time!
Bud Greenspan, in partnership with General Motors, invites you to join this historic effort. Cast your ballot and enter to win a trip to see the 2004 US Olympic Team compete in Athens.
ENTER SITE

The site's first screen (which Thoughtbubble calls the "prologue") sets the scene. Here, visitors are introduced to Bud Greenspan and told about the two activities on the site: entering the sweepstakes and voting for their top ten Winter Olympians.

Sports broadcasters CNNSI (Cable News Network–Sports Illustrated) teamed with sponsor General Motors (GM) to offer an Olympics-flavored sweepstakes in the days leading up to the 2002 Winter Olympics in Salt Lake City. Visitors to a special Web site could register to win a trip to the 2004 Summer Olympics in Athens, Greece. At the same time, they could participate in another GM-sponsored promotion: the naming of the ten greatest Winter Olympians of all time, as determined by Bud Greenspan, a sports historian and documentarian who would announce his own top ten at the Olympic games.

For Thoughtbubble, the challenge was how to bring the site's separate goals together into a coherent presentation. "'Sign up here to win a trip' doesn't tell a great story," says Jonathan Heck, Thoughtbubble's chief development officer and co-founder. "We made a case to our client that they had a significant opportunity here to capitalize on their relationship with the visitors to the site."

The resulting site did indeed gather names for its sponsors, but that wasn't the main event. Instead, visitors were drawn into the electronic equivalent of a coffee-table book on historic Winter Olympians, with an added interactive element: They could register their opinions about the athletes by voting for their own top ten.

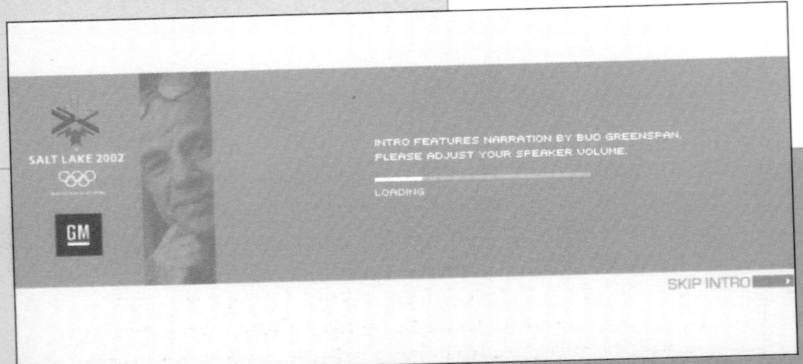

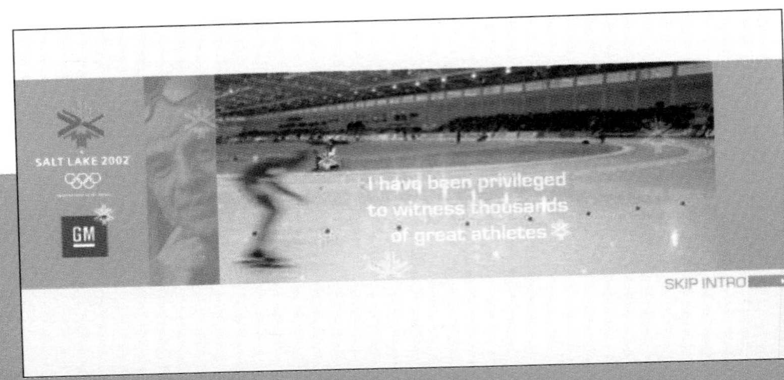

As the introduction loads, a screen advises users that audio is on the way. "It was a way of letting people know how to get the most of what's coming up," says Dave Carroll, Thoughtbubble's director of multimedia. Even users without sound get the information, though, thanks to the text of Greenspan's narration that is displayed over the photos.

> A Complex Task

When Thoughtbubble analyzed the task before it, the company found that the site needed to accomplish three distinct jobs: It needed to introduce Bud Greenspan and draw an audience to his announcement of his own top ten Winter Olympians. It needed to let users vote for their own top ten choices. And it needed to promote the sweepstakes. The trick would be to meet these goals in a way that wouldn't be confusing to the site's users.

"It was a complicated scenario in that users voted for their top ten and then Bud Greenspan had his own top ten. And there wasn't a direct relationship between voting on your own favorites and being concerned with Bud Greenspan's," explains Dave Carroll, Thoughtbubble's director of multimedia.

The twofold answer to the problem hinged on carefully layering information as the user enters the site, and meticulously planning the layout and interactivity of the site's main screen.

> One, Two, Three

Entry to the minisite was carefully paced. Most visitors would arrive from a banner ad promoting the sweepstakes. When they clicked the banner, the site would pop up in a new window that contained the prologue—a page introducing Greenspan and the chance to cast your vote for the top ten athletes, in addition to entering the sweepstakes. "The prologue was a way of forcing people to find out about the complexity," says Carroll.

When you click Enter the Site from the prologue, a montage featuring Greenspan's voice and stylized scenes from past Olympics fills the same screen. The images, accented by falling snowflakes along with Greenspan's nostalgic narration, create a somewhat elegiac mood. Here's where the site begins to build a relationship with its visitors—with all the emotional capital of the Olympics brought to bear. When the montage ends, the screen fades away, to be replaced by the interaction screen, on which all of the promised activities take place.

"The introduction presents Bud Greenspan as the authority on Olympian biographies," explains Heck. "His name carries a lot of currency in the sports world and in the documentary world."

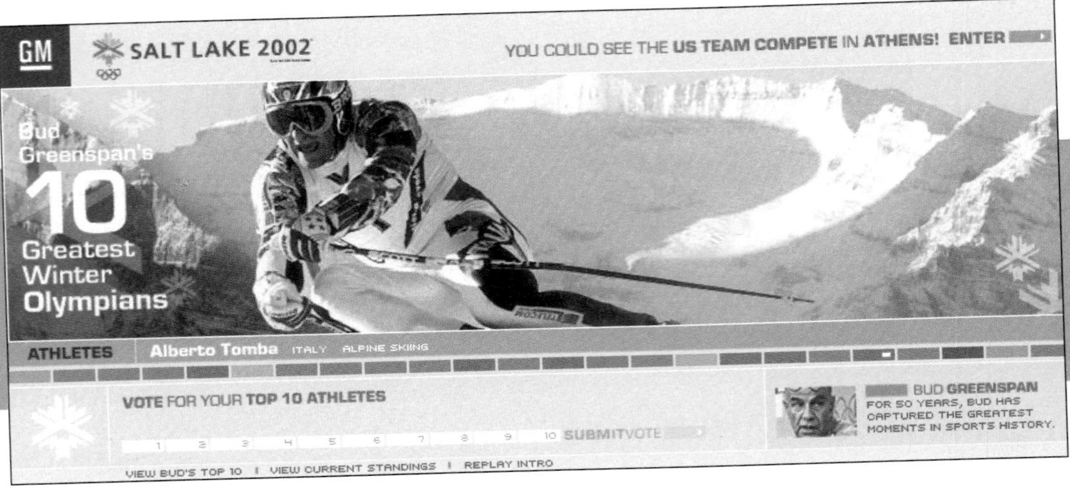

On the main screen, the information comes into view dynamically, focusing the visitor's attention on one item at a time. First, photos of the athlete slide in (right and facing page, top), then the athlete's story appears (facing page, bottom).

> Focus on the Athletes

Once you've arrived at the main screen, the site homes in on individual athletes. After a short load time, two photos and a text block featuring one of 24 preselected athletes slide into the center of the screen.

The Thoughtbubble team admits that the focus on the athletes rather than the sweepstakes was a bit controversial. (An invitation to enter the sweepstakes appears at the top right of the screen.) In the first layouts, where the call to enter was at the bottom of the screen, the client objected that it needed to be more prominent. In the end, though, everyone was happy with the result, with the sweepstakes text in the top-right corner. "We made the font a little brighter and a little larger, but we didn't want the first thing in your face to be 'Give us your information,'" says Kevin Cavallaro, Thoughtbubble's art director and lead designer. "We felt that the more we give the user something to engage in, the more they'll look for." And, the team reasoned, visitors would already be on the lookout for the entry information, since they got to the site by clicking an ad promoting the sweepstakes.

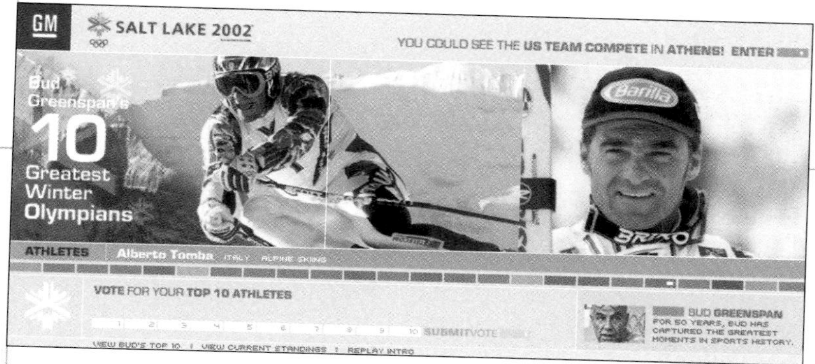

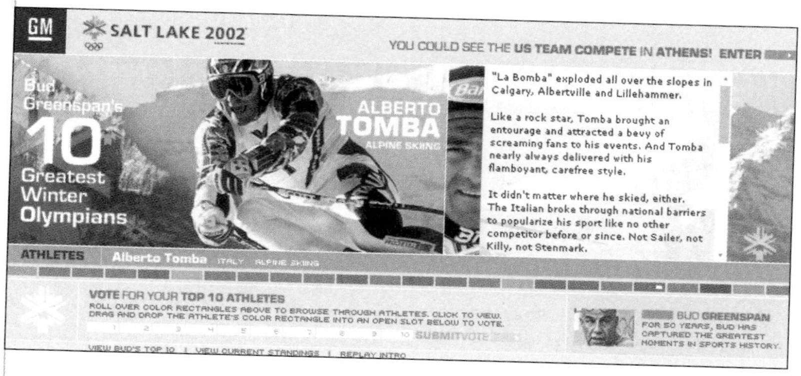

The presentation is elegant and efficient. Two photos of the athlete—a longer shot, of the athlete in action, and a close-up, in repose—then a short text biography move from right to left in layers, offering a full view of each photo before it is overlaid by the next piece of information.

By using time and space thoughtfully, the studio achieved all three site goals without causing confusion. The two screens that introduce the site let the visitor understand what's going on without getting in the way of the main action. The layout of the main action screen reflects the designers' view of what's most important (the athletes). The dynamic presentation of the key information there (skillfully paced introduction of photos and text, followed by instructions on how to use the page) lands the visitor softly in what might otherwise be a confusing landscape.

Finding, getting permission to use, and then giving a coherent look to photos that ranged in quality and over 50 years of styles called for careful art direction and Photoshop work.

> Managing the Assets

Marc Goldleaf, the project's producer, laughed ruefully when I complimented the team on the effectiveness and economy of showing each athlete in long-shot and close-up views. "I lost that battle," he says, explaining that Cavallaro felt strongly about having multiple photos of each athlete, but that he resisted, thinking of the complicated task of managing all the photos. "We were working with assets from 50 years ago, and a limited number of images were available," Goldleaf explains. And once the images were found, they needed to be approved by the surviving athletes, GM, CNN, and the athletes' national Olympic Committees.

The work didn't end when the images were finally authorized. "It was a lot of work making them look the way they do," says Cavallaro. "There aren't a lot of images there that don't have at least an hour of art direction involved."

To give the images—ranging over 50 years of styles and quality—a clean and coordinated look, the team had to change the photos' backgrounds and airbrush out competing logos, "even entire people," Goldleaf says. Thoughtbubble had to collect releases from everyone in an image—or from their estates, if they were no longer alive. If releases weren't available, that person had to go.

> Dynamic Exposition

After the bio and images are in place, text begins to appear below the photo. Under the title "Vote for Your Top 10 Athletes" are just two lines of instructions: "Roll over colored rectangles to browse through athletes. Click to view. Drag and drop the athlete's color rectangle into an open slot below to vote."

A Flash animation that types the instruction text one letter at a time is a simple but effective way of drawing eyes to what would otherwise be just another block of text. "In writing classes, they always say you need to make your exposition dramatic," laughs Heck. Flash makes it possible to do that, literally.

Carroll says he got the idea for typing out the text from futuristic screen interfaces portrayed in films like *2001: A Space Odyssey.* "The screens in those films look eerily like Flash interfaces," he notes. However, Carroll says, screen interfaces in films are typically a lot more active than those on our own computers. "In movies, it has to be engaging," he says.

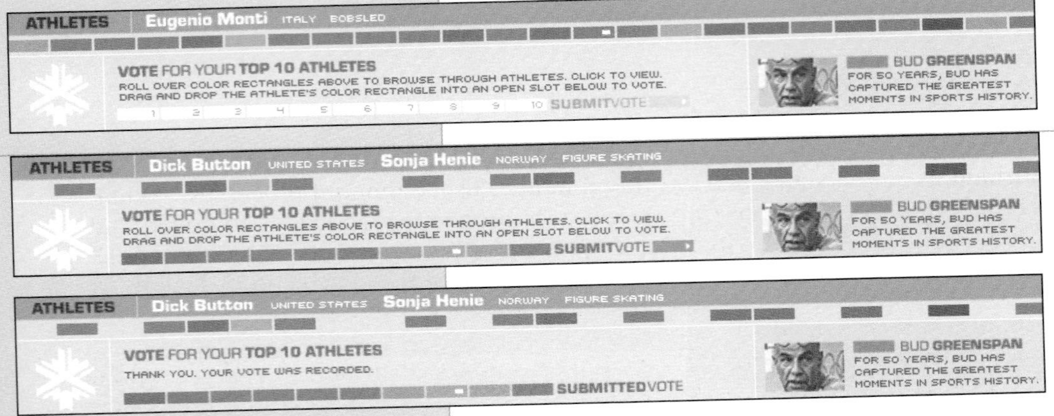

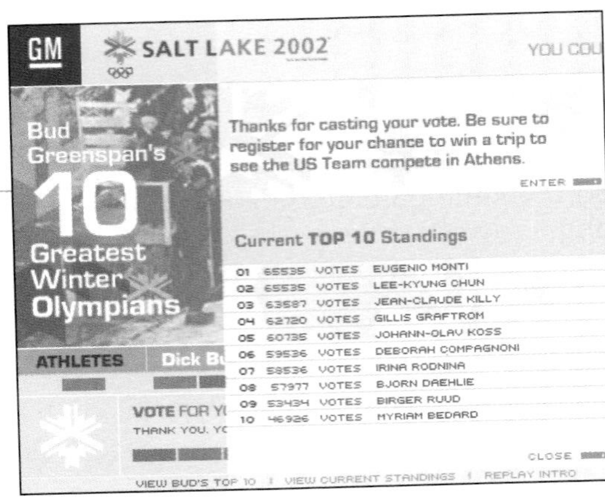

Colored tiles represent each athlete. The currently chosen one is indicated by a dot on his or her tile (top). Rolling over other tiles displays the name of the athlete represented by each one. Clicking a tile calls up that athlete's info. Users vote by dragging an athlete's tile into position in the voting bar. When all ten slots are filled, the Submit Vote button is activated (middle). When Submit Vote is clicked, the text changes to a label, Submitted Vote (bottom), and a list of the current popular vote standings is displayed, along with another call to enter the sweepstakes (right).

> Managing the Vote

Thoughtbubble put a lot of thought into the deceptively simple voting process.

The need to present a level playing field for the athletes resulted in a number of decisions. For one, the first athlete name you see changes each time the site is loaded. Carroll created a `RandomAthlete` function to select a number between 1 and 24 and an ActionScript `LoadMovieNum` function to load the correspondingly numbered athlete's movie.

The need for parity also legislated the horizontal layout of the tiles that represent each athlete, as well as the use of rollovers to show the athletes' names. "Putting crucial information in a rollover is generally risky," says Carroll, because users may simply never see it. Here, though, the designers found it the only way to avoid a stacked layout that gave precedence of position to one athlete or another. In the horizontal layout, the tiles are organized alphabetically by last name, but users won't necessarily scroll through the names from the beginning; they're just as likely to choose an interestingly colored tile or one next to the current tile.

"We had the intuition that drag and drop was the way to go for the voting," says Cavallaro—an intuition that was confirmed as the team designed the implementation. In the final design, you drag the athlete's tile into one of ten voting slots to create your personal top ten.

"There were a lot of nice things that happened by accident," says Carroll. Because each tile is positioned on the stage dynamically with ActionScript, and each is assigned the properties of the athlete it represents, the chip's behavior is the same whether it sits in the navigation lineup or in the voting slots. You can still click them to call up the athlete's information, or drag them out again into the roster in the same way you dragged them in. (The tile snaps back to its original position in the line.)

The Thoughtbubble team says that all the comps it showed included some version of drag and drop. "One design had you drag the photo into a ballot box," says Cavallaro. "It took the idea really literally."

"When we were putting together the drag-and-drop interface, we were concerned whether people were going to get it," says multimedia designer Paul Gomez. The typed instructions were designed to make the interface clear. But he also points out that you can get a lot out of the site without even getting to the voting. Carroll agrees: "We wanted to introduce next-generation interactivity but not make it necessary for using the site."

> Hidden Significance

Heck believes that the design of the voting system owes its success to the way it mimics users' thought processes. "What we're asking the users to do here is somewhat complex," he says. "Consider 24 possible choices, evaluate the individual merits of each, and then keep all those facts and opinions in their heads long enough to choose their ten favorites."

The tiles, he says, serve as useful *aides-memoire*. "Each colored tile represents everything the user knows about the individual athlete, whether learned from the site or from previous experience," he explains. The voting mechanism allows the users to organize each of those individual ideas, compare them, group them, and sort them. It's a process, he says, "that mimics the countless cognitive evaluations and comparisons that go into every decision we make." Users are able to reevaluate and reconsider their choices by rearranging the tiles as much as they want before committing to a final vote. The information about each athlete remains associated with its tile no matter how the user organizes it, just as a host of associated information and ideas connects to an item.

UNDER THE HOOD
THE TYPING EFFECT

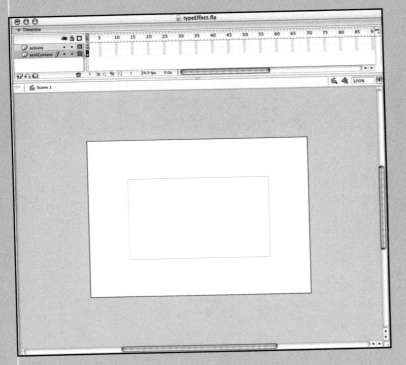

Figure 1

The dynamic text field, with its size and formatting, is defined in Frame 1.

Thoughtbubble used a dynamic effect to draw the visitor's attention to important text in the Greatest Olympians site. As the screens load, the text is typed into the screen letter-by-letter for a dramatic, *Mission Impossible*–type entrance. Thoughtbubble produced the effect by creating a script that can animate any text, in any position and formatting required.

Using ActionScript functions, rather than keyframing the animation, not only took far less time to implement, but also made it easy to change the text in response to the client's feedback, and to reuse the effect in different areas of the project without recoding.

When they developed this site in Flash 5, the programmers attached the ActionScript to frames inside of a movie clip, which loop in order to update a dynamic text field according to the movie's frame rate. Thanks to Flash MX, Thoughtbubble can now take advantage of the new object event model to define a function and trigger it programmatically, rather than from a timeline loop. The new `SetInterval()` action defines how often the function is called.

To create the effect, Dave Carroll, Thoughtbubble's Flash developer, created two layers on the timeline, naming one `actions` and the other `textContent`. On the `textContent` layer, he drew a rectangular text field that would define the area that the type would take up on screen. He then used the Properties Inspector to make it dynamic and multiline, and to assign the instance name textContent, along with the type font, size, color, and other formats (**Figure 1**).

```
initTyper();
function initTyper() {
    // Determine text to be animated and store in a new String object.
    textString = new String("Who would you select as the 10 Greatest Winter
Olympians? \n\nAt February's 2002 Olympic Winter Games, renowned sports documentarian
and historian Bud Greenspan will reveal his Top Ten list for the very first time!
\n\nBud Greenspan, in partnership with General Motors, invites you to join this
historic effort. Cast your ballot and enter to win a trip to see the 2004 US Olympic
Team compete in Athens.");
    // Determine the length of the text in characters.
    charNum = textString.length + 1;
    // Declare a variable to count through the characters.
    theChar = 0;
    // Declare an array to contain each character.
    words = new Array();
    // Loop through every character and store character sequences into the array.
    for (i=0; i <= charNum; i++) {
        words[i] = textString.substring(0,i);
    }
    // Determine speed of text animation in milliseconds.
    typeRate = 10;
    // Establish the interval to call doTyper and animate the text sequences.
    typerLoop = setInterval(doTyper,typeRate);
}
//
function doTyper() {
    // Compare the character counter against the total number of characters.
    if (theChar == charNum) {
        // Kill the function interval that's animating the text.
        clearInterval(typerLoop);
    } else {
        // Pass current array position value to the dynamic text field on the stage.
        textContent.text = words[theChar];
        // Update the graphics on the stage.
        updateAfterEvent();
        // Increment the character count.
        theChar++;
    }
}
```

Next, he selected the actions frame and entered the code shown in **Figure 2** into the Actions window. The code has two parts: a function called `initTyper`, to initialize the function, and another called `doTyper`, to run it. The `initTyper` function creates a string variable (`charNum`) to count the number of characters in the text, and another (`theChar`) to save the current character number. Then it creates an array variable (`words`) to store the text and uses `setInterval` to pace the onscreen typing.

The `doTyper` function determines whether the end of the string has been reached. If it has, it stops the `setInterval` action. If it hasn't, it passes the next character in the array to the dynamic text field, updates the stage, and sets the character-counting variable to the next number.

Because Thoughtbubble used a single text field for the entire text string, Flash was able to handle all the line wrapping during the animation. This effect was an unlooked-for benefit of animating the text this way, avoiding the need to add extra code (and reduce the modular flexibility of the script) to control the word wrap.

Figure 2

The script that types out the message creates two functions: `initTyper` and `doTyper`.

```
if (status == "success") {
    gotoAndStop(9);
} else if (status == "failure") {
    gotoAndStop(11);
} else {
    gotoAndPlay("checkServer");
}
```

When the Submit button is clicked, it collects the votes from an array on the root where they are stored and sends the ten values to a Java servlet. The servlet returns `success` to the `status` variable. The movie loops between the frame that holds the button and a frame that checks for `success`. When it hears `success`, the movie displays a message to the user, changes the button to Submitted Vote, and displays the current standings.

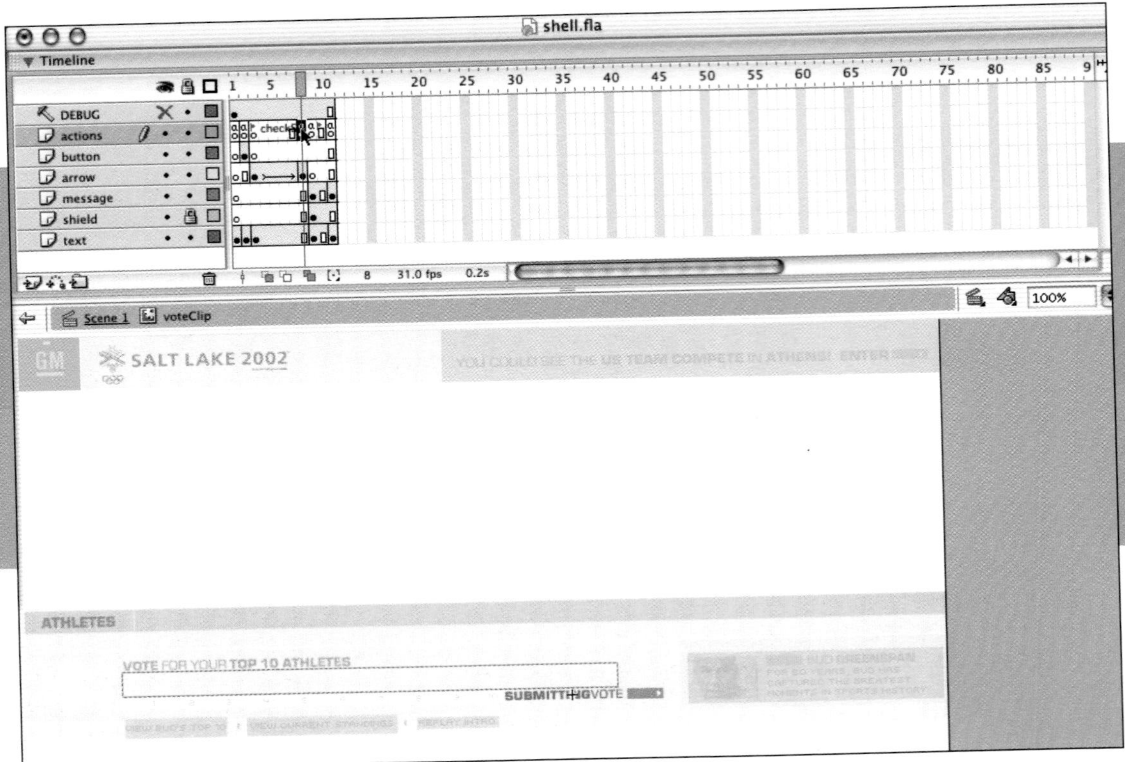


```
_root.voted = 1;
loadMovieNum("standings.swf", 30);
stop();
```

> Flash Plus Java

Once the voting line is filled with ten tiles, the Submit button next to it becomes active. Clicking Submit Vote activates a movie clip that collects the data and stores it in a database. Clicking View Current Standings activates another servlet that returns a string of data reflecting the current vote. Senior Programmer Robin Curts notes that the design of the front end actually made the back end simpler and less expensive to code—in addition to enforcing a fair vote. Because the Submit button doesn't become active until all ten slots of the voting line are filled, and because each athlete is represented in the interface by only one tile, users can't vote for a single athlete over and over again.

A third servlet managed the clicks on View Greenspan's Top Ten. To build tension—and encourage return traffic—Greenspan's own top ten were released over time, with a new athlete announced about every two days. The programmer created a servlet that would handle the time release on its own. When the button is clicked, the servlet checks the current time and date and sends out only the part of the list that is to be publicized by that time. Using a servlet to manage the timing of each announcement was a way of making site maintenance as easy as possible, says Goldleaf.

> Components in Flash 5

The Thoughtbubble team coded the project in record time: Five days after the approach was approved, they had a working site. Using Flash 5 ActionScripting, the team made sure that the site was coded for maximum flexibility and quick changes. Rather than place objects in frames, the team created every possible piece of the interface as a scriptable movie clip. "Everything was defined as a function in the first frame of the movie," says Carroll. For example, since the team didn't know at the outset how many athletes would be featured or what colors they would finally use, the color chips that stand for each athlete were created as objects with variables for their color and position. "Each tile knows who it is and what its x-y position is, so that it can snap back when it's moved," says Gomez. The content area was also created as a template so that the designers could swap out images as needed. The text is a dynamic text field, so when the client or the athletes wanted to make changes to it, those changes could be made rapidly.

The "typing" effect used for site instructions was another example of the effective use of ActionScript modules to make changes easier and the code reusable (see "The Typing Effect," page 186). "We could feed it any text, and it would be typed out," says Gomez. "It wasn't a tweened animation. If that text was keyframed out, we would have gone crazy reanimating the text every time a change was requested." As it is, the text can be changed almost instantly in an external text file. "I think it's the smallest thing we ever built," says Gomez. "It's something like 400 bytes."

"We tried to make sure that in this design, the things that we needed to change were changeable and the things that weren't going to change were not changeable," says Gomez, noting that things like the overall grid and the position of items like the logos and voting mechanism were fixed.

"We used a SmartClip user interface module for the biography-text scroll bars. We could customize the look and feel to match the final design, but the functionality was set beforehand," explains Gomez. The scroll bars work similarly to Flash MX's components, although the Thoughtbubble team created them by assembling and modifying public code available from Flash-community source-file exchanges.

GM SALT LAKE 2002

Registration Prize Rules

Enter Below For Your Chance To Win A Trip To Watch The US Team Compete In Athens!

You must be 18 years or older to submit information. The information submitted will be available to CNNSI, GM and Sports Illustrated . CNNSI will not sell or otherwise transfer to unaffiliated third parties any personal information submitted to us in connection with entering this Contest; although, we may use the information for our own statistical analyses or other uses consistent with our Privacy Statement. Please note that CNNSI does not control the use of this information by GM or Sports Illustrated. For more information on CNNSI's policies regarding user information, please read our CNN Privacy Statement. For more information on GM's policies regarding user information, please read its Privacy Statement. For more information on Sports Illustrated's policies regarding user information, please read its Privacy Statement.

Click here for more information on GM products and services

FIRST NAME*

LAST NAME*

ADDRESS*

CITY*

STATE* Alabama

ZIP*

PHONE

EMAIL*

DATE OF BIRTH* (MM/DD/YYYY)

Please update me as Bud Greenspan chooses his Top 10

The only HTML page on the site is the sweepstakes registration. People coming to the site without the Flash 5 plug-in are directed here.

> Only in Flash

It took a little convincing to get the client to agree to use Flash for the site, says Heck, but the team felt that Flash was the only way to achieve what they wanted to do. The team also knew that with careful file setup, they could actually make the site load faster than it would in HTML.

Using the SmartClip coding was one way Thoughtbubble kept download times short. "The heaviest thing in terms of file size is the intro," says Carroll. "But we don't force people to download the whole thing. We buffered it just enough to load smoothly on 56 K." Each athlete movie weighs in at about 20 K to 60 K. "We made the case that Flash movies don't have to take forever to load,"says Carroll. "In the end, what we've done is actually more efficient than Web pages, where every time you click you have to download the HTML and the formatting information."

The team also convinced its clients that the Flash 5 plug-in was ubiquitous enough that most of their audience would already have it. For those who don't, the team didn't even try to replicate the Flash experience with HTML. Instead, users who come to the site without the plug-in are directed to a page that gives them the opportunity to download the plug-in or go straight to the sweepstakes registration, which, after all, is what they came to find out about. To make sure that nobody misses it, the sweepstakes entry form is coded in HTML. ■

SPOTLIGHT
SKIP THE INTRO

Many Flash sites feature an animated introduction, a sort of video played to a passive audience, extolling the qualities of whatever the site is about. The problem with the intro is that it assumes a style of interaction that is the opposite of a user's natural attitude toward a Web site. Web sites are about interaction. At each moment, users are actively searching for their next move—the link or button that will take them on the next step of their journey. An introductory animation assumes an opposite attitude: one of patient passivity.

I'm prejudiced against animated intros as a rule, but three sites featured here use them—and I have to admit that each provides an economical and well-integrated presentation of key information. Most important, they also all offer Skip Intro buttons, which let users hunting for a goal go quickly on their way. The Skip Intro button gives users a choice. Those who have the patience, or interest, will view the introduction. Those who don't, won't—but they'll be satisfied users, and that's what you're really after.

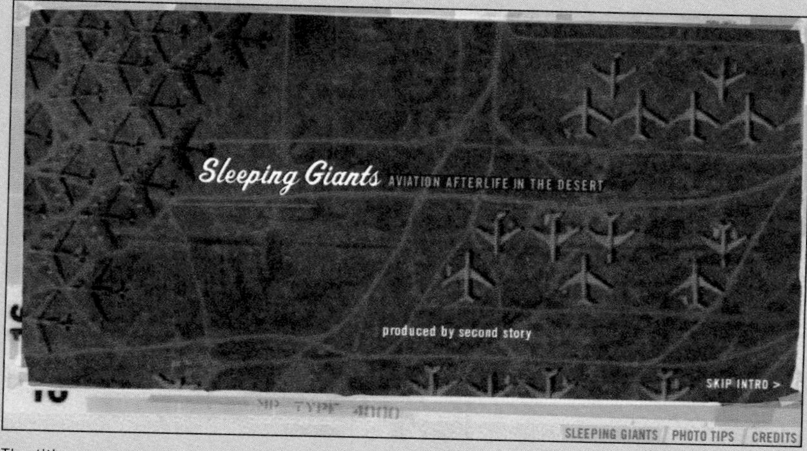

The title sequence that opens Sleeping Giants is effective actually because it thwarts the user's hunting approach. The movielike opening prepares the user for the cinematic presentation of the main site, which asks users to sit back and be passive for once.

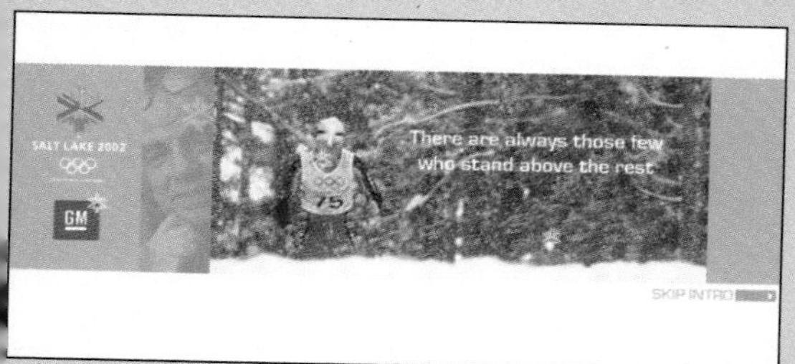

Bud Greenspan's Ten Greatest Winter Olympians uses a poignant voice-over by Greenspan and the slow fade-in and fade-out of vintage images to build up the elegiac tone that is key to the site.

The intro for KQED's Beautiful Bay Area lasts just long enough for all of the page's elements to assemble. In those few seconds, it economically introduces the area's range of scenery plus the graphical and navigational vocabulary of the site.

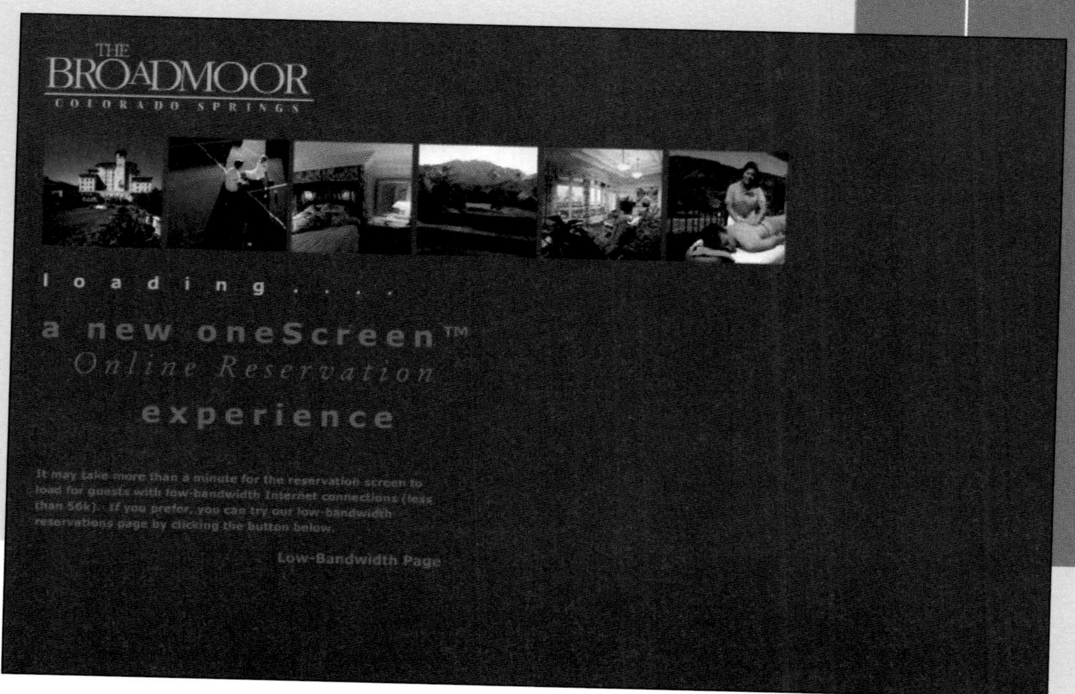
THE
BROADMOOR
COLORADO SPRINGS
l o a d i n g . . . .
a new oneScreen™
Online Reservation
experience
It may take more than a minute for the reservation screen to load for guests with low-bandwidth Internet connections (less than 56k). If you prefer, you can try our low-bandwidth reservations page by clicking the button below.
Low-Bandwidth Page

CHAPTER

iHotelier OneScreen

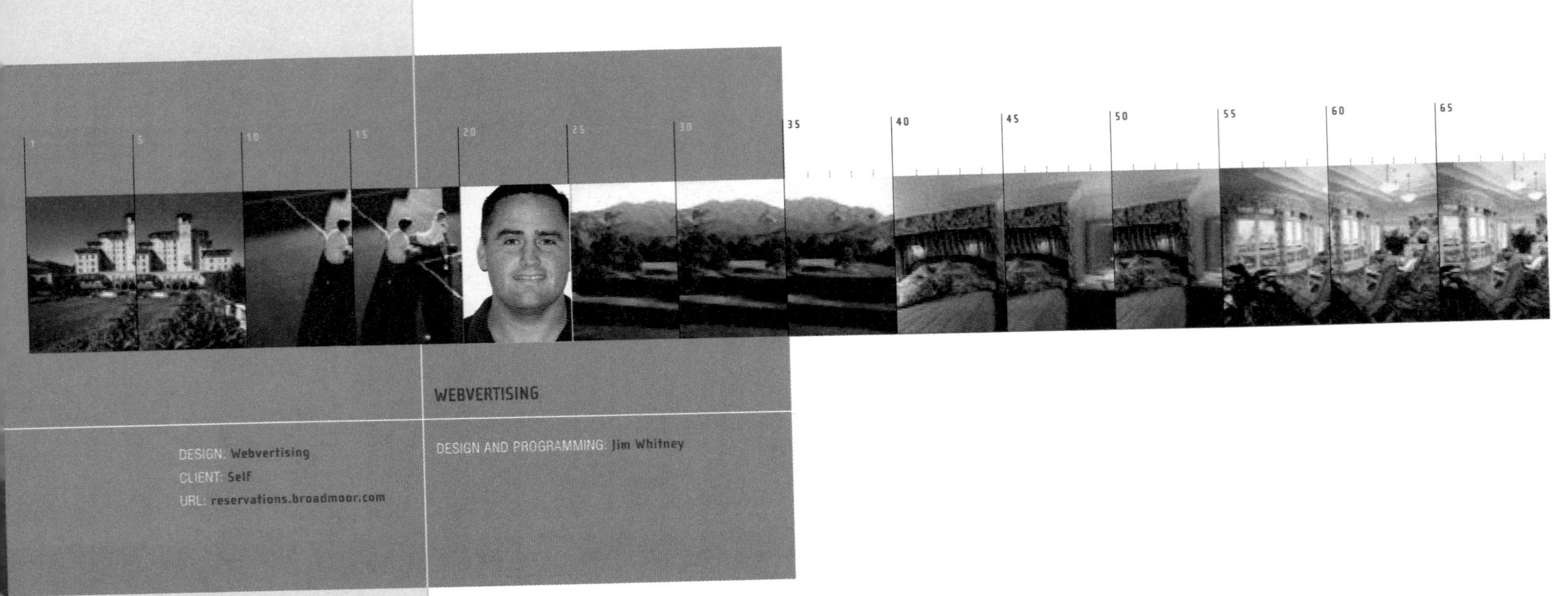

CHAPTER

iHotelier OneScreen

INTRO

Webvertising had created hotel-booking systems for several clients. But only when it tried a Flash front end did the firm find the approach that it felt put it head and shoulders above the competition.

Pictured: Jim Whitney

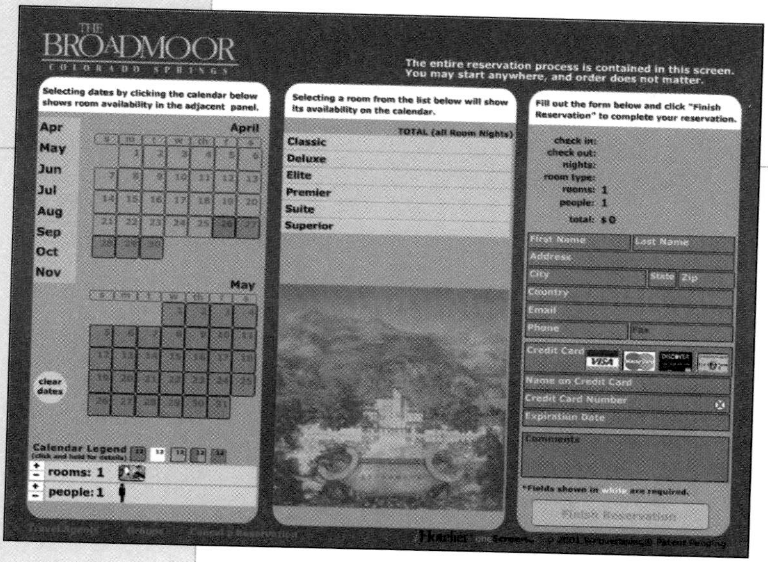

The iHotelier OneScreen interface lets users make their choices—room type, dates, number of rooms—in any order. Each choice updates the other sections automatically.

More than 300 hotels across the country use a Web-based room-booking application created by Webvertising, a Houston-based Web development firm. The company's first effort, a site created with Macromedia ColdFusion in late 1997, booked more than a million dollars online in its first year. Following that success, Webvertising began offering the service to more hotels, and in 1999 it launched a suite of Web-based hotel-management products called iHotelier.

To turn its services into a product, says Webvertising's chief technical officer, Jim Whitney, "we spent lots of time with the code and turned it into something that could be customized and sold over and over again." That fine-tuning included attention to the front end as well as the database; the company was pleased to have gotten the booking process down to a streamlined five steps.

Then, while surfing the Web, Whitney ran across a Flash guest-book application that called a database, saw another Flash site that used a calendar interface, and put the two ideas together. He began experimenting with a Flash front end to his product and was amazed to find that not only could he cut the interface down to a single screen, but this single screen could work in a way that was both a lot clearer to the customer and much more likely to result in a successful booking.

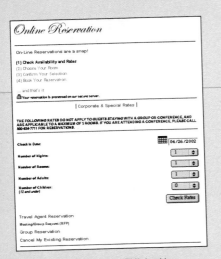

Users must complete the HTML booking interface in order, a page at a time.

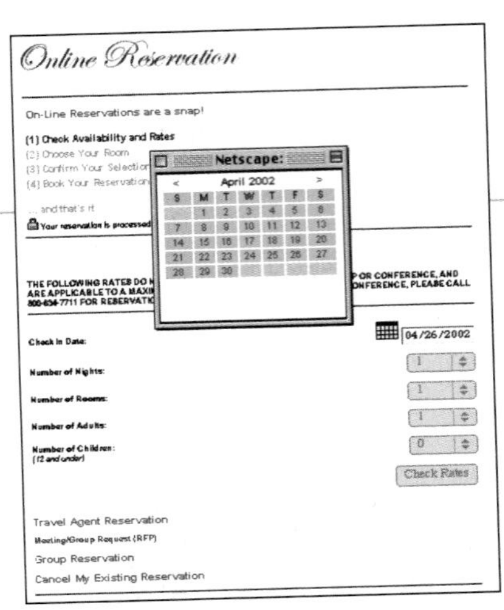

An extra click (on the calendar icon) brings up a calendar in a new window.

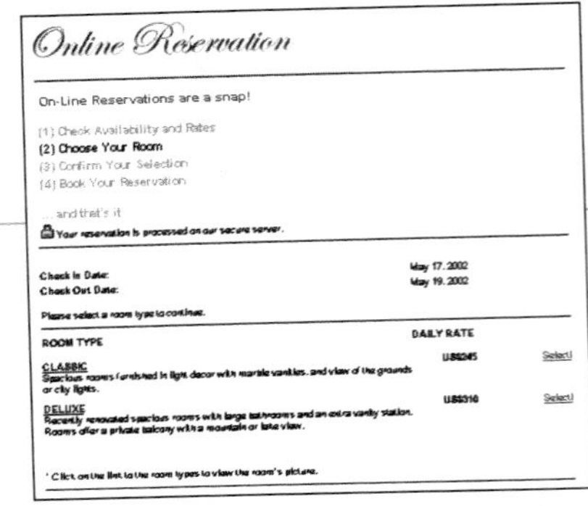

A new page is needed each time the system requires a call to the database. After submitting your room request and dates (in screen 1), you choose an available room type.

> The Pitfalls of HTML

Plunging into a standard HTML-based reservation system requires a leap of faith. Most involve multiple screens, which allow the system to submit your request to a database that parses out the many variables that go into a booking (room rates depend on day of the week, room types depend on availability, and so on). As you click through, you wait with bated breath for the next screen: Will your request be accepted? Will two rooms be available on that date? Then, after you've submitted all of your information, will you find out that the only available rooms are too expensive? Or worse, will the system be "unable to process your request" and invite you to return at a later date or ask you to call an 800 number?

"In an HTML system, if you can't find something in your price range or on your date, you have to go back and just try to guess" whether another date or another room type might work better, says Whitney.

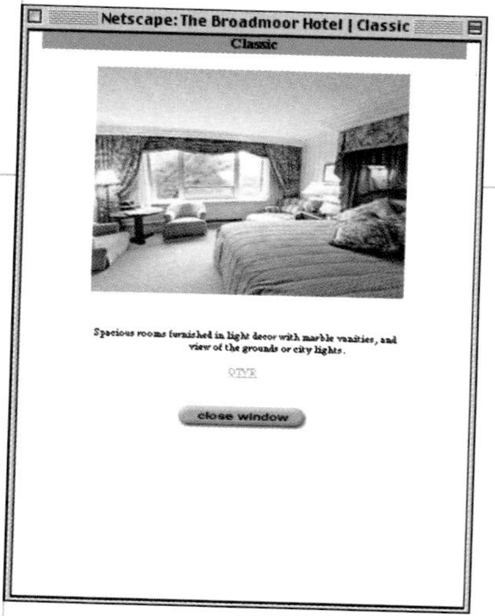

A room photo pops up in a new window if you click the Photo link on the previous screen.

When the system is sure there's a room for you, you input your name and credit card info.

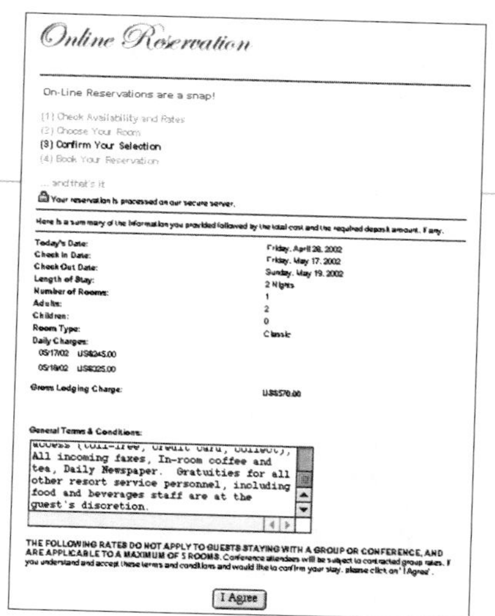

A confirmation screen puts all the information on one page, with the total cost, and displays terms and conditions.

Webvertising spent a lot of time fine-tuning its HTML-based system to make it as trouble-free as possible: Its five screens were the minimum required to make the necessary calls to the database. The order of the screens was carefully thought out to minimize user annoyance—for instance, the system doesn't ask for credit card information until the user has confirmed room choice and dates. And an outline of the required steps is posted at the top of each screen so that users know what the process entails and where they are within it. Even with all that, though, the system is unable to avoid the pitfalls common to any such HTML-based system.

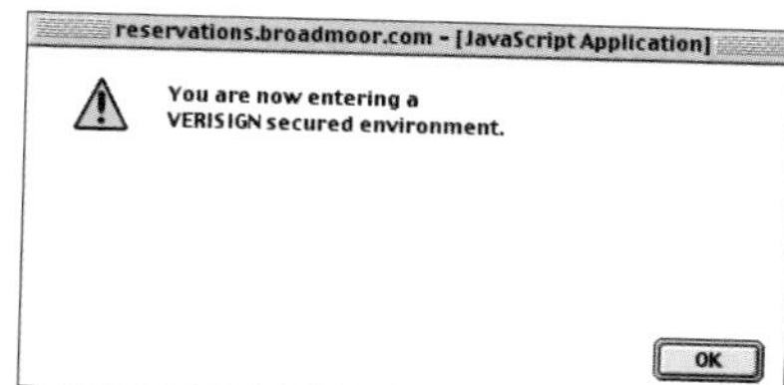

But wait ... you need to click again to get past the notification of the secure transaction.

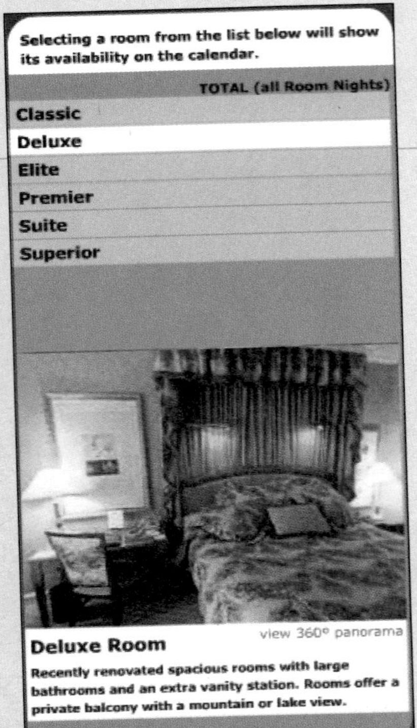

Selecting a room from the list below will show its availability on the calendar.
TOTAL (all Room Nights)
Classic
Deluxe
Elite
Premier
Suite
Superior
Deluxe Room
view 360° panorama
Recently renovated spacious rooms with large bathrooms and an extra vanity station. Rooms offer a private balcony with a mountain or lake view.

On the Broadmoor's OneScreen page, clicking a room type brings up a photo of the room, with the option to use Quicktime VR for a 360-degree view.

> The OneScreen Interface

The Flash interface that Webvertising finally settled on for iHotelier managed to put all the required input fields onto one screen. Users can see at a glance what type of information is required and what types of selections they need to make. And if room type is more important to you than date, you can select that option first—or call up photos of the different room types to see if there's anything to your liking. Webvertising named its new Flash product OneScreen—in recognition of the fact that a single-screen interface was an important advance in hotel-booking software.

There are no calls to the database in response to user input. Instead, the room data is uploaded along with the Flash movie to the user's system, so that all the calculations take place in Flash, on the user's own machine. If you choose a Deluxe King, the calendar updates to show what dates that type of room is available. If you choose a holiday weekend, OneScreen's options change to show the room types available and the prices in effect for those dates. There's no wait for calls to the database or for new screens to load.

In addition to being more flexible, OneScreen is also faster to use than an HTML system, claims Whitney. In its new MX version, the OneScreen download is about 50 K to 100 K (depending on the hotel and its options), and the time spent waiting for that to load is far less than the time it takes to load five separate screens with the associated calls to the database, he says so. And that doesn't even count the time you don't spend second-guessing the inventory.

Whitney says that the biggest challenge in creating the OneScreen interface wasn't the Flash coding. It wasn't even developing the database. It was figuring out all the reservation logic. He developed a matrix that described every possible starting condition and what should happen in response to every possible user action. For instance, what should happen if no dates are selected, a room

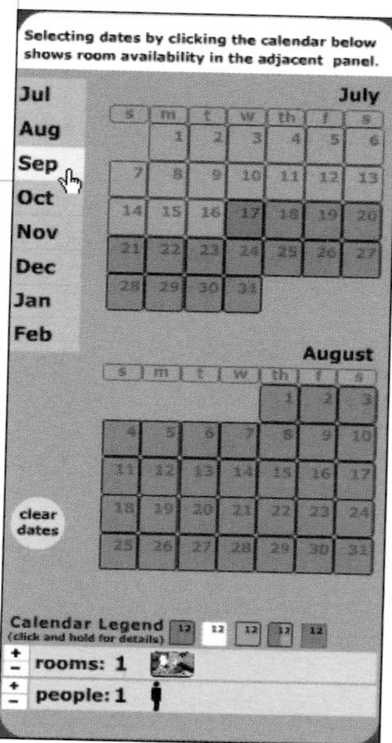

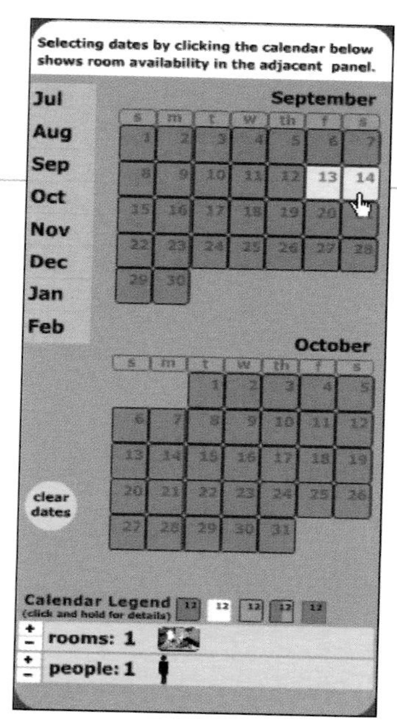

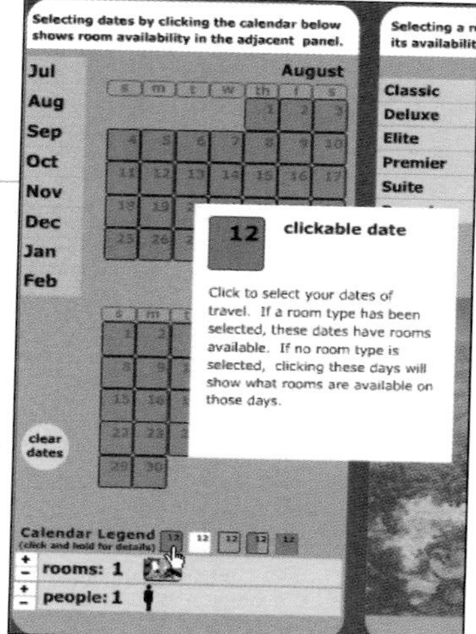

Left, the calendar opens to the current month. Clicking a month on the left shows later dates.

Center, clicking dates on the calendar selects the nights of your stay. Clicking again deselects them.

Right, a color key below the calendar describes the meaning of the different shades. A click on the legend pops up the description.

type is selected, and the user adds to the number of rooms? In that case, the program checks inventory and blocks the selection of any dates that don't have the requisite number of rooms available. The same types of hypotheticals had to be traced for more than 500 different cases.

> Calendar as Interface

Whitney feels that a key to OneScreen's success is the central interface of the calendar. Although a calendar is a familiar and efficient method of choosing dates, Whitney says few if any sites were using it when OneScreen was launched. More often, he says, you see two sets of pull-down menus to choose dates from. Common sense and his industry contacts told him the calendar was the way to go. After all, isn't that what clients have in their hands when they're making a hotel reservation?

The calendar in OneScreen is color-coded to indicate room availability. Each hotel has its own color scheme (adjusted to match the design of the hotel's own site). One color indicates dates with available rooms; another indicates dates on which nothing is available. A half-shaded square means that date can only be a check-out date. Another color shows dates the user has selected. And an outlined date shows other dates you must select if you've chosen a date that requires a minimum stay (common for weekends at resort hotels). As the user selects other options (room type or number of rooms), the calendar's shading is updated to reflect the new choices.

All this interactivity wouldn't be feasible on an HTML site, says Whitney. "You'd have to store the start date and the end date. You'd have trouble highlighting the dates. And it would be hard or impossible to take those inputs and show the consequences of those choices on the availability."

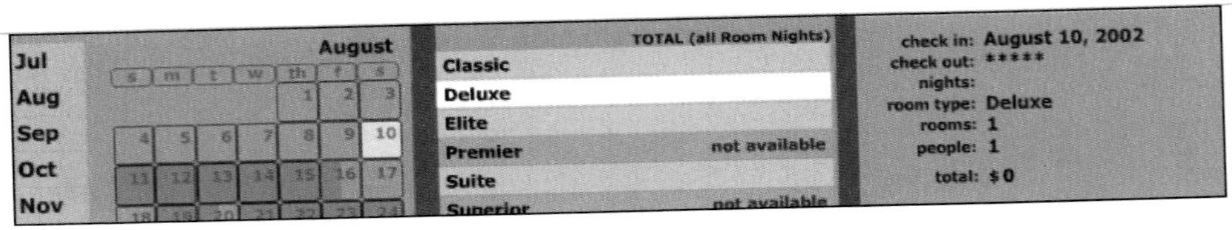

Clicking one night on the calendar results in the confusing sum of $0 for your Deluxe room. User testing found that most people think of their stay in terms of check-in and check-out dates. When you click Submit, you get an error message indicating you must choose a check-out date.

> How Many Days Is Two Nights?

I was surprised by the way the OneScreen system logged dates. Choosing a three-day stay included just two nights; the three days were counted from the check-in day to the check-out day. Although it seemed counterintuitive to me, Whitney says the system is based on user testing.

"The original version didn't operate that way," he explains. "But we did some informal research and some focus groups, and people were confused. They would say, 'I'm coming in on the fifth and leaving on the sixth,' and click two days."

Whitney says that programming the system to manage days according to the user's behavior caused development complications, but he felt it had to be done. "If you just think in terms of nights, the inventory check is very easy," he says. "If the availability is zero, the day isn't clickable." With the check-in/check-out calculation, the day is clickable if it's the last day in a range, a conditional he says more than doubled the complexity of the code.

As one of those people who would have clicked the dates representing the nights I wanted to stay, I was at first confused by the interface. Selecting one night resulted in a $0 charge, which left me wondering what was wrong until I figured out the system. I wondered whether using the already established half-shaded day to show rooms that were only available at the end of a range, or to

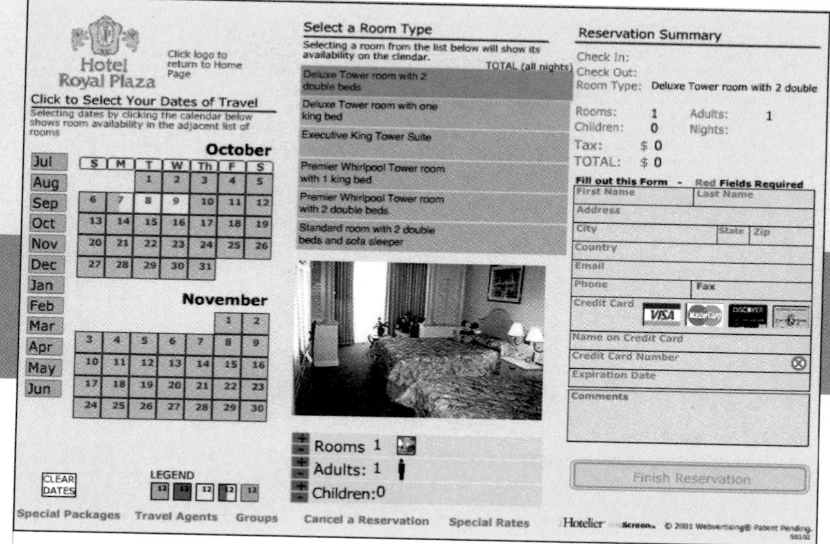

The OneScreen interface for the Hotel Royal Plaza shows how the basic OneScreen layout can be adapted to fit the style of a different hotel by changing the colors and graphics.

show days chosen at the end of a range, might solve the problem for both types of user. The day would be clickable if it were at the end of a range, and the half-shaded day would have made it clear that it was a check-out day.

Whitney says that his experience over the last four years has led him to believe that there is no way to make the system absolutely clear to all users—there will always be those two ways of thinking. To deal with this ambiguity, the system relies on instructions and error-catching in the interface: the legend, the summary area (which includes separate lines for check-in and check-out), and the pop-up window that appears if no check-out date is selected to tell users that information is still needed.

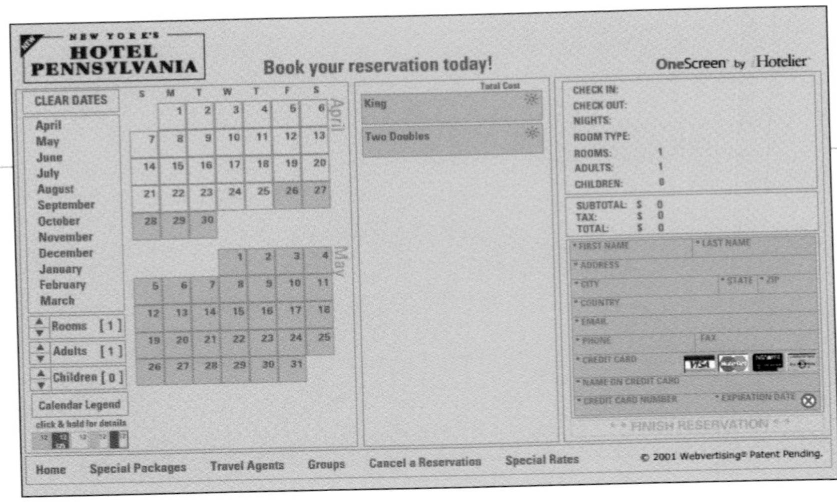

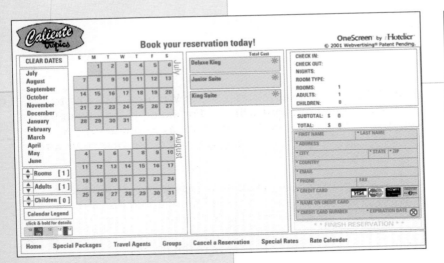

These hotel sites all subscribe to the "standard" package, which offers custom colors and graphics, but no other customer-specific features. The central column is designed to accommodate the wide range of room types for different hotels, ranging from two for the Hotel Pennsylvania (above right) to the dozens that may be available at another hotel.

> Standardization and Its Discontents

Webvertising focuses on a certain segment of the hotel market, which Whitney describes as "mid- to upscale, independently owned hotels." (Chains generally have their own reservation systems, he says.) This specialization allows the company to tailor its services to the needs of that group, designing a solution that should meet most needs of most clients right out of the box.

Yet the system still needs to be customized for each client, according to Whitney. "After 300 hotels, we've got most of the variables, but every hotel has some idiosyncrasies," he says. He gives some examples: "Some hotels don't want to show tax in the room total. Some hotels charge different rates for children and adults."

Differences in the way hotels handle their rates can be dealt with in the ColdFusion database and in the ActionScript that totals the charges. Other differences have a greater impact on the interface.

Webvertising offers hotels the option to customize the OneScreen design in any way they see fit. The three-column interface is the

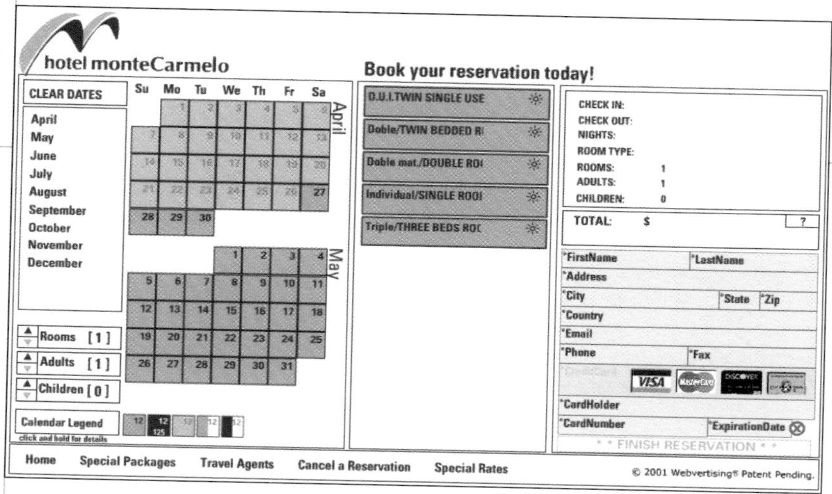

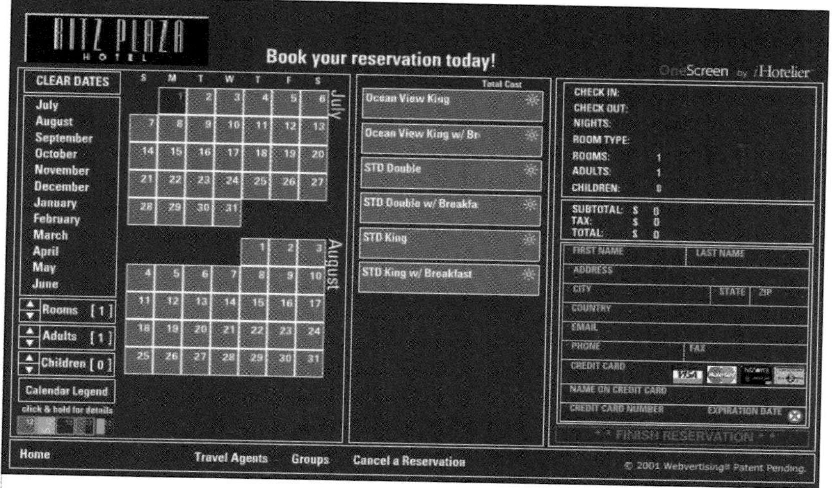

default, but "it's not set in stone," says Whitney. "We like to see people doing fun stuff with it." For example, one potential client, a casino, is talking to the company about adding a roulette wheel to the interface, giving users the chance to win a free stay.

Webvertising also offers a plain-vanilla model, using the client hotel's own color scheme and room information, but without extra customization. In some cases, this results in layouts that aren't as well tailored to the content as the Broadmoor's, where every inch of the window is optimally used.

Whitney explains that those cases are inevitable compromises. The standard template has to allow for a range of cases. When I asked why the center column on the Hotel Pennsylvania's site was empty, he explained, "The Broadmoor has six to eight room types. The Greenbriar has 42 room types. You have to figure out where all that information goes. In the standard template, the center column is reserved for that."

Such standardization is key to making the business work. Spending too much time on customization would compromise the company's economic model, and at press time, Webvertising was focused on fine-tuning the customization process.

"With the Broadmoor version, we could take the application and redo the interface to fit another hotel in about six hours for me (since I'm familiar with it) or about two days for a designer," says Whitney. "But recall that we have about 350 clients, with only about 30 of them using OneScreen so far. Two days times 300 hotels is a whole lot of time." Webvertising's goal is to create a version it can customize and deploy in 30 minutes.

l o a d i n g . . . .
a new oneScreen™
Online Reservation
experience
It may take more than a minute for the reservation screen to load for guests with low-bandwidth Internet connections (less than 56k). If you prefer, you can try our low-bandwidth reservations page by clicking the button below.
Low-Bandwidth Page

As the Flash 5 version of OneScreen loads, users are asked to be patient—or just go to the HTML version. The smaller size of the MX application may make the escape route obsolete.

> The MX Version

OneScreen's latest version is coded in Flash MX, an upgrade that Whitney credits for a number of improvements to the application's responsiveness—and, not incidentally, for the team's ability to streamline its customization procedures.

"With Flash MX, we have greater ActionScript control over things like text styles and movie-clip colors," says Whitney. In studying ways to deploy sites faster, the team made a list of every item in the application that had to be customized for a new client. Then they designed the code so that all of those features were controllable through ActionScript. "For example," says Whitney, "there is a thin line that borders each area of the interface. Instead of having to drill down into the Flash file to change this color, we can now define a variable to hold that border's hex color value." All that would have been impossible without new Drawing API, text-field features, and Color object MX's.

Next on the agenda is building an interface that noncoders can use to manipulate the code. "Now that we can change the 'skin' of OneScreen by changing values stored in variables," explains Whitney, "we can load those values from a database. And if we can load them from a database, we can create an interface that enters them into a database." The control interface is itself in Flash—a dummy version of OneScreen with pop-up color-picker panels. The result is a system that lets anyone—designers, sales people, and even, potentially, the clients themselves—customize the OneScreen interface.

Coding OneScreen in MX also has advantages for the application's users. Whitney says that in the original, Flash 5 version of OneScreen, the application's file size was between 160 K and 210 K (depending on the specific hotel's features). Coding it in MX reduced the application's size by about 50 percent, bringing it down to between 50 K and 100 K.

Whitney says that the MX version also performs faster—about 40 percent faster than the Flash 5 version, due, he thinks, to the code efficiencies gained via new MX features such as the `LoadVars` object, which makes it possible to reach directly into a database with less overhead than the old `MovieClip.loadVariables()` function.

> MX Only?

In moving so quickly to a version of the site that requires Flash Player 6, Webvertising is a bit ahead of the curve. Just four months after the release of Flash Player 6, Macromedia reported 30 percent penetration of the plug-in, but most publishers are still playing it safe, and won't require the new version until the penetration percentage hits the 90s. Webvertising, in contrast, is now offering the MX application as its standard version.

To ease the transition, Webvertising offers its clients a range of options for handling users who come to the site without the needed Flash player installed. Generally, the company suggests that the site test for the Flash player on a visitor's machine, then send users who don't have it to a backup HTML system. For the Broadmoor and others, even those who do have the plug-in are offered the option of going to the "low-bandwidth" (HTML) version if they become impatient as the Flash application loads. With the application's new smaller size, though, Whitney is confident that most customers will wait out the download. He's even thinking of presenting a Flash-only option to his clients as a feasible approach.

"The other day, my wife's grandfather had me put something on his computer, that needed Flash MX," says Whitney. "Up popped the window, and he just hit Yes. He didn't even know what happened, and the plug-in was installed." The ease of downloading the Flash plug-in has made Whitney think that some of his clients may be able to get away with offering only the OneScreen Flash version.

While moving to the Flash MX version of OneScreen has clear benefits for Webvertising—it means the company only has to support one version of the site for the client—Whitney feels the MX version offers benefits to his clients and his clients' customers as well. "The new version is just so much faster," he says. ■

UNDER THE HOOD
SPACE-SAVING INPUT FIELDS

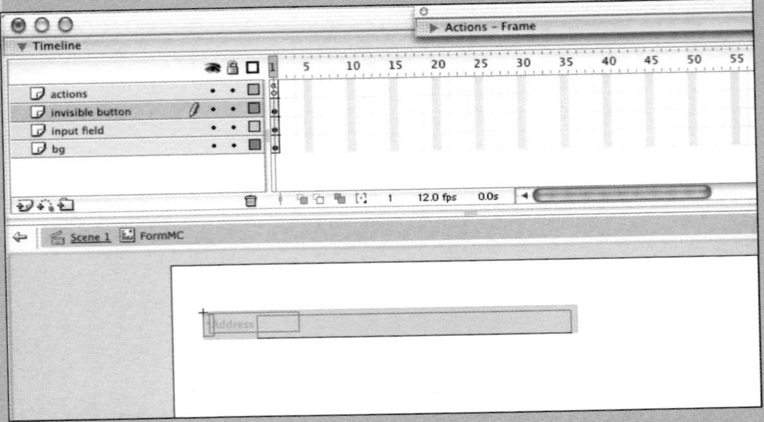

Figure 1

The movie clip holds the input text field, covered by a button, and the bg movie clip (see **Figure 2**).

Figure 2

The bg movie clip includes the different states of the field, each in its own frame. Frame 1 (top) is the empty, unfocused state. Frame 2 (middle) holds the focused state. And Frame 3 (bottom) holds the unfocused, filled state.

Getting everything into a single screen for the OneScreen interface was no easy task. But out of that necessity was born a compact, clean interface for form input that would not otherwise have been invented.

"In our initial efforts, we set up the form fields the same way we would set up fields in HTML, with the field label outside the input field, either above it or to the side," says OneScreen's developer, Jim Whitney. The problem with that approach was the room it took up. With the field labels above the input fields, the form was too long for the page, forcing the user to scroll. With the field labels to the side, a column had to be set aside on the screen just for the form, which would have forced Whitney to reduce the calendar or room-type size beyond what he considered acceptable.

It became apparent that the only solution would be to place the field labels on top of the input fields, then somehow move the label out of the way when an input field is in focus or filled. There was some debate among the team about whether this practice was acceptable from a usability standpoint, but Whitney believed he could make it work.

Whitney determined that he had to consider four states for the form fields: out of focus and empty, out of focus and filled, in focus and empty, and in focus and filled. Flash let him handle the different states by using different frames of a movie clip.

For each input field, Whitney created a movie clip called FormMC (**Figure 1**) that contained a single frame with the input text field, an invisible button covering it, and a background movie clip, called bg (**Figure 2**), that handled the appearance of the different input-field states. (Instances of the parent movie clip, FormMC, can be created for each form field.) The bg movie clip has three frames, with a rectangle in each representing the input field to the user. The first frame holds the empty, unfocused state, with a larger field label. The second frame holds the focused state (for our purposes, filled and unfilled are the same). And the third frame contains the unfocused, filled state. A smaller field label spans the two last frames of the movie clip, positioned within the outer rectangle so that it does not overlap the input text field in the main, outer movie clip. The rectangle in the first and third frames is in color, signifying an out-of-focus state, while the in-focus state in Frame 2 has a white background rectangle.

An onRelease function attached to the button (**Figure 3**) controls the behavior of the input field. When the user clicks the field, the bg movie clip moves to Frame 2 (the in-focus state), and the focus is set on the clicked-in input text field in the outer movie clip. If another field were in focus, that field would be turned off. Whitney stores the currently focused movie clip in a _root.focusField variable, and the variable for the value of the current field in _root.focusVar—which allows him to remove focus from one as another is selected. An "if" statement checks to see whether the field is empty, and sends bg to Frame 1 (with the larger field label) if it is, and to Frame 3 (with the smaller label) if it is not. Finally, the current input field and its parent movie clip path are set in focus.

This approach, conceived to save space, has another, unlooked-for benefit: It lets Webvertising customize the behavior and appearance of the form for each client.

```
on (release) {
      bg.gotoAndPlay(2);                    //in focus
      Selection.setFocus("CardNumber");  //place insertion point inside input text field

      if (eval(_root.focusField add "." add _root.focusVar) == "") {
            eval(_root.focusField).bg.gotoAndPlay(1);    //unfocused, empty state
      }
      else if (eval(_root.focusField add "." add _root.focusVar) != "") {
            eval(_root.focusField).bg.gotoAndPlay(3);    //unfocused, filled state
      }

      _root.focusField = this;              //stores this mc as in focus
      _root.focusVar = "CardNumber";      //stores this varable or text field as in focus
}
```

Figure 3

The onRelease function, attached to the button in the outer movie, controls the behavior and appearance of the input field.

SPOTLIGHT
MAKE THE WAIT COUNT

Sometimes it's unavoidable: You're going to have to make your user wait while your site, or part of it, loads. Luckily, there are ways to mitigate the boredom and annoyance of the wait.

Divide your site into sensible components. Wait times will be noticed least if they're short. Keep all your movies as small as you can without breaking your site into illogical parts. Wait times are most annoying if they come unexpectedly, so take advantage of times, such as the click on a new section, when users expect to wait, and download a new section then.

Preload. Flash *streams*, meaning it doesn't need to download a whole movie before it begins playing the first frame. Take advantage of this capability, but use it wisely. Use a `stop` action in the first frame of the root movie to keep the movie from playing until enough of it has loaded to avoid the annoying stuttering that occurs when Flash plays while waiting for frames to download. Test your movie using Flash's Bandwidth Profiler to determine how much of it needs to download before you can set the playhead free again.

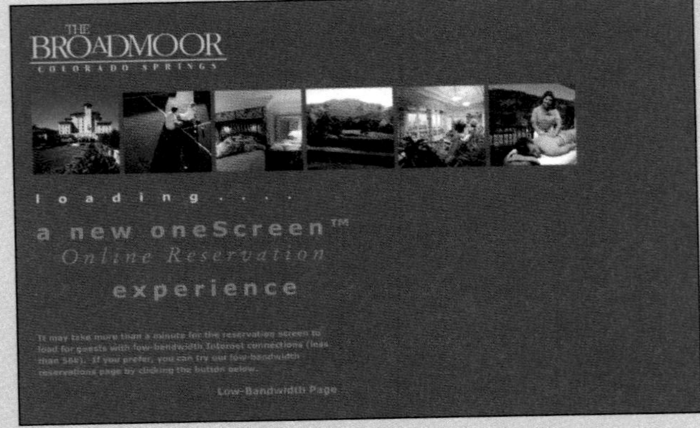

The iHotelier site gives users the option of jumping to the HTML version of the site if they become impatient during the initial load.

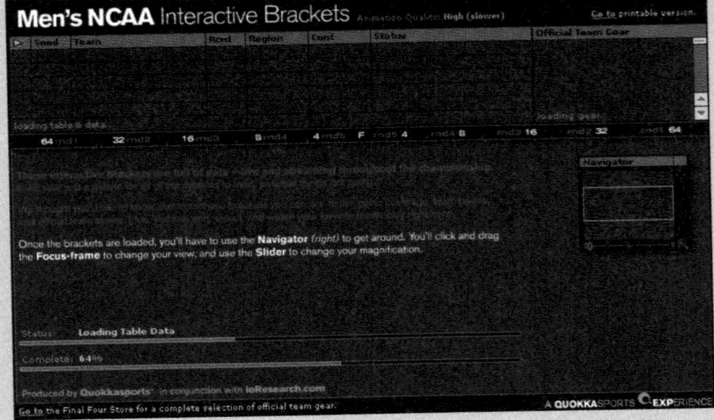

The NCAA Interactive Brackets uses the initial load time to run a quick tutorial explaining how to use the site's controls.

Keep users apprised of the progress. It's easy to put up a progress gauge, showing either the number of kilobytes loaded (out of total kilobytes to be loaded) or the percentage of the file loaded. This reassures users, first, that something is happening, and second, that the wait won't be interminable.

Use the time well. Preload something that the user will find useful or interesting. A looping animation does the job, but it's hardly scintillating viewing. Take a cue from the sites here that fill the time in interesting and appropriate ways.

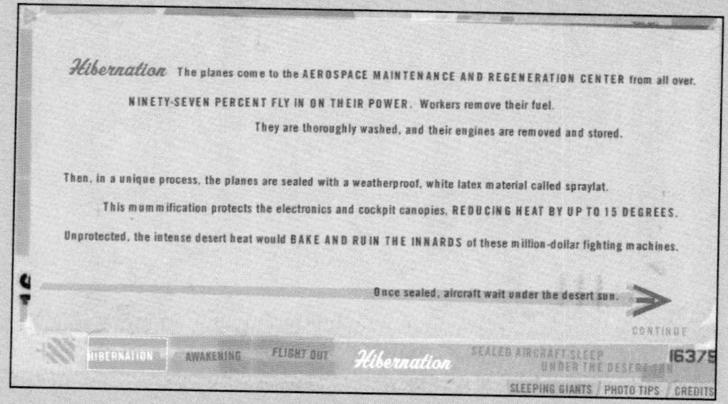

Sleeping Giants provides introductory text to occupy the user as each section loads.

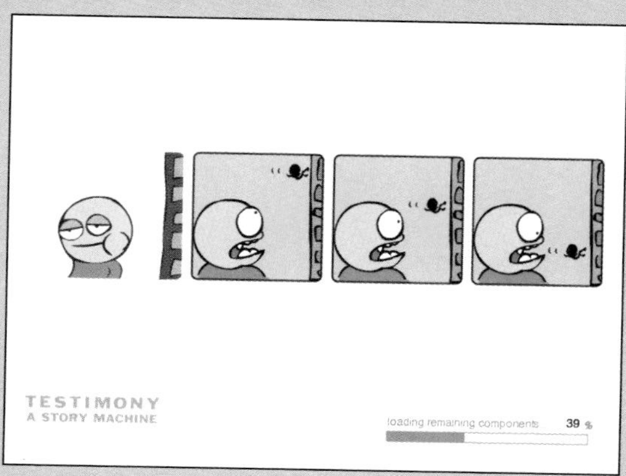

Testimony: A Story Machine breaks its initial loading sequence into two sections. After a very short preload, a short sequence of animation and sound teases the user into continuing.

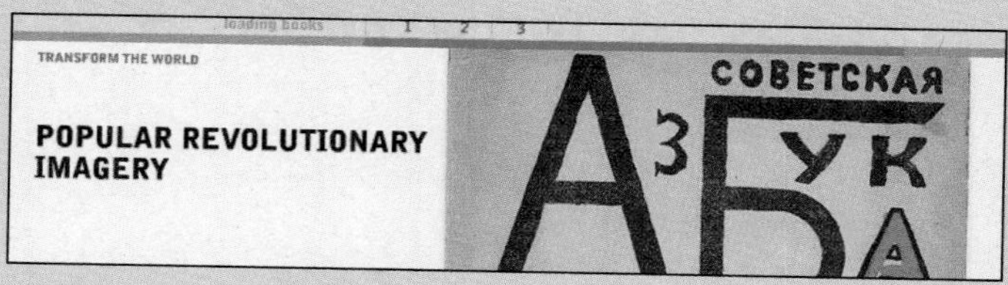

MOMA's Russian Avant-Garde Books site uses the loading time to display a preview of what's being loaded.

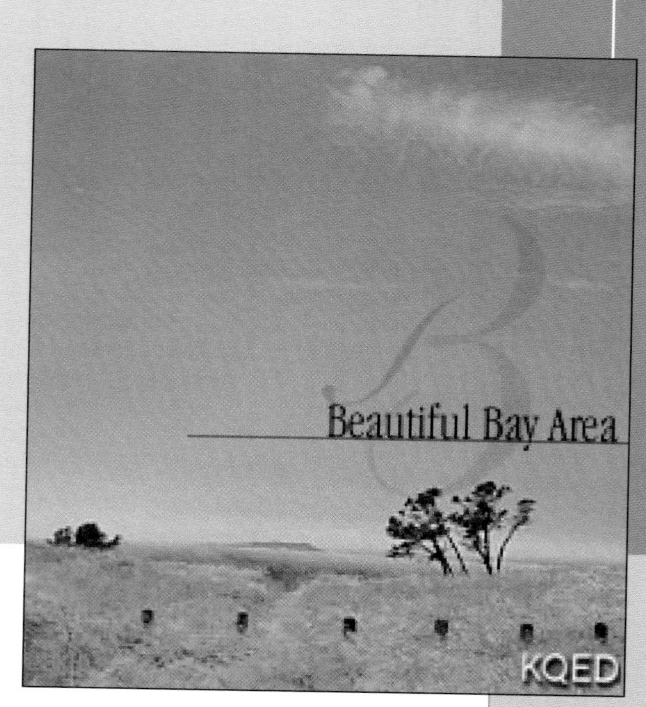

CHAPTER

BEAUTIFUL BAY AREA

DESIGN: Tractor Studios
CLIENT: KQED
URL: www.tractorstudios.com
KQED
DIRECTOR OF NEW MEDIA : Richard Dean
TRACTOR STUDIOS
PRINCIPAL: Steve Huber
INTERFACE DESIGNER: Dave Dieter
DEVELOPER: Jason Linder

CHAPTER

BEAUTIFUL BAY AREA

INTRO

For public-television station KQED, Flash provided the platform that made it easy to move information from the station's Web site onto a Pocket PC. The process was as easy as expected from a technical point of view, but more complicated in terms of interface design.

Pictured: [from left] Dave Dieter, Jason Linder, Steve Huber

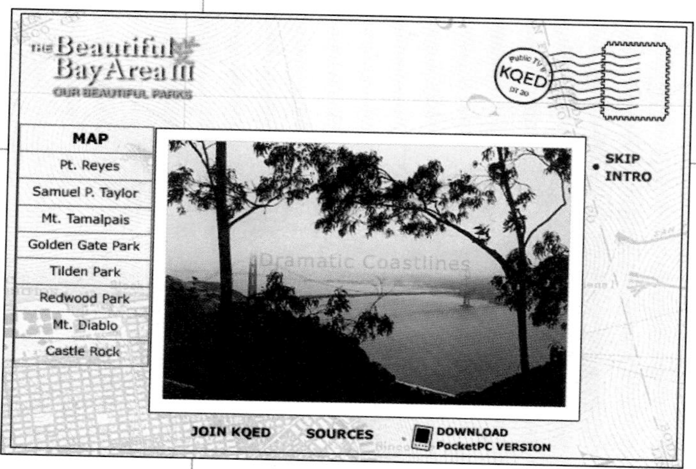

The Beautiful Bay Area Web site (above) opens with a panoramic view overlooking the Golden Gate Bridge. The site menu stays at the left. In the restricted real estate of the Pocket PC version (left), a transparent menu overlays a tighter-focus photo.

"**Public broadcasting should be** driven by local initiatives and local support. Our mission is to get people interacting with their environment," says Richard Dean, director of new media at KQED, a public television and radio station for San Francisco and Northern California.

As part of that initiative, the station produced a television show called "Beautiful Bay Area," showcasing the area's national parks. A companion Web site displayed photos and visitor information on the profiled parks. Next, Dean saw the topic as a perfect opportunity to try to extend the station's reach onto palmtop computers, too.

"Our idea was to get our audience out from behind their computers to experience the things on our Web site," says Dean. "Beautiful Bay Area was our first shot at it." The station decided to target Compaq's iPAQ palmtop, the leading hand-held model running the Pocket PC operating system, which has a Flash plug-in.

Dean went to Tractor, a San Francisco–based design studio, with the task. Given that the Web site was already in Flash, he expected a quick move to the new platform. "I thought they'd be able to port it over, and it would just work—maybe they would flip it on its side or something to get the right aspect ratio," Dean laughs. In fact, the team learned that it needed to design the new version from scratch.

The Compaq iPAQ had the high performance and color screen that Dean felt were necessary to achieve the effect he wanted.

> Picking a Platform

"I realized we could do this when I saw the performance of the iPAQ," says Dean. The Compaq palmtop had all the ingredients he had been waiting for before attempting a version of any of his projects on a handheld device. "In order to have a good experience, I felt you needed a fast processor and a color screen—and of course the availability of Flash," he says. The iPAQ is the most popular handheld running the Pocket PC operating system, the only handheld operating system (OS) for which the Flash plug-in is available.

"If Flash hadn't been available, we wouldn't have done it," Dean says. Not only did Flash allow for the kind of interactive experience he was aiming for, but Dean figured it would be the only way to do the job within a reasonable budget. Without Flash, the development team would have had to create a Flash-like environment in C++ or another programming language, in addition to creating the site itself without the benefit of Flash's authoring tools. "We talked to people that did things like this in C++, and it was a nightmare," says Steve Huber, principal at Tractor.

Although iPAQ is the leading Pocket PC system, it has still garnered only about 10 percent of the handheld market, far behind the leader, Palm systems running the Palm OS. Dean says that in deciding to develop for the iPAQ, he didn't worry much about the sheer number of users it would gain. Instead, he just wanted to see how the process would work. "We did this in large part to learn, what would it take to do this in Flash and on a Pocket PC," he says.

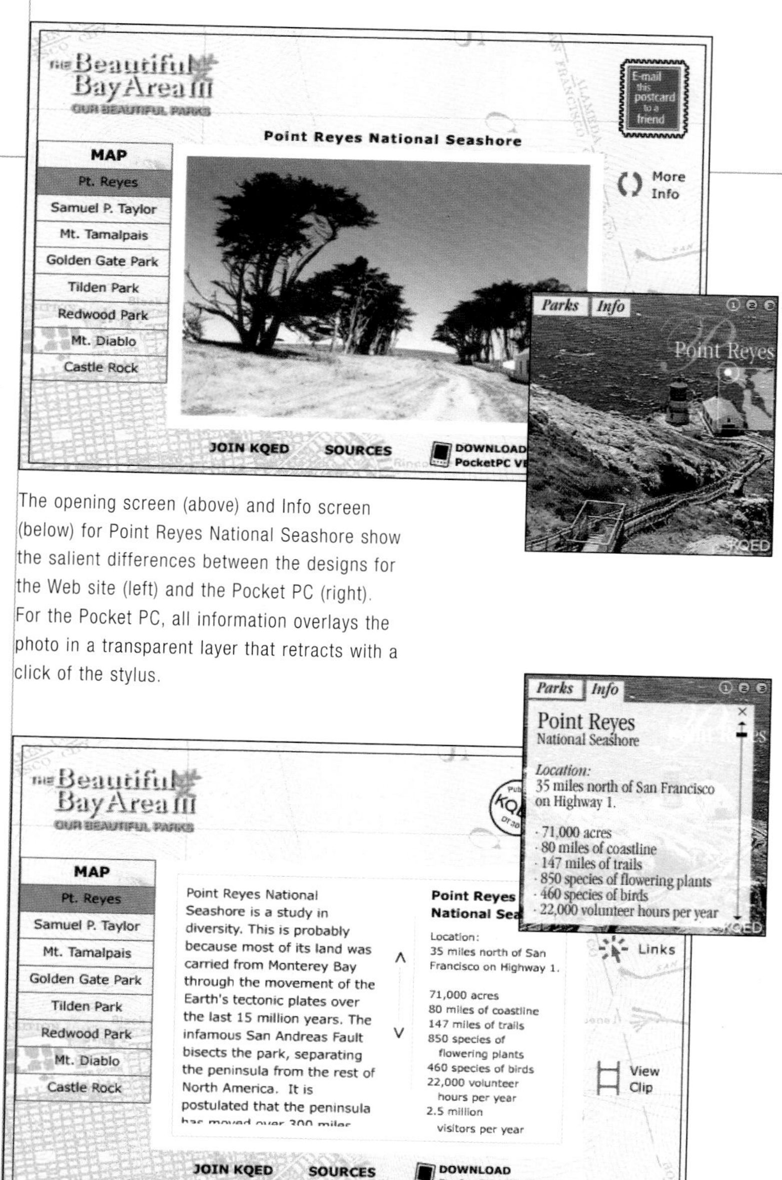

The opening screen (above) and Info screen (below) for Point Reyes National Seashore show the salient differences between the designs for the Web site (left) and the Pocket PC (right). For the Pocket PC, all information overlays the photo in a transparent layer that retracts with a click of the stylus.

> Discovering the Differences

Recognizing his beginner status, Dean says his instructions to Tractor were simply, "Here's our Web site. We want to move it to the Pocket PC."

In fact, Tractor was approaching the Pocket PC for the first time, too. The firm referred to Macromedia's Web site for the information it needed to apply the team's Flash expertise to a handheld interface. Armed with that help, the Tractor team spent the next month experimenting with different approaches. Then the team presented its recommendations to Dean and his team at KQED.

The two significant differences between the Pocket PC environment and the PC, says Dave Dieter, a principal at Tractor and lead designer on the project, are the screen (its size, resolution, and aspect ratio) and the fact that on the Pocket PC, the user makes selections with a stylus rather than a mouse. Those two differences, though, were enough to make Tractor rethink everything about the site.

In the end, the Web site and the handheld version have little in common besides their raw assets: the text and photos used to describe the parks. Everything else, from typography to the navigation system, was newly developed for the handheld.

The 230-by-250-pixel content area of the iPAQ called for a very economical use of screen space, forcing the designers to rethink what was and wasn't crucial in the Web site's interface. It also called for larger type, to keep things relatively sharp with fewer pixels.

Tractor deemed the photos of the parks to be the heart of the site. The photos appear close-cropped and full-bleed on the iPAQ. Numbered buttons at the top-right corner let users move among the photos of a particular park—a more efficient navigation device than the "next" arrow on the original site.

A few elements of the Web site were left behind, mostly, says Dean, to save money and time. The Web site's classically scored videos of each park and the Send a Postcard feature were left out of the iPAQ version.

Developing for the Pocket PC also forced the team to step back a bit in its development habits. At the time the team created the site, the latest Flash plug-in for the Pocket PC was version 4; version 5 was available for PC browsers.

> Imagery Front and Center

In honing the site for the iPAQ's small screen, the designers quickly made a decision. "The imagery was the focus of the whole interface," says Dieter. "That was the most interesting and most useful thing in the interface. That drove how the rest of it was built."

Images that were framed by a background pattern, navigation, and site identity on the Web site bleed full screen on the Pocket PC version. Those images remain onscreen at all times, though they are sometimes covered by a transparent layer containing the site menu or information about the current park.

Tractor's team had to doctor the images to suit the new environment. The designers brightened and saturated each photo to suit the characteristics of the iPAQ screen. They also reoptimized them, making sure that the reduced colors in the files were those that worked best within the color gamut of the iPAQ. "We did a lot of juggling and testing," says Jason Linder, Tractor's developer.

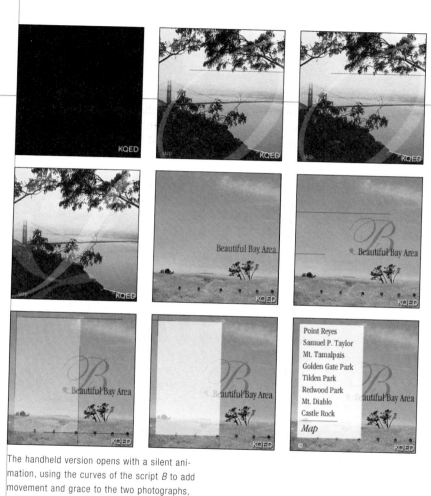

The handheld version opens with a silent animation, using the curves of the script *B* to add movement and grace to the two photographs, which emphasize the area's diversity by contrasting a water view with one of the dry inland hills. Grid lines then cross the photo to create the menu layer.

In the end, the site's entire interface was created with images, even the text. "We found that the iPAQ with Flash was rendering the text a little too slowly," says Linder. The team also found that the serif typeface it was using didn't anti-alias well in Flash. Pre-rendering the text as a GIF image solved the problem.

> Gentle Movement

Once the designers realized that the site would need an entirely new interface, the Tractor team essentially left behind the old site design. In thinking about the iPAQ version, the designers say they looked to the television show, rather than the original Web site, for inspiration.

Following that guide, the Pocket PC version opens with subtle movement designed to draw the viewer into the scene. "We wanted a cascading feeling," says Dieter. A graphic swirl from the script *B* in the title floats down into the photos, which change from a scene overlooking the Golden Gate Bridge to a golden hillside. Rules draw themselves across the screen to form a transparent rectangle, in which the menu appears.

The site's typography was developed to evoke the same sense of gentle beauty. A large script capital softens the display type. The Kuenstler Script used there and the Garamond used for the rest of the text were chosen to accentuate the site's humanistic quality, says Dieter.

UNDER THE HOOD
PREPARING GRAPHICS FOR THE iPAQ

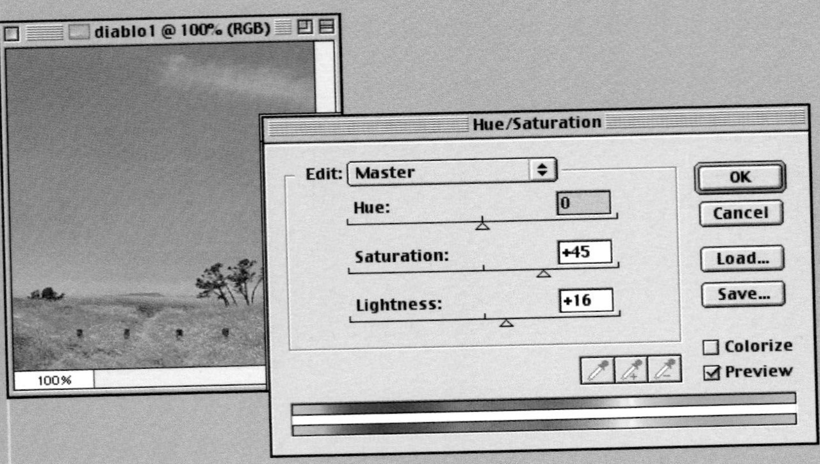

Figure 1
Linder used a standard set of Hue, Saturation, and Levels settings as a starting point for his image adjustments. He saved the settings in Photoshop using the Save and Load features in those dialog boxes.

Although the graphics for Beautiful Bay Area on the Pocket PC were Web-ready (since they were inherited from the original Web site), the Tractor team found it had to rethink and reprepare them all for use on the Pocket PC.

"The main problem on the Pocket PC is that images tend to look dim and desaturated," says Jason Linder, Tractor's developer. "It was obvious that we'd need to boost the colors and push the brightness." Using Photoshop, he followed a process of trial and error until he achieved an effect that looked good on the iPAQ. Then he saved the Hue, Saturation, and Levels settings (**Figure 1**) and applied them to each of the images, using Photoshop's Actions feature. Each image still needed minor adjustments, which were made on a case-by-case basis.

The next step was cropping the images to suit the iPAQ's screen. The panoramic views favored on the Web site were transformed into tighter-focus scenes more suited to the 230-by-250-pixel area available on the handheld computer.

Last, using Photoshop's Save For Web command, Linder saved each cropped image as a JPEG, deciding on the proper compression settings on an image-by-image basis. Viewing the JPEG preview in the Save For Web dialog box, he set the compression level as high as he could without introducing too many artifacts in the image (**Figure 2**).

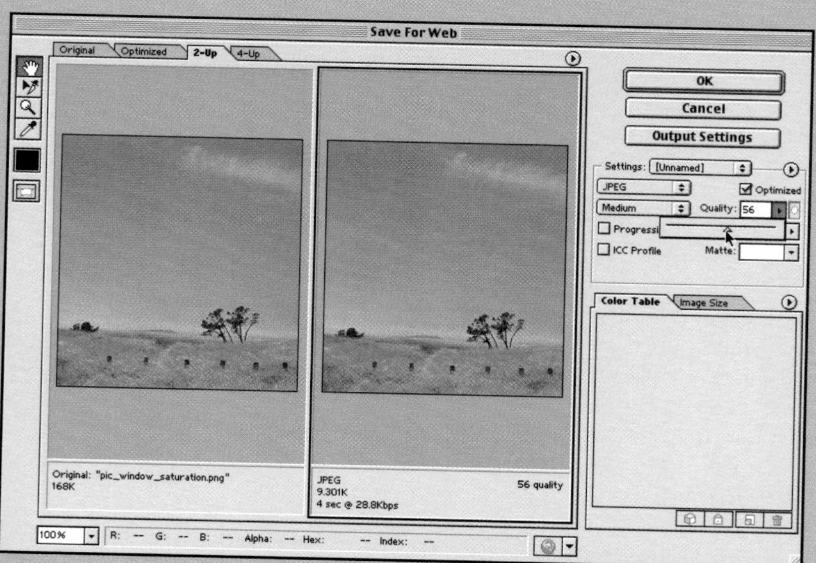

Figure 2

Photoshop's Save For Web dialog box shows the image before and after compression. Linder selected the highest compression setting that didn't create visible artifacts.

To bypass Flash's text-rendering feature, which ran unacceptably slowly on the iPAQ, Linder pre-rendered the menus and information text as transparent PNG files. PNG was chosen, says Linder, for its full alpha-channel support, which allowed the text to blend seamlessly into the transparent backgrounds. To create the text sections, he simply typed the text into Photoshop as the sole file in the layer (with Photoshop's checkered transparency indicator as a background), and used Save For Web to create a transparent PNG. "The files were a bit large—up to 64 K," says Linder, "much larger than they would have been with internal Flash text. But in this case, the file size was less important than the need for good scrolling performance."

On the Info layer, the two columns from the original Web layout are consolidated into one, with general park information at the top. Tractor tested the scroll bar control to make sure it was big enough to manipulate easily with the stylus.

> Stylus Navigation

For an interaction designer, the single most unfamiliar part of a handheld system probably is working with the stylus as a pointing device. The main difference, says Linder, is that there are no rollovers—an item is either selected or not. Other conventions that designers have grown accustomed to on the Web are different on the palm as well.

In the iPAQ version, navigation is pared down to two main buttons, Parks and Info. The Parks button causes the main menu to drop down. Info reveals information on the current park. Within each park section, numbered buttons at the top-right corner let the user move among different photos.

A map of the Bay Area (accessible from the Parks menu) provides a different way to move among the parks, letting users make their choices based on proximity or other location considerations. Interestingly, the Map command was moved to the bottom of the menu from its place at the top on the original Web site. This recognizes that the map is a slightly less efficient way to get to park information—two clicks from the menu rather than one.

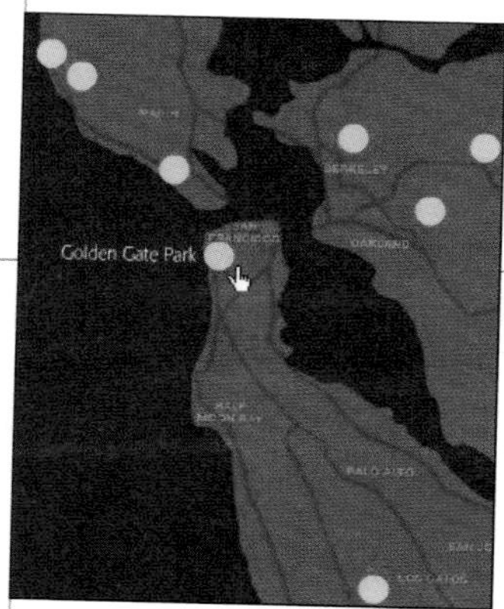

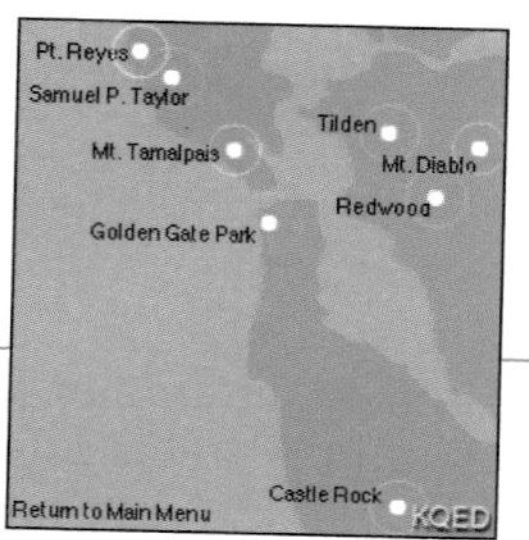

The map on the Web site (left) was redesigned for the iPAQ to work without rollover actions. On the iPAQ version (above), the park names are always visible, but here as elsewhere, less-critical information (city names) was stripped away, and colors were brightened to suit the iPAQ screen. An added animation draws attention to the different locations.

Linder says that another artifact of design for the stylus was the need to make everything a little bigger than one might on a Web site. In addition to upping the type size to work with the iPAQ's tiny resolution, Tractor had to consider the sizes of different controls, such as buttons and scroll bars. The team experimented with various sizes for the scroll control in the park Info sections, for instance. "We had to make it large enough so you felt like you really had your stylus on it, but without making it so large it got in the way of the design," he says.

> Lessons for the Main Site

Considering that the amount of information is essentially the same in both versions, I asked Dean whether he thought that the minimalist design used on the iPAQ could be just as effective on the Web. He says no: "If I were to put the Pocket PC version on a Web site, people would say, 'Where's the navigation?' " On a palm device you're used to having to hide and reveal things; it's part of the operating system. Hidden navigation wouldn't work as well on the Web site." When I probed a bit deeper on that, though, he laughed, and admitted, "We'd probably be better served by having a more minimalist approach on the Web site, too."

The iPAQ version on the Web. Tractor framed the movie in a digital photograph of the iPAQ and put it on its Web site.

> Lessons for the Future

Although relatively few copies of the Pocket PC version of Beautiful Bay Area are in circulation (about 1,000 copies have been downloaded), Dean counts the experience a success. "The point was for us to experiment," he says. "How is this going to work? How long is it going to take?"

Dean also says he gained the knowledge at a cost far lower than what he expected. Once the initial direction was approved, the team was able to develop the site in about a week. "It probably cost about half of what I thought it would," he says.

Now that his station has forged the way, Dean says that other public-television stations are looking to his team for information on handheld development. "Other PBS stations started to ask, 'Is this something we should emulate?' "

The answer Dean gives now, he says, is no: "The handheld market hasn't taken off the way it was expected to." In the longer term, though, he plans more along these lines. The programs that the education-minded KQED produces from its interactive division, like the shows it creates for television, aren't designed to attract the biggest audiences, he points out. Their measure of success is different: The question they ask is, "Does it serve the community?"

As part of the station's goal of encouraging its audience members to interact with their city and environment, Dean sees more opportunities for handheld Flash programs. By the end of 2002, he says, his department will probably start a series of Flash-based walking tours, beginning with one for Alcatraz Island. In his dreams, he envisions tourists renting iPAQs loaded with the tours, just as they rent headsets and audiotapes now.

The main lesson he learned, says Dean, is that when his division plans a site with a handheld component, the team should devise the approach for the two sites side by side. "You can't just say you'll port it over as an afterthought," he says. "When we plan a site, we'll have to say, 'This is what we want for the main site, and this is what we want for the Pocket PC.'"

And Back to the Web Again ...

Although interaction design and site goals may not be easily transferable between a regular Web site and a handheld version, Flash code is.

Readers who don't have a Pocket PC but want to see the iPAQ version of this site can view it on the Web. A testimony to the portability of the Flash code can be seen at Tractor's Web site. (Look under KQED in the Clients section.) There, you can run through a fully interactive version of the site, framed in a digital photo of the iPAQ. ■

INDEX

N

O

P